THE
DEAD
JANITORS
CLUB

PATHETICALLY TRUE TALES OF A
CRIME SCENE CLEANUP KING

a memoir by
Jeff Klima

sourcebooks

Published by Sourcebooks, Inc.
P.O. Box 4410, Naperville, Illinois 60567-4410
(630) 961-3900
Fax: (630) 961-2168
www.sourcebooks.com

Library of Congress Cataloging-in-Publication Data

Klima, Jeff.
 The dead janitors club : pathetically true tales of a crime scene cleanup king / by Jeff
Klima.
   p. cm.
1.   Crimes--California--Orange County. 2.   Crime scenes--California--Orange
County. 3. Orange County Crime Scene Cleaners (Firm) I. Title.
  HV6533.C2.K55 2010
  338.7'6136325--dc22

                            2010001458

        Printed and bound in the United States of America.
           VP 10 9 8 7 6 5 4 3 2 1

For my boss…
He pushed me to write this book—
Now I bet he's sorry I did.
Also, for Happy.

All of what follows is true, but my apologies if my memory of chronology or events differs slightly from your own. It mostly shouldn't, though, unless you're a liar.

Maybe something good can come out of all this evil?

from wine to spine

Man has to suffer. When he has no real afflictions, he invents some.

—José Martí

I WALK INTO THE LOBBY of a shockingly splendid hotel, and the wheel on the cash register in my mind is clicking audibly upward. I anticipate leaving this place a few thousand dollars richer than when I walked in. So many factors are at play here; I am chomping at the bit, trying to discern them all.

French doors gilded with a gold overlay breeze open effortlessly before me, working off unseen sensors and a pneumatic arm. Caucasian employees stare pleasantly at me from behind the counter. From a financial standpoint, this is a good thing.

White people are terrified of death. An overabundance of detachment and safety in our culture has resulted in "whitey" becoming a benign collective of soft-shelled whiners, people who understand pain only in terms of there not being three-ply toilet paper on sale at the supermarket closest to their condo.

Ethnic folks are confronted by death more frequently than white people, and that numbed acceptance of it can mean a lot less money for a guy in my line of work.

I stroll around a polite setup of stain-free and richly upholstered dark couches arranged around a coffee table holding stacks of newspapers from various regions of the world. The smell of breakfast fills the lobby. Whether it's pumped in or they have a café tucked somewhere, it still means that they give a damn about their multisensory first impression, and that is good news for me.

I set my clipboard on the counter and straighten my black polo shirt so that the biohazard symbol is smartly on display.

"Hello, sir. How can I help you?" the attractive, brunette counter girl asks. The orange script practically glows off my chest, screaming out what I do, but her eyes never waver from mine, not once. She's been trained well.

"I'm looking for Gary," I say.

"Right away, sir." She picks up her walkie-talkie, blocking out her mouth, but I can discern the same clipped and effortlessly polite tone with which she addressed me.

I feel good…important…larger than life, and regret not parking beneath the valet awning, right in the middle of the lane, my car torqued at a hard angle to create an impasse, letting everyone know the *Crime Scene Cleaner* is here. It is the sort of dick move that I typically do these days—carefree, powerful me.

What stopped me on this occasion was that my car had the misfortune to be parked the previous night under some sort of avian toilet. A ridiculous amount of white bird shit, speckled with the green remnants of devoured insects, gave my red car a rather polka-dotted appearance.

I pick up my clipboard and step over to the coffee table to scan headlines from the news of the world, hopeful that the *Orange County Register* will scream about mass death and murder in its banner headline. But probably not, because I would have already known about it.

Gary appears from behind me, looking dapper but terribly ethnic, which yanks several thousand dollars off what I was hoping to make the price tag. I curse silently behind a confident and winning smile.

"Hi, Jeff Klima from Orange County Crime Scene Cleaners," I say, extending my hand and speaking first to inform him that I am the alpha male.

"Hi," he says, a bit puzzled, and I suddenly hope I am in the right place.

He introduces himself and looks around ashamed, as if I were a homeless urchin who had obstinately wandered into the ornate lobby and began snacking on the odds and ends in a trash receptacle.

"I understand you have some sort of scene…" I query further, losing some of my swagger, and I can't help but note how two years on the job suddenly doesn't feel like that much experience at all. Shit, I might as well have acne and a pubescent hard-on, considering the detectable quiver in my voice. It shocks me how quickly my overwhelming shyness can come roaring back to capsize my confidence.

He politely shushes me with one raised hand, vibrating softly, panicked. I understand completely but say, "A suicide, maybe?" a bit loudly, as if I didn't, comfortably reestablishing my authority. The same trembling hand waves me out of the lobby and away from the guests checking in, who can undeniably read my shirt.

We step out into the courtyard, a lush open-air affair, where hotel workers are scrambling to set up for some speaking engagement to take place a little later in the day. None of them make eye contact with me; they've been well trained. We wait in silence for a short eternity, though I'm eager to persist, having had to wake up well before noon to ready myself for this gig.

Another man, also ethnic (and more money off the bill), joins us. I don't remember his name, so we'll call him Osama. He is better dressed than Gary, and I clue in to his seniority when Gary quickly moves aside, his eyes slightly downcast. I introduce myself to this man as well, comfortably meeting his gaze through his executive eyeglasses. This guy may be a fearsome boss to the minimum-wage herd working here, but to me he's just another jerk who needs my skills. It further empowers me.

Osama shepherds Gary and myself quickly along manicured stone pathways past doors with placards that refer to the rooms beyond the doors as "suites." This is usually good news for me. This place, in its self-congratulatory way, considers itself a "nicer" establishment. I bet I can get some good money out of them after all.

The elevator is farther away from the lobby than I would like, though, which is a glaring indication that this is an older hotel with fresh polish—not a good sign. It was built when places put less consideration into guest needs, and more into overall aesthetics and intent. Old hotel casinos do this, making guests walk through the main casino floor en route to their rooms, hoping the whirling lights and cheerful pings of jackpots being wheedled out will entice the guests into making a long detour at their expense.

Stepping into the elevator further confirms my suspicions. The elevator, with its glass paneling staring out into the courtyard, has threadbare and nappy carpeting that would be completely *verboten* anywhere near the entrance or lobby. The elevator buttons, once a trickle of elite white circles, have faded to a stale version of their past glory. The elevator buttons run from top to bottom, though, with the higher floors listed at the top, convincing me that the hotel started off as a glitzy, hip place some time ago.

We head for the third floor, the elevator doors closing around us like a tomb. I tap "Another One Bites the Dust" on my clipboard with my fingers as the elevator chugs upward, its pneumatic lift struggling far more than its brothers operating the front doors. Nobody speaks and nobody looks at each other, which is fine with me.

The elevator halts with a lurch, and the doors swing open to reveal a maid's cart jutting obstinately across the pathway, completely oblivious to would-be passersby. The fat cats share a collective acknowledgment over this, and I develop the melancholy opinion that this year some woman's kids aren't going to have much of a...however you say "Christmas" in Spanish.

The doors here, each similarly designated as suites, belie the fact that this hotel has no real suites, only standard rooms. It's one of those places that refer to every room as a "suite." This hotel lures guests in, rather like insects to a bug zapper, by using an alluring lobby complete with an English-speaking counter staff to make tourists feel comfortable—like they are going to have a high-dollar hotel experience.

Once guests check in and take the walk to their "suite," however, they realize they've gotten the bum's rush, and similarly, so have I. This job practically feels now like I will be doing it for free.

We step to a door conveniently located a short distance from the elevator, good for me on the likely chance that I will have to move a stain-mottled bed, flush with leaking guts and malodorous chunks, through the hallway. Few things are a bigger pain in the ass to a crime scene cleaner than a crime scene on the upper floors of a multiple-story establishment.

I wait apprehensively for one of the two suits to open the door, but nothing happens. Glancing right to left, I suddenly feel like it's all a trick and I've been led here to be whacked, Mafia-style. (Since I dropped acid in college, my mind occasionally leaps to these extremes.)

"We wait," Osama says mysteriously. I step over to the railing, wondering if there is anyone around who will hear the gunshots and react appropriately, but there probably isn't. My jaded experience over the past couple of years has taught me that precious few people react appropriately to the sound of gunshots anyway.

"Did a man kill himself in there?" I ask, adopting a slight person-to-an-affected-child voice.

"Please, we must wait," Osama maintains, and I look to Gary for some semblance of understanding. He is deathly silent and subservient to his master; he, too, has been well trained.

The doors to all the rooms face inward, open to the courtyard air, and it is warming up quickly. It will be a hot day, and I pray the job will be over quickly. Working in a protective biohazard suit normally makes all the sweat from my body collect and slosh uncomfortably around me. In the July heat, though, it makes the sweat stink. I need the money, because summers in the crime scene business are always slow, but craving even more than that, I need a few extra hours of sleep. I think I'm still drunk from a party the night before.

The clip-clop of quickly approaching executive shoes drums out the nearby freeway sounds and I look up. A third man, dressed better still than Gary and Osama, has arrived and has an assistant in tow, showcasing his importance beyond what a mere suit could achieve. Real power players have assistants, you see. Not that I care. I'm done introducing myself. Now I only want answers, not new friends to add to my Facebook account.

The top cat apologizes briefly and instructs Osama to unlock the door. His assistant steps forward nervously, holding a small handful of painter's protective breathing masks, but the master waves him back. The top cat then simply states that they will be downstairs when I am through and stands by the open door to let me pass, which is definitely a good sign for my pocketbook. He doesn't want to see anything more than a bill.

I step past him into the room, not waiting for the others to join me. They don't. The room, which is more opulent than I had anticipated, stifles the clip-clop of executive shoes moving away from the door in unison.

Decorated to allow for the matched prestige of the lobby, the suite is three rooms—a living room, a bathroom, and, down a slight hallway, a bedroom. I check first for the presence of a minibar that I could get into trouble with, but finding none, I plunge down the hallway toward the bedroom.

The place doesn't have the rank odor of death attached to it, which is nice but mostly expected. Unlike homes or apartments, which can be left unchecked for months in the right circumstances, hotels have a quick drop-to-flop ratio (that is, from the time the bodies drop to the time the maid comes in to flop out the bedding and the towels and then cross herself while jabbering hysterically at the sight of some ruined and eviscerated ex-human).

I check the bathroom en route to the bedroom. The bathroom is immaculate, much to my dual relief and concern. Concern because the tiled multi-surfaces of the bathroom are generally conducive to easy cleaning. Relief at the overall cleanliness of the bathroom, however, because I indulged in a meal of Jack in the Box late the night before, and it is beginning to push its way out. Few things are more of a bummer than having to take a dump amid the unsanitary and potentially disease-riddled innards of some jilted, joyless corpse.

Walking into the bedroom, I can scarcely contain my glee for the moments it takes to complete my survey of the room. It is clean, save for the bed, which is a king-size wreck of tangled sheets, dark-red blood (which means the unlucky fucker bled through), and one very, very soiled remote control. Finally I can laugh, exhaling a great torrent of cheery exclamations, doubtlessly heard through paper-thin walls.

It is a dream scene. This wrecked life, its remnants spread gashed before me on the large bed, in its temerity was probably too miserable to run screaming through the room splaying its hacked-at wrists outward, polluting the walls with its cherry-red essence. No, whoever it was stayed perfectly still, mummylike in the center of the bed, bleeding slowly out into the night, the linens catching the life that he or she let slip away.

I even flip the mattress upward, as experience has taught me, smiling broadly when I ascertain that nothing has even leaked down to the box spring. Sometimes when people rot, their guts collect inside the mattress, and when you go to move the damn thing, all their guts go splashing out onto the flooring. But that isn't the case here.

So as I wrap up my inspection and get ready to start cleaning, I'm feeling pretty good about this one. It's a simple job that will net me five hundred or so dollars for less than an hour of work. I bet they even have HBO on the living room TV that I can kill time with so these sharply dressed ethnic men will feel as if they have gotten their money's worth. Too bad about the lack of a minibar, though.

• • •

Of course, I wasn't always this way—this racist, uncompassionate whelp who sees dead bodies as dollar signs and trauma as a means to a fancy dinner out with my girlfriend. No, I wasn't always like this. I used to be unhappy.

Picture yourself standing in a line at a retail store. It's a long line, and the clerk has to wrap and bag every item of the customer several people ahead of you. You grow irritated because the store hasn't bothered to open any other checkout counters, even though there are three people ahead of you and two people behind you.

All the customers are equally displeased, as they all have many places to go and this particular clerk seems to be taking forever. It has easily been six minutes since you got in line to check out, and you need the items that are in your cart, so you can't just step out and refuse any further patronage of said nameless store. You're also tired from having to navigate your SUV all over town and deal with traffic and other hazards of shopping. You just wish the clerk would hurry up.

Finally it's your turn and the clerk apologizes politely, if not seemingly a bit insincerely. You let him reach over the counter and into your cart to grab your purchases so he can scan them, refusing him any help whatsoever. All the while, you tell him how irate you are at having been so shabbily treated. He apologizes again and offers to get the manager to help make it right, but you are tired, and the manager will most likely just be a more slovenly, older version of this idiot who stands before you.

You aren't going to go down that road again, and you tell the clerk this in a biting, grating tone that perfectly conveys how you feel. As he sets the last of your bags in your cart, you make a tart aside about how you don't know if you will be a repeat customer anymore. He blinks a couple of times and the corners of his mouth twinge, and yet he says nothing other than to wish you a better day in a flat, emotionless tone.

Mostly forgotten, you steer out of the store, pushing your cart away and feeling better now that you are almost finished with your day and had the chance to do a little venting at some moron's expense. Really you aren't a bad person, or even a mean person, but sometimes life doesn't go your way and you have to let someone know it.

If you can picture that scenario perfectly, then know that I, Jeff Klima, hate you. I more than hate you, in fact. If you had tried that scenario outside of that retail environment, I would have beaten you to death. I still might. You see, for two and a half years I was that clerk at a Beverages & More, an upscale chain of wine shops in Orange County, California.

You mistakenly thought that the clerk, me, was responsible for the corporate policy that understaffed the store and required that the glassware bought by the customers preceding you had to be wrapped nicely in bubble wrap or paper bags to avoid breakage.

Know that while you had to stand there inconveniently for ten minutes or less, I had been standing there for five hours. And the bullshit amount that they called my paycheck didn't make it any more pleasurable or tolerable. And believe me, I was trying to do something about my situation.

But I didn't have an SUV—I was in debt up to my ears from rent and school tuition that didn't come anywhere near getting paid on what I made in a month or a year, and it wasn't easy trying to be responsible and stay alive free of mom and dad while driving around in a beat-up Chevy Cavalier that I paid for myself.

And you didn't make it any easier on me when you were buying Bordeaux that you didn't need to add to your collection. You made me feel on the outside what you must feel like on the inside: a real miserable son of a bitch.

If, on the other hand, you can't picture that little scenario, then welcome aboard. You seem like a friendly, cheerful person, and I can definitely deal with more of that in the world of the living. So if you're interested in blood, guts, funny stories, and the crazy couple of years I had going from being a shat-upon liquor store clerk to becoming a bad-ass crime scene cleanup guy, then hang the fuck on, because I've got a hell of a tale to tell you.

CHAPTER 2

so you want to be a crime scene cleaner

All paid jobs absorb and degrade the mind.

—*Aristotle*

THE NUMBER-ONE QUESTION I GET asked about the crime scene business is "how can you do it?" Typically I give the polite, short answer: "Someone has to," accompanied by a wan shrug. But in truth, that isn't even the tip of the iceberg. I do it for two very good reasons, and though I can't pretend they are the main reasons, they definitely are part of it.

I was born on September 11, 1981, the son of a magician and a psychologist. My father was a stage performer, and my mother was a school psychologist who analyzed the inner workings of children's minds, so it was no surprise that I wound up a bit odd.

In fact, my whole family is a bit odd. Everyone is on medication for a myriad of very real disorders, with the exception of me. And I probably should be, too, but I'm terrified that medication will dull the spark that makes me the individual that I want to be. Or at the very least, I'm worried that medication will shrink my penis.

There are six people in my immediate family: my parents, who are still happily married; my older sister, Shaine, one of those religious types with a bipolar disorder; me; and my younger brothers, Chris and Ben, both creative types like me, who are prone to bouts of depression, anger, and attention deficit disorder. We're probably bipolar-lite, the lot of us.

We grew up in Sun Valley, California, a suburb of Los Angeles, in a house my mother inherited when her parents died. While it had been an ideal place for my mom to grow up with *her* brothers and sisters, the neighborhood had long since been seized by gangs, and I don't mean those crazy-fun dancing gangs from *West Side Story*.

By the time we were born, the area had become a dangerous place to live, a ghetto, where bullets zinged down alleys in pursuit of victims and street brawls with chains and bats were commonplace.

My parents once told me a story of how my sister Shaine and I, roughly aged three and four, were playing in the backyard of our little house on Haley Street. They say I walked into the house asking my parents where the kitty cat was. My mom wanted to know why.

"Because a man out back wants to see Shaine's pussy," I said.

My dad flew outside in time to chase some creep back over our six-foot concrete wall. It wasn't the last straw, but it was damn close.

In January 1990 we packed our bags and moved north to the very top of California. Eureka was a charming little burg, nestled between the mountains and the bay, with a population somewhere around twenty-eight thousand. My mom had visited Eureka in her youth and had always wanted to move there. For better or worse, it was the polar opposite of Los Angeles.

In Los Angeles I had been a popular kid on the playground, funny and well liked by the ethnic mix of low-income urchins who attended Canterbury Elementary School. But those Eureka kids were different. To them I was just another poor, big-city kid from far away, looking to get invited to their birthdays and clog up the dodgeball court with my presence. The elementary school in Eureka already had plenty of well-liked, funny kids and didn't seem to want to welcome another one, so I switched to the second most natural role for me, the quiet loner.

Ricky Moses was one of my first friends in town. We met at a Mormon church. We were just five days apart in age, but we truly bonded over religion...or, rather, our dislike of it. Both of us were raised Mormon, and our parents made the two of us attend the church services, which was an absolute ruin of a beautiful Sunday. So naturally we clicked in thinking up methods to find our way out of the church and into the redwood forest surrounding it.

Ricky was a bad kid in a good way. His round face, overloaded with freckles that ran clear up to his curly red hair, always reflected the fact that Ricky didn't give a damn about authority, which was something that impressed me immensely. I instantly became the Tom Sawyer to his Huck Finn.

Religion hadn't been a problem for me in Sun Valley, because none of my school buddies' parents allowed them to come over to my house, thanks to its ghetto location. So church was where I went to be with kids my own age. I didn't like getting dressed up every Sunday morning, but I didn't know any other reality.

When I moved to Eureka, though, my eyes were opened to the splendor that was a Sunday afternoon. Kids were out riding bikes, exploring, signing up for peewee football, or just lounging and basking in their freedom. At the Klima house, however, Sunday was "family day," a day when we all hung out with each other, couldn't have friends over, and couldn't leave the house, other than to go play among ourselves in the backyard.

Church evolved from my social life into my social prison. Worse, with the exception of Ricky, all of the other kids at church whom I could socialize with were feebs and wieners.

But Ricky was like a twelve-step program for me that combated my naturally shy disposition, a personality trait that I inherited from my mother's side of the family, one that hadn't yet formed while I was living in Sun Valley. My brothers and sister were all performers, taking after my father, so they had all adapted and made friends easily in Eureka. Ricky was all I had. So when Ricky joined Boy Scouts, I joined Boy Scouts, too, even though my heart wasn't in camping or tying knots or earning merit badges. Eventually scout campouts became cathartic for me while giving Ricky all the more opportunity to get into trouble through such activities as pooping where we shouldn't or stealing other troops' tents. Fishing poles were another frequently heist-worthy item, made easier by the fact that they could easily be thrown away after use. Ricky was a hell of a friend and got me into some crazy (and scatological!) adventures that, left to my shyness, I would otherwise not have known.

Ricky got into drugs at a ridiculously young age, though, which was an adventure that I was too afraid to join him on. When I was just out of the sixth grade and just through my school's anti-drug D.A.R.E. program (which had made perfect sense to me), Ricky brought a bag of marijuana along on a campout.

He was insistent that we smoke it, but I only knew enough about marijuana to know that smoking it at age eleven was pretty much the last thing we should do. Instead, I coerced Ricky into selling it to the two teenagers who ran the campsite where we were staying. Needless to say, they were all too delighted to indulge in what was probably mostly just stems and trim.

The end of our friendship pretty much came when we were about thirteen and Ricky's dad accused me of breaking into his garage and four other garages along the six-block span between our houses. It was a fair assumption at the time, because I had turned into a pretty reckless kid with a sneering attitude toward any authority figures in the church. His parents and my parents forbade us from seeing each other, and apparently I was still just enough of a mama's boy to obey.

Ricky and I fell out of contact, although I occasionally ran into him when we both had the small-town good fortune to attend the same high school. He had been held back in first grade or kindergarten at the elementary school he attended, so I was already established by a year in high school when I ran into him again.

He had made further exploration into the drug world, and we had become two vastly different people, as I was still happily drug free and writing for the school newspaper. Still, we always said hi to each other when we passed in the halls.

By the time Ricky's sophomore year rolled around, he was trying to get back with his ex-girlfriend and kick the drugs, which seemed like a pretty good move for him. So it was an enormous surprise for me to arrive at school one morning and find out that Ricky was dead.

The previous day, he had called the fire department, where his father worked as a volunteer fireman, and asked them to come clean up his body before his mom got home and found it. Then he shot himself. He was sixteen years old, younger than me by five days no longer.

After the funeral, his father and I talked for the first time since he had accused me of B&E all those years before, and we made everything as right as it could possibly be under the circumstances. Now every time I go up to visit my parents, who still live in Eureka, I stop by Ricky's grave and marvel about all the wonderful things that I have seen and done and learned in the years since his death, and that I wish he could have experienced as well.

Ricky made a choice, though. Christopher Simons never even got to do that much.

• • •

Finally having decided that small-town life was too small for me, I moved down to Santa Clarita, a northern suburb of Los Angeles. For the nineteen-year-old man that I was, full of piss and Fritos, Southern California had always felt just a bit more like home. All my aunts and uncles lived there, and besides, I knew that if I was going to become a bigwig in advertising, like I planned to, I'd have to be in a major metropolitan area.

The move also completely freed me from the indoctrination of the church, which was, in hindsight, the sweetest part of all. Once I had turned eighteen, I was no longer required to go to church by my parents, who hoped that by my eighteenth birthday I would have discovered my spiritual side and would want to go willingly. Nope, I was a non-Mormon on midnight of September 10.

By the morning of the 11th, I had practically forgotten what a Mormon looked like. I escaped before they could get their "secret underwear" on me. Mormons are friendly people who mean well, but I smoke cigars, drink whiskey, and cuss like a shit farmer with a sore dick. I like to think I was rejecting them before they could reject me.

The first opportunity I had upon moving back to Los Angeles, I got a job at a porn shop. My parents weren't all that happy about it and chalked it up to petty defiance, but they were seven-hundred-plus miles away and I was looking to sow my wild oats.

Porn fascinates me. My relationship with porn is one-sided (as most relationships with porn usually are, ba-dum-chee). Strangely, I'm not that interested in actually looking at the porn itself. Watching some party girl get anally reamed from multiple angles by a bunch of well-hung meatheads, I just end up thinking about whether or not that girl will have to wear a diaper when she gets older.

It's just the idea of porn and the world of people who watch or participate in it, or both, that I love. I don't know whether it is the effect of porn's forbidden aspect on my force-fed religious soul, or whether it is that I have always been shy and awkward around girls and am shocked to witness folks who had no shyness or inhibitions whatsoever.

At the porn shop, we had a DVD player beneath the counter to make sure that the DVDs people were returning were really defective and not just boring. The other employees used to sit and watch porn on it for hours. On my shifts, I would smuggle in Disney musicals.

Don't get me wrong; I've happily watched far more than my fair share of porn and have seen some shit that would make you want to wash your eyes while viewing it. But for me it was always enough to just be around naked people getting fucked. I didn't have to watch them. I knew they were there.

The store was a really nice place, surprisingly. It was nestled in a little strip mall between a tattoo parlor and a bunch of auto part stores, and the clientele was mostly comprised of upper-middle-class types, both male and female.

Doctors, lawyers, Hollywood laypeople, and some of those auto part store employees made up the customer base. Frequently, they were more than happy to oblige me, solicited or not, with tales of their sexual misdeeds and fantasies that they probably wouldn't even tell their psychiatrists.

Average couples came in frequently, and on several occasions normal people in the throes of an affair would frequent the place with their lovers one week and their husbands or wives the next, throwing me a pleading glance not to betray their secrets. It was a high-dollar place, and I sold many women of all ages their very first vibrator, patiently, calmly explaining the sizes and shapes and functions of each, doing my damnedest to make sure their first porn-shop experience was a pleasant porn-shop experience.

"Dirty Pete," the owner and my boss, was something else entirely. He was an ex-rocker from the eighties whose band had opened for some really huge acts, though he himself had never made it big. With longish, dirty-blond hair that looked like it had been washed with beer more times than with shampoo and a small hoop earring to let the "youngsters" know he was still "with it," Pete had the sad scowl and chubby cheeks of a party animal gone stale. He had drifted into porn and, somewhere along the way, opened up a shop of his own in Santa Clarita.

Between the drugs he doubtlessly still indulged in and his creepy and constantly suspicious Asian girlfriend, Dirty Pete was an increasingly paranoid individual. On the day after he hired me, he installed closed-circuit video cameras throughout the store that he alone could watch from a briefcase monitor. He somehow "forgot" to tell everyone that the cameras also secretly recorded audio. In addition to being paranoid, Pete was scummy, anal retentive, and prone to yelling at everyone and then apologizing to their faces before talking bad shit about them behind their backs. He was one of those people who would promote you the day before he fired you, just to keep you guessing.

He was also incredibly secretive and instructed that if anyone called or came in the store looking for "Dirty Pete," I was to say I had never heard of him. I'm sure he was in trouble, but I didn't want to guess what kind. I worked for him for two years and never even learned his real last name. But I guess he trusted me somewhat; Dirty Pete had plans to one day run a porno empire and promised me that if I stuck with him and remained loyal, he would make me a millionaire.

I had other plans, though.

• • •

After two years of dually managing Dirty Pete's Santa Clarita shop and another one that he owned down on Melrose Avenue in the heart of Hollywood, I was burned out on the porn industry. If you let it be, porn and hanging out with the porno crowd is a twenty-four-hour party that would have thrown even Ricky Moses for a loop. Everyone parties with everyone, and almost everyone fucks everyone else and does drugs. Fortunately, AIDS was a nonissue because of tight regulations created out of the industry having learned its lesson in years past.

During those two years, though, even just existing on the fringe of things, I met porn stars, got high, saw many uninhibited customers naked, and learned to use the word "cunt" in a casual conversation about fucking.

Girls at bachelorette parties at the store, drunk or on drugs, or both, would frequently try to get me to whip my cock out for their delight. But what with me genetically having a fat upper-penis area (or F.U.P.A.) that made my dick look small, particularly in the presence of the monstrous polyurethane-molded cocks I sold, I frequently said no. For a shy, small-town, ex-Mormon, it was an electric, Technicolor, blistering jack-off experience (and that's a good thing).

I wanted to go back to college, though, and focus on getting my degree in advertising, where I would put my creative brain to the test in minting millions of my own dollars. I love advertising. It is a weird hybrid of psychology and creativity that sums me up completely. I am advertising personified, I will explain to you if I get drunk enough.

Advertising makes sense to me in a way that few things in America do. What other occupation in the world allows you to find ways to sell cigarettes to children the day before you write a jingle about diarrhea medicine? Maybe an elementary-school custodian, but that's about it.

Yet as underhanded and manipulative as Dirty Pete was to everyone who worked for him or had been fired by him, he had still given me a job and eventually trusted me enough to give me managerial experience. Perhaps I'm a softie, but I didn't want to leave him high and dry when I left town to go back to college, so I set out to hire someone honest to replace me.

Christopher Simons wasn't even looking for a job when he strolled into the porn shop with his fiancée, Janine. But he was a friendly guy who loved porn and made the mistake of complimenting me on how cool and classy the store looked. I hired him on the spot.

He was a thin black guy and, based on his light skin, probably had some white guy thrown somewhere into his ancestry recently. He wore baggy jeans to match his baggy sweatshirts and smoked cigarettes incessantly. Personable but poor, he was the kind of guy who, if there weren't any people to bum cigarettes off of, would grab a used one out of the ashtray to light up.

Over the weeks that I trained him, Christopher and I would sit and talk about life and what we wanted to do with ours. Christopher wanted to be a record producer and was working with a buddy who had studio access to help move his dream along. I just no longer wanted to work in porn.

One day Dirty Pete and I had a falling out over some money that had gone missing. Whether it really was missing or he was just setting me up as the fall guy that all previous managers of the store had been at one time or another, I'll never know. I set the keys on the counter and walked out. The stores were now under Christopher's command.

I moved down to Orange County, a culture clash of the extremely poor and extremely wealthy, and would never have looked back, except for the day I read in the newspaper about Christopher's murder. He was working my old evening shift, around New Year's Day, when a young man walked in with a gun. The punk stole a two-hundred-dollar Jenna Jameson fuckable pussy and anus mold, complete with a fake pubic-hair landing strip, and on his way out shot Christopher in the chest.

The man shot two other people in the surrounding shopping strip with his small-caliber rifle before returning to the store, fearing that Christopher might have lived. Leaning over the counter, the bastard shot Christopher in the face, finishing him off. The guy then went to a nearby fast-food restaurant, called the police, and shot himself. He lived.

Dirty Pete, the class act that he was, taped down cardboard over the blood and bits of Chris's skull that the coroner couldn't get out of the carpeting and was open for business the next day.

While I had indirectly caused Christopher's death, I never thought I felt guilt over it. But as I'm sitting here typing this now, the article about his death hangs framed on the wall behind me.

At the time, I was angry about what Dirty Pete had done. He was crooked and always terrified of old business partners whom he had doubtlessly screwed over coming and finding him. I knew he was dirty, because I frequently had to commit mail fraud for him, shipping strange packages out to Australia for him and lying to the post office about the contents. I don't know what was in the packages, but it wasn't the clothes and schoolbooks he instructed me to tell the postal clerks that it was.

In the aftermath of Christopher's death, I wanted to bring Dirty Pete down. He'd eighty-sixed his humanity long ago and needed to be taken down a peg. I wrote a letter to the FBI detailing the numerous boxes I'd sent, the days I sent them, and the addresses to which I'd sent them. I didn't know what I hoped the Feds would do, if anything, but I was angry for Christopher and probably for me, too.

The letter sat on my desk, printed and ready, for weeks. I just couldn't commit to dropping it in the mailbox; it felt too much like I was being a rat. I never, ever wanted to be a rat. Finally I destroyed the letter, dropping it into my aunt's paper shredder.

That action didn't feel too good either, so to compensate, any time I told people about Christopher's death, I told them I mailed the letter and that the Feds hadn't done anything about it. That way, at least in the eyes of the people listening, I didn't come off like a coward.

So when people ask me why I got into the crime scene business, I can't say that Ricky and Christopher instantly pop into my mind, but they are definitely baggage that I pull along with me on every scene I work.

It probably was only an intense yearning to finally rid myself of the misery that was retail employment that prodded me into the business of scooping up the dead, though. I had my thumb out on the employment expressway, and crime scene cleaner just happened to be the truck that stopped.

a new hope

Don't worry about life. You're not going to survive it anyway.
—Unknown

THE TWO AND A HALF years I spent working at Beverages & More after leaving the porn biz were dismal, a real drain on my soul. That fact really bummed me out, considering that working in a wine shop was probably the best retail job on the planet. To me, though, that only made it the cutest girl in an ugly contest.

I wanted to be a good and exemplary employee, one of those guys who whistled while he worked and always had a grin ready, no matter what the situation. But retail was retail, no matter how much "sampling" we were allowed to do at the liquor store. All too quickly, the work once more became mind-numbing and repetitive.

I needed something more challenging, more creative, and with my school loans completely wiped out for the year, something better paying. By then, fall of 2004, I was back in school at California State University, Fullerton, working toward my advertising degree. BevMo was flexible around my class schedule, but the well of my humanity was drying up quickly.

While toiling at BevMo, I had begun to grow surly toward the customers and increasingly lazy in my job performance, which swerved violently against everything that I had resolved to do as a retail employee. During the day, while the manager (shockingly, a really good guy) was there, I would perform above and beyond expectations in my menial tasks as a way to endear myself to him.

The second he was gone, though, I would head into the stockroom and crack open a few German beers while whiling away the hours playing mini-golf on the store's inventory computer. If the night supervisor was finally able to convince me to get off the computer, which he frequently couldn't do, I would go outside under the guise of gathering shopping carts, only to disappear into a nearby Circuit City for an hour to browse their DVD selection.

It was as if I was subconsciously begging to get fired but smart enough to realize that I needed the income, so I would eke out what needed to be done while the manager was around, just enough good work to make him think that the night supervisor was full of shit.

I was living in a one-bedroom apartment in the ramshackle, dust-bowl north territory of Orange County. The Joads would have flipped their shit if they had moved from the scenic Midwest and wound up in dismal North Orange County. The more prototypical Orange County residents derisively referred to the area as "NORCO." It's the industrial sector of Orange County, a place mostly left out of that show *The O.C.* A lot of the folks who cleaned estates and mowed lawns for the elite living in "South County" commuted down from their homes around me in NORCO.

I was living with my brother Chris, four years my junior. He wanted to follow in my father's footsteps and be an entertainer, maybe the next David Letterman or Jon Stewart. Chris was a tall, handsome but chubby kid who spent hours every day on a skateboard until he thinned out. He worked at Home Depot, and Disneyland before that, while attending a junior college in the area with an emphasis on TV and radio broadcasting. Chris and I were not all that close growing up, but as adults struggling to survive on our own, we were bonded in the manner of best friends. Lacking money, know-how, or experience, we forged an existence that was both sour and sweet, taking on adversity headlong because we knew no other way.

When we moved in, there was no refrigerator in the apartment. Neither of us had a truck or knew anyone in the area, so we ended up buying a fridge at the local Goodwill store and pushing it on a dolly the two and a half miles through the ghetto streets and hills back to our apartment, mocked by thugs and passersby along the way, only to find out the fridge was too big for the kitchen. As Charles Dickens wrote in *A Tale of Two Cities*, "It was the best of times; it was the worst of times…"

We lived in Sycamore Terrace, the most affordable apartment complex in town. Well maintained, the complex was built on the edge of the dangerously seedy area of Fullerton, the kind of place where white guys had no business jogging or riding skateboards at night. But for two brothers sharing one bedroom, the price was right at nine hundred dollars a month, plus utilities.

The neighbors were nice folks, if not all a bit clichéd. Across from us upstairs, we had the snooty couple who never talked, even when we said "hi" to them. Downstairs from them was a hardworking Mexican family with a young son who rode his plastic-molded car up and down the cracked pavement of our shared walkway.

Next over was the fitness addict, Doug, who could never remember our names and always had ridiculously hot-sounding women over to his house for drinking, smoking weed, and sex of the rough variety. We rarely saw the women, but through concrete walls that were more water than rock, everyone could hear them. Regularly, Doug would strut around the complex, shirt off to showcase the thin, red slits raked the length of his back that could only have been made by fingernails in passion.

Chris and I spent many nights on the patio, drinking beers, playing chess, and enjoying the company of the occasional passerby. It was a nice place, maintained by maintenance guys who looked like ex-cons and made you want to hide your electronics equipment before they came to service your apartment. I could have called it home for a long time.

• • •

But the good times couldn't last. I was enrolled in school, working as many hours as I could squeeze around my class schedule, and paying monthly dues to a school fraternity I had joined to make friends. I had barely enough cash to survive as it was—the proverbial weeks of eating nothing but ramen noodles and drinking non-Blue-Ribbon Pabst (yes, they have another, *cheaper* brand) were a big part of my life. And then the apartment complex raised the rent.

I didn't like to think it was a personal attack; I'm sure they raised everyone's rent. But it was a little suspicious, because not too long before the rent change, the apartment complex had stolen my car.

Let me explain: I raced out of the apartment one morning, fairly running toward my car, already close to being late to work at BevMo. I was in the midst of an experiment to time out exactly how long it would take me to get to work and punch in with not a moment to spare. This particular morning, I was already playing to the late side of things.

Stopping short of the parking area, not quite seeing my car in the space where I thought I had parked it, I was nonplussed. During this period of my life, days and nights were a little blurred together, and as a result, I wasn't always sure where I had parked my Cavalier.

I jogged around the perimeter of the apartment complex twice, frantic now as I became certain that the car was no longer there. The place had an electronic gate around it, so I was doubly worried about the abilities of high-tech thieves preying on shitty red sports coupes. Sweating, gasping, and desperate to remember if I had paid the anti-theft insurance premium that month, I floundered into the complex office to report my vehicle stolen.

The assistant manager, a fat lady with eyeglass lenses doubtlessly made from the viewing ports on a space rocket and nappy hair that would have been a delight to Don Imus, sat behind a desk glowering, almost awaiting my arrival. I told her my plight, and she splayed a collective of Polaroids on the desk between us.

"Was it one of these?" she cackled.

The Polaroids were close-up photos of car license plates that looked trapped in the square frames of their pictures. One of them was indeed mine. I nodded my head yes.

"The car's registration was expired, so we had it towed," she said cruelly.

My car's tags had expired in October, and this was now the first week of November.

"I thought you guys were an apartment complex, not a tow company," I said, incredulous. Other than mentioning that towing companies paid a nice kickback to apartment complexes to have vehicles towed off their property, she didn't feel like discussing the matter. Then she told me where I could pick up my car. It didn't seem to matter to her that my tags were, in fact, paid up and somewhere in the mail.

I was able to catch a ride to the tow company from my sister, who was in town meeting a potential roommate. To both of them I looked like a total loser. My boss at BevMo, good guy that he was, ended up being completely understanding.

At the beginning of the next month, when I paid our rent, I underpaid by $210, the cost of the towing fee, which I felt I had been improperly charged. I included a letter in the rent envelope "from my attorney" detailing how the apartment complex had wronged me and how the cost of the tow was theirs to pay.

I thought I had gotten away with it, and that the karmatic powers of the universe had sorted themselves out. However, a couple days later I received a call from the apartment complex manager. She was a curvaceous Latina girl with big boobs and low-cut shirts to match, and she definitely had the fiery temper to round out the equation. To this day, I can't explain quite what she said to me, but her tone was that of wicked and icy non-restraint, full of innuendo for a fate easily worse than death.

My only response was something to the effect of, "Ma'am I am terribly sorry about all this. I will come in this evening and give you a check for the remaining balance."

It was like getting chewed out by Satan. I wanted to continue my crusade and fight the good fight, but this bitch had caught me off guard and knocked me cold. I had never considered myself a pushover, but here was a test of manhood, and I was evidently lacking. With one phone call, she had reduced my sensibilities to that of a child's. My will defeated, I paid up.

Amazingly, though, I received a check from the tow truck company a couple weeks later, compensating me for the full amount of the tow. I think it was the apartment complex's way of admitting that they'd been ticky-tack assholes, but it was the sweetest moment of my life up to that point, and I would have framed the check were we not running precariously low on that aforementioned Pabst.

When the apartment complex suddenly raised our monthly rent by more than $170 a month, I couldn't help but wonder if that apartment complex manager wasn't Satan after all. She had placed what I thought I had wanted in front of me, only to snatch away something far more valuable, my home.

Chris and I couldn't afford that kind of increased payment, and our options seemed to be: 1. We could crawl back home to Eureka, defeated, or 2. Be homeless. My brother was enthusiastic about the second option, having always wanted to embrace his earthy, hippy side. I, on the other hand, was more inclined to create a third option.

My fraternity had a large house on Fraternity Row that was essentially four two- and three-bedroom condos linked together. I knew they had a single empty room, and Chris and I could be just the guys to fill it. The fraternity graciously suspended their bylaws to allow my brother, a nonmember, to move in. Chris and I were now officially and unofficially frat boys.

While the rent was cheaper living in a single room of the frat house, the kitchen wasn't something you wanted to cook in, due to the high proliferation of cockroaches and ants constantly investigating any and all food items. And so the cost of eating out for every meal put us right back in our original quagmire. We were also having a fine, drunken time on a nightly basis, which further drained the wallet. So the bottom line was that not only did I need to find a new job, something out of retail, but it had to pay better, much better.

• • •

Dirk Whitmore was a sheriff for the Orange County Sheriff's Department, working in the evidence storage rooms as a property handler, one of those "civilian cops" who didn't seem to want to walk a beat and be a real cop. Dirk also had a side job as owner of a DJ business that he managed on nights and weekends. But Dirk, like me, was after more money, and had grown weary of spinning "Celebration" for drunken revelers at graduations, birthdays, and funerals alike.

Somewhere along the way, he had happened upon a fairly new industry that was poking its uncertain head around Orange County, crime scene cleanup. Always having been more of a doer than a thinker, Dirk immediately contacted one of the forefathers of the crime scene cleaning industry, a guy named Schmitty.

I don't know how the industry started, but the occupation of crime scene cleaner seems to have emerged out of the late eighties or early nineties. Like a teenager's acne, at first there were no crime scene cleaning companies, and then suddenly there were several, each spawning itself and wholly independent from other companies in other cities.

Schmitty himself got the idea around 1995 from watching the movie *Pulp Fiction*. In one scene a character called "The Wolf" aided the protagonists after they'd accidentally shot someone's head off in a car. The Wolf showed up and discreetly helped them clean up the mess. Schmitty wanted to be The Wolf.

Schmitty had been running a crime scene cleaning business out of Oakland, California (a dynamite place to have a crime scene business, considering the 145 murders there in 2006, not to mention suicides and other deaths). He agreed to let Dirk attempt a franchise in Orange County.

For a week, Dirk trained with Schmitty's crew in Oakland, during which time he witnessed them charge a little old lady in excess of twenty thousand dollars to gut her home after a police raid. A criminal had broken in while she wasn't home; a standoff with the police had occurred; and gas pellets fired into the house by the officers pretty much made the place and its contents uninhabitable.

Dirk realized there was money to be made, especially in Orange County, where the rich are very rich, and the poor are very armed and jealous. Dirk sold the DJ business to an employee of his and offered the rest of his employees a stake in his new business. The employees, being more comfortable spinning records than sweeping up what was left of someone's grandpa, all declined the invitation.

I was interested in crime scene cleanup the minute a BevMo coworker told me it existed. The coworker introduced me to Dirk, and I was on board right from the first call he made to my cell phone in late November. I neglected to tell him that I had never seen or smelled a dead body, but I figured it wasn't that important. Anyway, I had a secret.

When I was about ten and my mom was in college, looking into getting her doctorate in psychology, she and I would go on road trips to the University of Oregon to assess their doctorate program. These were special bonding trips between mother and son that the other kids in my family were either too young or too busy to go on. I liked the trips because I got to miss school and feel for a couple days like I was the favorite kid. But more importantly, on one of these trips I realized my life's work. I was going to be a serial killer.

Before my mother met with professors, she would drop me off at the school's library, leaving me with hours to meander through the shelves and read to my heart's content. I was a prodigious reader, so getting dropped off to wander the U. of Oregon library was something akin to being the proverbial kid in the candy store.

There, in my hunt for Stephen King books that I hadn't yet read, I happened upon a tome much more sinister in nature. It was an anthology of serial killers, complete with gruesome crime scene photos. I was blown away and yet oddly titillated by the grainy black-and-white photos of dead bodies under sheets, skeletal remains, blood, and larger-than-life mug shot photos of men the book described as monsters. Forgetting Stephen King and his now-mundane chills, I curled up as best I could in one of the library's stiff plastic chairs and got to learning.

The killers were a mix of fascinating loners and well-liked funny men, but they all shared characteristics that made my budding pubescent hair stand on end. Serial killers, according to the FBI's psychology files, typically shared three common traits in their history. They were bed wetters; they were attracted to fire; and they were cruel to animals. I had found my people.

I had been a bed wetter, to my immense shame, for most of my early life, right up until my early teens, older than most bed wetters had been when they stopped. In fact, I thought I was going to wet the bed forever and would live alone in mortification for the rest of my life on rubber sheets.

I also delighted in maiming insects, as all young men did, but I made it into an art form. I couldn't wait to get home from school each day so that I could spend my afternoon torturing flies and ants and spiders. At one point I came up with the brilliant idea of spray-painting red ants blue and then depositing them in spider's nests. The spiders, much to my delight, would then descend godlike and bite the struggling blue ants, poison themselves on the paint, and drop down dead, their bodies falling from the web as their silk webbing unspooled slowly behind them. Everybody died, and it gave me enormous pleasure. I was also quite fond of pouring wood glue on anthills to make huge collages of twitching ants intermingled with the dried glue and sand mounds of their homes.

And as for fire, my friends and I once set fire to the back of our house by touching a match to a bowl of gasoline. The fire grew faster than anticipated, and one of my idiot friends kicked the bowl in fear, spreading the burning liquid onto the painted wood panels comprising the exterior of the house. Spraying everything down with water from a nearby hose squelched the fire, but we had to rub mud on the blackened scorch marks to cover up the evidence.

Reading that book, though, everything clicked for me, the bed wetting especially tying me in with the killers and providing a kinship I had never felt before, an understanding of loneliness that no one else could fathom.

When my mom picked me up that day, I wisely told her that I wanted to have a career *catching* serial killers. (My serial-killer cunning and strategizing was already at work.) She promptly drove me to a bookstore, where she bought me a book about serial killers to have for my very own.

The more I read, the more I believed in my destiny. It was almost too logical: profile after profile documented men like Albert Fish, John

Wayne Gacy, and Ted Bundy, and each one was shown to have a higher-than-normal IQ. In fact, serial killers are routinely shown to be smarter than most people, and I was sharp enough to discern what that meant. If these men were proven to be smarter than normal people, their capacity for understanding far exceeded that of a normal person.

Society was clearly flawed in locking up America's intellectuals! It was typical bureaucracy at work when the stupid, terrified of the intellectual, isolated and executed them to maintain the ignorant status quo. At the tender age of ten, I realized that the serial killers were, in effect, the victims. And I was determined to be the most intellectual serial killer of them all.

Matters were made only more concrete when my mom underwent regression analysis therapy and discovered repressed memories that led her to believe that her own father, who had worked for a time as a grave digger, was, in fact, a serial killer who had never been caught. Certain factors, such as locations, a string of unsolved murders in the area at the time, and her father's fascination with death, compounded her belief and increased my joy. It was all a dream come true.

The end of the dream came a few years later when I came across an FBI behavioral list regarding my future line of work. That list basically divided serial killers into two groups: the organized and the disorganized. The organized were the intelligent ones, who kept their rooms and work spaces very neat. They were usually very social and were characterized by how they killed their victims in one place and then left the bodies elsewhere.

The disorganized, on the other hand, were messy, dirty individuals who were most often portrayed as the loners and chronic masturbators. They were more apt to spring out, animal-like, and ambush their victims, leaving them for dead where they were attacked.

Almost as much as I respected serial killers, I respected the FBI and its accuracy in profiling said killers. And to me that FBI behavioral list was absolute. I couldn't help but notice that most of my demeanor put me on the wrong side of the list, the *disorganized side*...the chronic masturbator side. I would be lost among obscure killers like Carlton Gary and David Carpenter.

To me, at the mature age of twelve, being a largely forgotten and, therefore, lame serial killer was a more embarrassing fate than working some bland office job for the rest of my life, high-fiving coworkers and being unnecessarily self-satisfied. I decided to break from my fate, forget the serial killing business, and become smug and boring.

But years later, when the offer came to work around crime scenes, the concept of being around the gore that had so fascinated me in my youth was too sweet to conceive—and part of me wanted to see if I could handle it.

• • •

My first meeting with Dirk didn't happen for several more months, but we eventually met up at a Starbucks by his house in late January 2007. I wasn't a typical Starbucks customer, since coffee tends to run right through me, but I could still pick Dirk out of the early morning crowd because he looked exactly how he sounded on the phone.

His round, observing eyes belied a silly grin, and he had the slightly bulging gut of a married cop who didn't report in the field very often. He looked to be in his late thirties or early forties. I finally sided with his forties because of the two clean bald patches peeking out of his short nest of hair.

"Hi, Dirk?" I inquired, giving him the benefit of the doubt. He beckoned for me to sit and offered to buy me a coffee, but I declined, giving him the same reason I just gave you. He started on a sales pitch, virtually the same thing he had done on the phone two months earlier. I stopped him as politely as I could, informing him that he already had an employee. Whatever crime scene cleaning involved, I was in.

He had a binder full of Xeroxed articles on crime scene cleanup, which he flipped through as he spoke. One headline in particular caught my eye: "Crime Scene Cleaner Makes Six Figures a Year." That was going to be me. That was where I wanted to be.

Our discussion meandered around different topics until finally we got to the money part. Because I was getting in on the ground floor, Dirk wanted to make me a partner, sort of. Since we were a franchise, Schmitty was to receive 50 percent of our gross profit, meaning out of all the money we made, before taking out anything for expenses, 50 percent of it would be shipped off to him. I found that a bit high and unfair, but I didn't have any money to invest or experience of my own to benefit from, so I kept my mouth shut.

Dirk and I would then split 50 percent of the net profit, basically any money left over after expenses. When I was in my late teens, I ran a small T-shirt business, so I knew full well how you could screw people on receiving "net profits." But again, I said nothing, because I was flattered that Dirk would even cut me in for an equal share, especially since I didn't have to put my name on any paperwork.

And besides, it was anything but retail. Half of the net profits seemed like a fair enough start toward making that six-figure income. What I didn't know, though, was that there were still ways to screw someone earning that 50 percent share. I'd find that out soon enough.

Dirk, apparently satisfied with me in person, took me back to his house to get me my crates. His house was on a quiet, curving street in a neighborhood filled with colonial-style homes, complete with grand Grecian columns and wrap-around porches. I would live in a neighborhood like that when I had my six-figure income, I decided.

Crates were the work kits of our business. The woven plastic kind, usually found stocked with gallons of milk at the supermarket, they now contained all we would need to enter the crime scene cleanup world. In the kits we had:

- A jug dispenser containing an enzyme that neutralizes blood-borne pathogens.
- Three color-coded spray bottles, the green one holding Simple Green, the blue one holding Windex, and the red one holding…bleach.
- A heavy silver flashlight with three settings, one for normal light and two for ultraviolet.
- A box full of extra-large black latex gloves, which protected us and made us look dangerously cool.
- A box of furniture-stripping brushes, basically small white brushes with coarse, stiff red bristles for heavy-duty scrubbing on fabric.

- Two rolls of industrial paper towels for heavy-duty wipe-up jobs.
- A bag containing cloth towels for heavier-duty wipe-up jobs.
- A razor for cutting through carpet and mattresses when the job was too heavy-duty for cloth and paper towels.
- Huge, thick, white full-body Tyvek suits for keeping the biohazards out and the farts in.
- Paper masks for breathing in case the smell was light.
- An industrial plastic breathing mask in case the smell was heavy.
- A box of industrial-strength deodorizers for covering up the smell of our chemicals and, possibly, the smell of decomposing bodies.
- A box of industrial-grade black trash bags for containing all contaminants.
- A roll of biohazard tape for marking the really oozy bags.
- Encompassing paint and a roller for when the blood just wouldn't come all the way out, which I didn't understand fully at that point but trusted I would when the time came.
- A bag of extra-potent marijuana for smoking in the truck after the job was over and we needed to "forget." (Actually, that wasn't really in there, but it should have been.)

I packed up my kit with Dirk's assurance that we would meet sometime in the next couple of weeks to do some basic training, where I would learn to use the equipment I had and how to conduct myself at a crime scene.

Before I left, Dirk reiterated the belief that because he was in the sheriff's department and had a lot of law enforcement contacts and friends, we were going to be busy right from the get-go, and I had better be prepared to work hard and make a lot of money. I was definitely prepared to do that.

• • •

My enthusiasm carried over back to the frat house, where I bragged to anyone who would listen about the loads of money I was going to make. "Six figures," I repeated confidently, finally feeling like some aspect of my life was going to have some stability.

The only one not swept up in the hype was my girlfriend of a year, Kerry, who barely acknowledged my enthusiastic slap on her ass. A sensible and fiercely intelligent girl, she was one of those overachievers, destined to do great things in life. She was so smart that Cal State Fullerton hired her to work for them the day she graduated. (Don't tell her I said this, but if she were really smart, she would have gotten into a better school than Cal State Fullerton.)

Kerry worried about AIDS and disease and my safety, and to a certain extent her safety. I laughed and patted her head, reassuring her that once you were making six figures a year, AIDS was basically a nonissue; ask Magic Johnson. She didn't look reassured, though. I had a stack of generic business cards and pamphlets that contained the 800 number for Schmitty's company, which I was instructed to hand out at all the businesses in the area that dealt with death, such as cemeteries, crematoriums, mortuaries, and funeral homes. Chris had nothing cooler to do, so he tagged along.

If I thought the reception to a new business in town that brought something different to the party was going to be a welcome one, I was dead wrong. The general reception at each funeral home and cemetery office was essentially that we were lepers selling hand jobs. They couldn't have been more repulsed if we walked in and told them that we were opening up a rival cemetery, complete with a salad bar, next door.

These people, who charged ridiculous amounts of money to put loved ones in the ground, felt that we, who cleaned up the mess made by those "loved ones," were vultures, feeding on the bereaved. After the tenth reaction that went pretty much the same way, I called Dirk and begged him to let us off the hook. These people were never going to call or refer any business our way, I argued, but Dirk demurred. It was a numbers game, and besides, as he didn't have to tell me, he wasn't the one out there doing it.

What was particularly depressing was the knowledge that there was no money to be made in this door-to-door work. Now that I was no longer retail, I was strictly commission, and in Dirk's eyes this was merely me "doing my part" to help make the company grow.

The last straw came when we visited a cemetery where a man was standing in the foyer crying. He was there to make arrangements to bury his daughter. The funeral director insisted that we say what we had to first, because working with the other guy was going to take a while. If there was ever a moment in life where I felt like a ghoulish vulture, that was it.

I merely nodded an apologetic glance to the man, thrust a pamphlet into the funeral director's hand, and walked out the door. Wanting the responsibility no longer, I threw all the pamphlets and business cards into a nearby trash can. Chris nodded a silent agreement with my actions, and feeling resolute, we headed back to the frat house.

Kerry made sure she was there to rub it in that I had saved myself from working in a miserable industry. I informed her that I wasn't done with the business; I was just done with the disgusted looks of people who weren't going to call us anyway. Besides, we had nothing to worry about: cemeteries and funeral homes were just the icing. The cake was going to be all those "sure thing" business contacts that Dirk had.

If only I'd known.

grandma got blown apart by a remington

Death waits for no man.

—Ancient proverb

ACTUALLY, DEATH WAITS FOR RIGHT before the beginning of a hockey game, an Anaheim Ducks game that I was supposed to attend. It had been well over a month since I had seen or heard from Dirk, and it was showing in my bank account. I couldn't afford rent at the frat house, so I hadn't paid it in two months, and I was still allowed to live there only because my drinking prowess was needed against the Chi Sigs up the block. Chris wasn't faring much better.

Having quit BevMo two weeks after "starting" the crime scene business, I was definitely at Kerry's mercy. My credit card payments had come and gone unpaid, and I was a shoo-in for debtor's prison. I no longer even had enough money to go out and eat, let alone take Kerry out on dates. Instead, I sat in my closet all day counting broken dreams and subsisting on expired bologna sandwiches and warm, flat soda. (That last part isn't entirely true, but it frames the context nicely.)

I was stuck in a new sort of prison, a type of hell that I wasn't sure I deserved. Around the frat, I was starting to develop a reputation as a user, a freeloader who talked a big game about a six-figure income. Feeling cheap, dirty, and nearly bereft of hope, I was tempted to start searching for another job. I still had faith, though, that somehow, someway, I was meant for this line of work.

Kerry and I had scored her parents' season tickets to see the Ducks take on the New York Rangers on March 14, 2007, in what was promising to be one hell of a game if you're the hockey sort. I had donned my J. S. Giguere goalie jersey and Ducks hat for the trip down to the Arrowhead Pond when my phone rang.

"Hello?" I mumbled, not recognizing the number on the caller ID.

"Jeff, it's Dirk," said the voice. I waited curiously, wondering who the hell Dirk was. "We've got one," he eventually said when I failed to answer.

"Oh, Dirk!" I said, the name having finally clicked. (In case you're wondering, his name's not really Dirk. Who forgets a name like Dirk?)

"Can you be at my house in fifteen minutes?"

Another silence, this one was shorter.

"I'll re-give you directions on how to get here." We never had bothered to get together for any sort of training, and now it was too late.

• • •

I arrived wearing my crisp, black polo shirt, smelling of newness. I had a jacket as well, one of those SWAT-style jackets in black with an "Orange County Crime Scene Cleaners" emblazoned patch on the back, but it was warm enough yet, even in late March, to forgo it. Plus, the jackets cost $150 each, and since Dirk hadn't told his wife he'd ordered them, he preferred if I would keep it on the down low.

Kerry had been a split decision on the news of my first job. She was relieved that she wouldn't have to pay the bills entirely but annoyed that I was missing the game. I would be damned if I irritated two women that evening, so I left the jacket in my car.

Dirk was loading his milk crates full of brand-new crime-cleaning supplies into the back of his extended-bed 2500 Chevy Silverado. His crates were black, mine were red, and the truck was gray. The color scheme looked like what I thought a crime scene might. I loaded my crates next to his and nodded, nervous but trying to look upbeat.

"Do we know what we're getting into?" I asked.

"Nah, the guy, Martin, didn't say. It's out in Riverside, though."

I maintained a positive outward appearance but groaned inside. Riverside was a dump. It was a dirty, dusty area from which the poorer people commuted to work cleaning houses for the poor people in Fullerton who were out cleaning houses for the rich people in Laguna Beach. Riverside made Fullerton look like Bel-Air.

It wasn't so much the poor part that got me, though; it was the knowledge that at 5:30 p.m. on a weekday, the freeway would be a parking lot. There was no chance I was going to even make part of the game. It was an hour drive to Riverside without traffic, so with traffic it was going to be misery, and I was already beginning to have butterflies about the mission ahead. Serial-killer leanings or not, this was real.

The most blood I had ever seen was when I was younger and my dad made me take down my tree fort, claiming it made the backyard look like shit. (Plus, at fifteen, I may have been too old for a "secret" tree fort.) I was pissed about having to rip apart the rotting planks attached to the overhang that I called my fort and was yanking at the nails angrily, forcing the crescent head of the hammer to act as leverage in prying the long lumber nails toward me.

One of the nails slipped out too easily, though, and the hammer careened around, completing its arc when its sharp claws stabbed into my forehead. The blood rolled slowly across my vision, dropping down like one of those grand theater curtains, and I was sure I had cracked open my skull like a hatched egg. Death was surely upon me.

I must have been shrieking, because I heard my father's voice below me, annoyed. He insisted that I climb down from the fort by myself, because there was no way he could come up and get me on the rickety ladder that barely supported my weight. I couldn't believe his ignorance; his eldest and most handsome son was going to be worm food in a place the worms couldn't possibly reach.

Neither of us was in the mood for rich irony at the moment, though. The blood had washed out my vision completely, so I carefully put my hand out where I remembered the rusty metal ladder to be, perched against a beam. Descending slowly, the wet red drops plunking down onto my hands, I wondered how much blood was in the human body and how much was left in me.

Guiding me into the house, my father was careful to keep me from dripping onto any carpeting or laundry between the bathroom and the back door, taking his time, unconcerned. I was melodramatic as hell, though, and crying out for last rites, which was a Catholic ceremony, but you couldn't have told me that at the time.

With a washcloth soaked in cool water, my dad absorbed the blood off my face, restoring my sight. With the first glances of my newfound vision, I looked upward, marveling in the beauty of colors that weren't red. It was as if I'd never really seen the world before. (Like I said, I was melodramatic as hell. At that age, my parents had voted me most likely to be a homosexual.)

As I glanced at my wound, I expected the puncture to be raw, exposed, and jagged, a bloody chasm with hints of white skull and pink, pulsating brain peeking through the punctured head vein. Instead, I was disappointed to see only a tiny ripple where the skin of my forehead had been nudged aside barely, resulting in something more akin to an acne scar.

"Where's the rest of it?" I wondered aloud, hoping for some complicated answer about impacted contusions and how sorry my father was for making me take down my childhood playhouse.

"That's it. Cuts on the head bleed a lot even when they're not serious," my dad said, matter-of-factly.

I was robbed. I felt like that kid who didn't get his BB gun on Christmas. Although technically I was doubly robbed, because I never got a BB gun for Christmas either. My parents didn't like guns.

• • •

We finished loading up the truck, adding a wet-dry vacuum and a broom, just to be safe. Dirk gave a quick kiss good-bye to his wife while I gave a long kiss good-bye to my hockey tickets, and we were off.

I could tell the traffic would be bad right from the outset. Lines of traffic snarled around the block, all cars impatiently awaiting entrance to the California 55 freeway heading north. We had a lot of time to kill but surprisingly little to talk about, both of us just exclaiming that we were glad to get a call, me especially.

"The first of many," Dirk said optimistically.

"The first of many," I agreed, daring to dream that it might be true.

I stared out the surrounding windows of the truck as we crept down the freeway, our brand-new tools loaded in back. I was in awe of the vehicles traveling next to us, purposeful, oblivious. They were full of dads and moms and teens and poor Mexican day laborers stuffed into rusty trucks, all headed for home. None of them knew anything about Dirk and me, where we were going, or what we were in for that night.

We finally made our way onto the 91 freeway heading east, and the traffic picked up a bit.

"Do you think you're going to puke?" Dirk asked, smiling.

"No," I said, suddenly uncertain. "You?"

"Nah. I've seen these things before, as a sheriff...course I never cleaned one up before," he added, suddenly uncertain as well.

The traffic let up further, as if God had cleared a path, special for us, understanding our divine purpose. Dirk geared down on the accelerator, nosing the large truck forward faster. I picked up the handwritten directions detailing how to get to the scene of the crime, consisting of a lot of off-ramps and streets I had never heard of before.

Suddenly the truck lurched slightly as we ran over the shredded remains of a big rig's tire, left torn in the road. Dirk yanked the wheel hard, sending the Silverado barreling into lanes of traffic that I didn't have time to hope were clear. I expected a flash of memories—me eating ice cream, my first love, me eating more ice cream, me wondering why my first love said I was too fat to date—but the memories never appeared. Instead, we ended up on the side of the road under a freeway overpass littered with trash, a twin line of tracks behind us, the skid in the dust barely visible in the waning sunlight.

"The tire's flat," Dirk said.

I thought he meant the piece of big-rig tire we had run over, until I noticed that my section of the cab had an unnatural lean to it. It was like God had airmailed a loogie from heaven.

"Shit," I said, cursing in front of Dirk for the first time and not caring how he took to it.

"Shit," he agreed. He hopped out and took the long way around to survey the damage on my side. I clambered out—my fresh, black shirt cool from the air-conditioning that had been blasting inside.

The outside of our large tire had ripped almost completely away from the rest of the rubber and hung down over the rim like a black bib.

"What now?" Dirk asked, unsure.

"We change it," I guessed.

"I've never changed a tire before." Dirk shrugged.

I couldn't believe that I was in the presence of the first forty-one-year-old guy who had never changed a tire.

"I think it's underneath the bed," he said, referring to the spare helpfully.

We both searched around for what I imagined the jack looked like, but we could find only a piece of it. With frustration and night setting in, I climbed under the truck, the dust settling a thin, dirty haze onto my new shirt, but found no conceivable way of freeing the spare tire from its locked mooring under the truck. The only car I had ever owned was my sissy little red Cavalier with its sissy little quarter-sized spare tire that any idiot could put on.

With our special, expensive, blood-detecting flashlights illuminating the phone's buttons, we dialed for a tow truck, Dirk now cursing up a storm.

"Make sure you tell them we're in a dangerous area...the tow truck will come faster," I said, but Dirk was in no mood to take suggestions. Cars whipped along the expanse of freeway beside us, late workers racing home to those warm meals, slowing only to laugh at us as they passed. Dirk called Martin next and assured him that we were still coming, failing to mention the holdup of the tire.

"Maybe Martin has a truck," I postulated after Dirk had hung up. "Maybe he knows how to get the spare tire down."

Dirk shrugged off the idea coarsely and, still not open for input, squatted to survey the pieces of jack we had to work with, mumbling to himself. I wiped the dust from my shirt and arm hair in vain, and wished I had my jacket.

Like a bald, chubby MacGyver fumbling with the pieces of tire jack, Dirk was able to jerry-rig a metal pole that would access the bolt securing the tire housing.

An hour later, no tow truck yet in sight, we had the new tire on and the old one taking up space in the bed, next to our crates. Dirk canceled the now unnecessary tow truck, and we rolled on in the darkness toward a scene we could only guess at.

• • •

The street signs of this particularly rural area of Riverside were handmade and impossible to see while driving at night, so once again our heavy, silver blood-detecting flashlights came in use as we stopped at each intersection and climbed out of the truck to read the murky print. I could imagine banjo-strumming inbreds hiding in the dark and eyeing my crotch like it was a plug of Skoal and some Lotto tickets. After we had passed his house twice going forward and twice in reverse, Martin called us and directed us through his gate at a little before 9:00 p.m.

He was taller and older than I imagined, a mostly bald white guy, most likely not inbred, standing barefoot on his gravel driveway in jeans and a white undershirt. Light blazed out of the front door ajar behind him, illuminating him and making him look angelic: our savior.

"I...I...I...don't know what happened, really," he rambled on, his composure fading in and out. "I went to the store...my wife was sick... has been sick...and well, I wasn't gone very long, but she got ahold of the shotgun, and she took her head off."

My first crime scene was going to be an old-lady shotgun suicide. I felt like I had swallowed a brick. I couldn't think of a more visceral introduction to my crime scene experience.

Tittering with awkward uncertainty, we followed the barefoot Martin across his yard and into his house. The exterior of his faded yellow stucco, ranch-style house looked foreboding among the pale, moonlit "Hoovervilles" of Riverside. It was a low, one-story spread that took up a fair length of land in the rural country. Somewhere in the distance, a coyote howled its presence.

Approaching the front door, a heavy wooden French job, I felt eerie and voyeuristic. Normally I would never see the inside of this home, and in that moment I realized what I liked about working in porn. It wasn't the act itself but the ability to see in past the window blinds and beneath brassieres and up dresses. It was like having superpowers, like x-ray vision or invisibility.

I could walk where others could not, enter where others could not, and do both with impunity. It wasn't the fucking I liked but the power to watch others do it without repercussions. This was an odd epiphany to have at that moment, but I knew that once I walked through the door, my life was going to take on an odd slant, and I anticipated future philosophies of the sort.

I had mentally prepared myself to mentally prepare myself once I got in the house, figuring that I had the time it took to walk from the front door to the bedroom to center my chi or whatever the hell it was that people did to focus for the unpleasant and the unknown. So when I entered the living room and saw the mess, I wasn't ready whatsoever.

Blindly I had assumed that she had killed herself in the bedroom or the bathroom, but no. The view from the front door was unmistakably red and unbelievably pulpy. My eyes may have bugged out, but my jaw stayed firmly in place, as did any bile in my stomach. If I was going to throw up, it would have to catch me by surprise.

My not throwing up was an important contribution to the team effort, as we were supposed to be conducting ourselves as if we did this all the time. I stepped from the front door across the foyer and down into the carpeted living room, which was streaked with red rivers fanning out in every direction.

She had been sitting in a recliner in the once-white room, next to a little table holding her eyeglasses, her pills, and her *TV Guide*, the three now streaked with a melon-colored, flesh-toned sponge that could only have come from an exploded brain. Similar streaks, in various sizes and distributions, were etched across the wall behind her and onto a framed pastoral scene of a deer or two. Funny, it wasn't the pink color I was expecting, and yet when I saw it, it was unmistakable, even in dime-size flecks.

The recliner had been hit hardest. Blood was soaking into the fabric, pooling in the corners and accumulating around more chunky red pulp. Starburst like, it had spread from there to stretch out and touch a couch up against the adjoining wall.

I turned to face Dirk.

"You okay?" he asked.

"Yeah…"

"Do you want to do this?"

"…Yeah."

I followed him out of the living room and into the dining room, where the old man had taken a seat at the dining room table.

"She was in a lot of pain," Martin said, and it took me a moment to realize he meant before the shotgun blast.

"It's a bad time, I realize, what with it being so recent," Dirk said, "but it's important that we start tonight to make sure that the stains will come out."

"I understand."

"The cost for us to clean all this up is $750, because we're going to have to take the carpeting and the recliner and the table and everything on the table near her, if that's okay…"

"Probably also the picture," I said softly in my most sincere voice, not quite sure about the correct way to extract money and justify the cost to the grieving.

"I can't pay that."

"We can work with the price…"

"No, no, no," Martin said, his lips and face tightening to reveal a momentarily stiffer, more youthful man, a military man with well-honed reserve. "Look, I'm sorry to call you out here. I know you drove a long way. Just forget it; I'll clean it up myself. I was a pilot; I've seen this stuff before."

My first crime scene wasn't going to be an old-lady suicide.

"Is it the price?" Dirk persisted.

There was a knock at the door behind us, and another old man walked in, this one a few years younger and with a lot more hair. Walking into the dining room, he put his arm around Martin. I turned to go back into the living room, feeling more comfortable with the blood and guts than I did with the human emotion.

"This is my neighbor, Fred," I could hear Martin announce from the next room. The rest of the house was clean but not sterile. It had a lived-in look that suggested that the folks who resided here had done so a long time. It was dark and the air smelled musty, like a comfortable cave.

Portraits of the couple hung on the opposite wall. I couldn't discern their features, but I recognized Martin's vague outline in them. There were also several metal placards advertising beer companies of which I had never heard. These accumulations of a full life lived made me feel a little better about the old lady's actions. If I had spent my life collecting as many metal beer signs as she had, I'd probably kill myself too.

I walked outside to suck in some night air and leaned up against the truck, not sure how to respond. I felt terrible that we were taking the old guy's money, but I was going to feel a hell of a lot worse if we had driven all the way out here only to stare at the scattered meat chunks of some old lady's face and not get paid, especially when I was undoubtedly worse off financially than the old coot. It no longer felt like this job was a divine mission from God to fill my bank account—hell, I couldn't decide if I believed in God at all anymore.

Dirk came walking out to me, nonplussed.

"We're going to do it," he said, emotionless.

"Yeah?"

"Martin's in shock. His neighbor convinced him to do it. But we're doing it for $435. I dropped the price because we're going to leave the carpet."

"Can we leave the carpet? Isn't that counterproductive to the whole crime scene cleaner philosophy?"

"No. We don't clean it if they won't pay for it." He grabbed his crate. "Let's suit up." I guessed I could believe in God for a little while longer.

• • •

The Tyvek suit—or "bunny suit," as we called them—was incredibly hot even in the cold air of Riverside. Stepping into the house covered up to my neck in a protective biohazard suit was like turning on a hair dryer in a pup tent. Sure the blood couldn't get in, but the sweat couldn't get out. Now I knew how the scientists who killed E.T. felt.

"Where do we start?" asked Dirk, suddenly nervous about things, which made me scared as well.

"I guess the recliner," I said, figuring that once it was out of there, the major part of the mess would be isolated.

"It's too saturated with blood to cut into it here," Dirk said, shaking his head. "We should carry it out intact and deal with it later."

Between us, we lifted the recliner awkwardly and then moved slowly, the weight of it more than we had anticipated. We heaved it out at last, though, through the French-door entrance and into the yard, where it sat in the dead of night for the neighbors to gawk at, and the coyotes to gnaw at, while we dealt with the rest.

With permission, we bagged up the pills, *TV Guide*, and eyeglasses for disposal, along with a trash can filled with wadded tissues that had caught some heavy hunks of grandma. We were going to toss the painting as well, but Martin begged us to clean it. "It was her favorite," he said, dazed.

I had just started on the walls, scrubbing at the crimson-splattered drywall with a furniture-stripping brush when I heard the sound of dialing from the dining room, followed by an echoed ring, eerily loud, and then another one.

"Hello?" The unassuming female voice came out of the ethers.

"Hi, sweetheart," Martin said slowly, loudly, unaware. "It's your dad."

"Hi, Dad, what's up?"

She didn't know.

There was a pause, and then Martin said, "Oh, your mom…she…accidentally killed herself with a shotgun today."

He was telling his kids via speakerphone while I was in the next room, scrubbing up mom's "accidental shotgun mistake." Worse than any part of the recliner and its gloppy, undermixed-paint look, worse than the thought of leaving the carpet, had to be overhearing that phone call.

"Oh, my God, what?" An instant release of tears mixed in, so that the words sounded fuzzy, but they were unmistakable and painfully horrible. I scrubbed harder, the coarse bristles doing their damnedest to drown out the rest of the phone call, but it came through crystal clear all the same.

"She loved you guys…you know that," Martin said gravely, and the shrill, unrelated cry of an ignorant and wanting child reverberated through the phone's receiver. "She was just so sick, and so tired, and she hurt, and it was just her time," Martin continued, his voice gravelly but unwavering.

I imagined I was listening to an iPod, the volume notched up, blaring out some rock song with thumping drums, but the only song my imagination could effectively conjure up was "The Star-Spangled Banner." It did the trick. I even hummed along aloud, wiping away the red blood from the white walls and feeling blue the entire time.

We had finished the wall and hit the spots on the couch that we decidedly weren't going to take, mostly because there wasn't enough room in the truck for it, and were starting to feel pretty damn done about things, when I noticed a wall in the hallway that somehow, some way had caught a good amount of the spray. The guts looked like caterpillars trying to inch into the darkness of the next room, but we used our flashlights and got them, too.

My suit was shredded at the knees from inching along the carpet to access the length of wall up to the brick fireplace. Blood had seeped into the fabric, and I prayed it had not breached the plastic lining separating it from my pants. But I still felt fairly good about the job we had done, despite the fact that the carpet still looked horribly streaked and bloody.

Regardless of it not being implicit in the contract we had drawn up, we removed any and all chunky spots from the carpet, leaving only bony branch lengths of blood soaked in. I stood, ready to carry out my crate, strip off my bunny suit, and find an all-night convenience store with a cooler full of Dr Pepper. Dirk had even managed to save the painting by decontaminating it with the enzyme and then scrubbing lightly at it with a brush so that only some of the oil paint smeared. I was proud of us.

Then I heard it. "We missed some."

I followed Dirk's finger, pointing at the ceiling, where, mixed in with the dust and stucco, there were some unmistakable chunks of that melon-looking brain matter, too high for us to reach safely without a ladder.

Exasperated, I said, "I got this," and stepped up the two feet of the raised brick lip of the fireplace. Holding on to the oak mantel with one hand so that I could hang off the edge of the fireplace and extend upward, I reached out over the carpet toward the ten-foot ceiling, with my free hand gripping my brush.

Stretching my left arm as far as it would go, I could just barely reach the ceiling. Scrubbing at the patches of brain, I rolled them into tight cocoons from the friction. Stucco dust dropped from the scrubbed areas overhead, and I blinked once while continuing my work, until as I opened my eyes, I felt the gentle, cold splat of something soft connect with the naked orb of my right eye.

Automatically, I blinked again, but it was still there. Dropping down, I reached my latex glove toward my eye but then thought better of it and stripped the glove off quickly. Trickles of sweat ebbed from my pale fingers as I shook loose the feeling of the powder resin from the glove. Using my thumb and middle finger like fleshy tweezers, I managed to extract what was undeniably a hunk of melon-colored brain that had become stuck to my eyeball. I stared at it, incredulous—praying the sweet little old lady with a table full of medicine vials didn't have AIDS—and then dropped it into the trash bag with its friends, Dirk staring all the while.

"I guess we should wear goggles from now on," he reasoned matter-of-factly. I couldn't decide how I should have reacted, so I just rolled with it good-naturedly. We were "professionals" after all, and this sometimes happened to professionals, right?

Bagging up the rest of the mess, we threw some black trash liners over the carpeting and once more tried to reason Martin into letting us take it.

"No, no…I'll throw newspaper over it," he maintained. Shrugging, we once more turned on our blood-detection flashlights, letting the intense ultraviolet purple beams wash over the area, showing Martin there was no blood left. "Good job, guys," he said softly. "Really nice work."

Hoisting the recliner into the back of the truck at 12:30 a.m., along with the bags and the little table, I was glad he didn't let us take the carpeting after all. I was sweaty, exhausted, and repulsed, and my new shirt hung wet and limp around my skin. Driving home with the blood-soaked, chunky recliner sticking out of the truck bed like a gleaming beacon, I was surprised that we escaped cop detection. Dirk being a sheriff or not, there had to be something not OSHA-compliant and illegal about our method of biohazard transportation.

The two of us were tired, so Dirk decided to leave the recliner and bags in the truck to deal with later, and let me go home. Soaked with sweat and dusty from the Riverside experience, I pointed my little red car in the direction of the frat house. Kerry and Chris were eagerly waiting for me on the front lawn when I walked up slowly, stumbling, dehydrated, and exhausted.

Kerry had taken Chris to the game in my place, introducing him accidentally throughout the night to her parent's seatmates as "her brothers' boyfriend." The Ducks won, but that story paled in comparison to my own, which I gladly regaled my listeners with, complete with photos taken specifically for this moment on my cell phone.

I hadn't made enough money to pay rent that month, much less my credit cards, but in the eyes of my doubters, I was vindicated for the moment at least.

the minister and the stairway to heaven

If Jesus Christ came back to Earth today, the last thing he'd be is a Christian.

—*Mark Twain*

VINDICATION DOESN'T BUY WHAT MONEY does. All vindication ever bought anyone was a little freedom. And I had too much freedom—so much, in fact, that my bills still weren't getting paid. Sure, I'd thrown small piles of cash in all of my creditors' directions, enough to let them know I wasn't trying to screw them, but not enough so that they would stop calling me.

I was confident, though. I'd broken my cherry, popped my bubble, shot my load—whichever sexual euphemism best applied to cleaning up "Grandma Shotgun," as I'd taken to calling her.

Another month slipped by, and I was still boasting about her to my frat cronies without a shred of new story material on the horizon. Dirk called me every other day to reassure me that he was working on scaring up new clients, but he was so tonally awkward about the lack of business that I didn't have the cojones to ask about his "surefire business connections" within the world of law enforcement.

He asked if I wouldn't mind calling a few of the law enforcement agencies in the area during our downtime to see if I could scare up some business on my own. Despite having cleaned up the splatter of Grandma Shotgun together, in my mind we still weren't fully in business together. As far as I was concerned, I was still more or less auditioning for the part of his partner.

"Sure," I said, trying to sound confident. "Send the list of contact numbers over on email."

I've mentioned that I'm shy, but let me convey to you the scope of my shyness. I hate talking to people. I can't make small talk; I can't chitchat. It's hard for me to even have in-depth conversations with neighbors. Job interviews have always been a nightmare. Typically, I just write off my chance of getting the job if there's more than a cursory interview involved.

I only got the job at the porn shop because after they interviewed me (an interview that, typically, went poorly), they hired some other asshole. And when the mother of that guy, who was in his thirties, found out where he worked, she came down to the store and loudly chewed him out. They fired him on the spot. The owners needed someone else quickly, and I was the first applicant to call them back.

I try not to go into stores alone; I don't eat in restaurants alone. I tend to avoid doing things that require me to talk to people I don't know. I'm like J. D. Salinger but without the talent. So imagine my excitement about trying to solicit business from policemen.

The police and I have had a rather *sturm-und-drang* relationship over the years. Authority, particularly when used with the word "No," has amped up my dislike for social interaction. The police, who always seem to secrete a sense of false authority, make me the angriest. Obviously they have a very real authority, no matter what I say about their secretions.

One cop in particular contributed to my sentiment for those boys in blue with their guns and rules. "Officer Butler" first came into my life when he stopped me for "driving erratically." I was eighteen and had my driving permit. (I never wanted to drive, but my parents were sick of chauffeuring me to work.) I was driving with a girl who was over twenty-one.

I wasn't driving erratically, but it was a Saturday night and I figured that Officer Butler created a reason to pull me over to see if I'd been drinking. (See also the famous police excuse that "The light over your license plate is out..." If they say that, ask if you can get out and check.)

I hadn't been drinking, but when Officer Butler found out I only had a learner's permit rather than a license, you could see the authority blast through him. Butler was the type of police officer who wore his riot gear all the time, even though that stuff was optional. For him, finding me with just a learner's permit was like Christmas in July or a Kentucky redneck cornering a "faggot."

A little sneering smile crossed his face as he said something about how I wasn't supposed to be driving with a learner's permit. I pointed out that I was over eighteen, my passenger was over twenty-one, and I was well within the scope of the law. Officer Butler didn't like that, but he evidently didn't know the law himself. He concluded our introduction by telling me sternly that he could impound my vehicle and arrest me if he wanted, but this time he was letting me go with "just a warning."

Over the years, he also handcuffed Chris and drove him home for skateboarding outside a bank, and then stopped my mother for driving at dusk without her headlights on and accused her of drinking. My mother is a lovely Mormon lady who absolutely does not drink—and he hassled her.

You might side with the policeman, saying he was just doing his job, but later Officer Butler shot and killed an unarmed man outside a grocery store. That tells you the type of policeman he was. So after he harassed my mom, who truly is the sweetest person on earth, I decided that forever after I hated policemen.

As I've matured, my opinion on policemen has changed somewhat. I recognize the good, even heroic, and other thankless things that they do. Now there are several whom I work with on a regular basis and some I wouldn't hesitate to call friends. But then, even though my new boss was a cop, I didn't want to call other cops and beg them to send us business.

Dirk, not noticing the reluctance in my voice (or more likely, choosing to ignore it), said he'd email the list of law enforcement agencies right over. Being the forthright person that I was, I printed the list and set it in my "Fuck That" pile, right under my subscription renewal for dick-enlargement pills.

• • •

In the meantime, the horror story I told people about my one and only crime scene was rapidly growing in detail and intensity. At this point perhaps I should mention that I have a tad of dissociative identity disorder, also known as multiple personalities. While I'm not as bad as my mother, who reverts to a childlike state of innocence every so often, for all my shyness there's another aspect of my personality where I turn into a complete chatterbox.

That aspect of my personality got me elected senior-class president in high school, nearly got me sued four times as a writer on the school newspaper, and had me give a hilarious speech at graduation while wearing a huge sombrero. The dichotomy of my two personalities is unsettling, to say the least. Basically, whenever I feel vulnerable, the shy guy takes over; when I have something to offer, I am untouchable.

So when I was before a crowd of peers telling my crime scene story, it grew to include my talking the old man out of killing himself and finding the dead lady's cache of Nazi paraphernalia. An attractive girl in the group would then ask for another story, and I had to awkwardly inform her that there weren't any more. I was a one-trick pony.

But that was about to change.

Dirk called me up out of the blue one day and told me to pack up my crates. We were off to Claremont. Claremont is a small city along a major highway about twenty minutes north of Fullerton, but more importantly, it's in Los Angeles County. That was the big time for us.

We had started a crime scene company in Orange County not only because my boss lived and worked there, but also because Los Angeles was teeming with crime scene cleaning companies. Mongol hordes in the form of rival companies virtually had the metropolis on lockdown. And now we were on our way into their outskirts to do their work and see what sort of crime scenes they had to offer.

We pulled up in the middle of a pleasant suburb, parking on a tree-lined and well-lit street that was the polar opposite of Riverside with its sewer breath. A small off-white home that might have housed Ward Cleaver and his brood sat proudly among other homes equally as proud. The police car out front was the only indication that something was askew in this charming little neighborhood.

At the front door, not knowing what else to do, we rang the bell, hoping that this was the right address. It would be very awkward if we'd gone to the wrong house and someone answered the door only to find two men standing there wearing polo shirts that read "Crime Scene Cleaners."

A pleasant policeman in uniform answered the door and led us into the well-lit home. This time I had prepared myself for the sight before we knocked, effectively readying myself for a scene where neither of us knew what to expect.

The house was immaculate, and I wondered how the owners had the time to keep it so clean. My first crime scene had been a well-lived-in ode to all things collectible, but this house was most definitely what I thought of as a home. Plain and uncluttered, it seemed as if it could be a showroom for other houses, featuring the dream layout your home could have if you bought one of the surrounding properties.

Only a few picture frames, not hung on the wall but instead standing freely on the polished tile countertop separating the kitchen from the dining room, indicated that anyone lived there. One picture in particular caught my attention. It was of a middle-aged man who was bald on top but had a crescent ring of hair that started above one ear and carried around to the other. The man's thick glasses made his eyes appear owlish and almost perennially surprised, and a short, small grin betrayed an otherwise serious expression. But it was the view over the top of that photo and into the kitchen that stopped me short.

A pond of blood, the circumference of a throw rug, lay on the smooth linoleum of the kitchen floor as though someone had dropped the world's largest red egg onto it. And in the center, comprising its yolk, was a piled-up, large crimson mass with a jellylike consistency.

Aside from the sight of the horrifically unidentifiable mass, which I speculated was a brain, and the pool of blood around it, the kitchen was as sterile as the rest of the house. I found it odd that there was no body, but residual trash from attending paramedics told me where it had gone.

"He was a minister," the older of the two policemen said, emerging from a back bedroom to fill in the blanks. "He shot himself in the head with a pistol."

"Who should we get to sign the invoice?" Dirk asked.

"Oh, the wife's down at the hospital. She took it pretty bad. They gave her something to calm her down, so…I guess we'll sign for it," he answered.

"It's going to be nine hundred dollars," Dirk said evenly, and I almost gasped aloud. In the car on the way over, we had talked about how we were going to charge more money for this one, regardless of the scene, because our half of $435 split two ways wasn't going to cut it. But nine hundred dollars? The scene was much less serious and still fresh; nine hundred dollars sounded like silly money.

"Not a problem," said the cop, signing off on the invoice. I exhaled slowly, hiding a smile, and got my game face on. It was time to clean.

The same two policemen had picked the minister up on a DUI charge the day before, and rather than face his congregation with the shame of having done wrong, he compounded his "sin" and shot himself.

He'd called his wife on the phone while she was at work in the morning and told her what he was going to do. She had begged him not to and said she'd come home and they could talk, but then she heard a popping sound. She called the police, who beat her to the house and then refused to let her go inside and see what her husband had done to himself.

I noticed that small traces of blood had been tracked onto the carpeting and a large rug in the dining room from when the paramedics, detecting a pulse, attempted to revive and transport the minister to the hospital. He arrived DOA.

Dirk and I suited up, nervous because the cops were hanging around, watchful and curious about what we did and how we did it. I had only a general idea of how to proceed, since my training was still nonexistent and I had only the one previous scene under my belt, a scene that was nothing like this one.

My eyes kept drifting back to that glob of crimson gelling in the center of the blood. It was missing that grayish, melon-colored consistency that I identified with brain after our last job, but I was quick to believe that, like jelly beans, brains came in many different colors.

As we hauled our crates into the house, Dirk whispered for me to follow his lead. We set up in the kitchen, keeping our supplies well away from the mess. Dirk pointed out where the bullet, from a small-caliber revolver, had exited the man's head and slammed into one of the wooden cabinet doors behind him. A small splatter of blood with some tiny chunks of head surrounded the hole, and a piece of the minister's hair hung through the opening like thread through the eye of a large needle.

I started my cleaning there, spraying enzyme onto the cabinet door and letting it drip down to the countertop, showing the policeman that we weren't stingy with our use of product.

"No, not like that," Dirk chided me, giving me the stink eye. He didn't want to correct me in front of the cops, lest the officers think us amateurs and refuse to let us continue. "You don't want to let the enzyme go everywhere and create a bigger mess." He showed me how to spray the enzyme into a paper towel and then wipe the stain away with super-absorbent towels. The Brawny man would have been pleased.

After the cabinet I set to work on removing the stains from the carpeting. Our furniture-stripping brushes handled the job more than capably by not only removing the bloodstains but also taking the color out of the carpeting. The biohazard was gone, but there were two noticeable patches of light carpet and a much lighter area on the rug than had been there before the blood.

"Looks good to me," the officer commented.

It was finally time for the big stain and, with it, that eerie mass of human-something. I tried to wrap my head around how, no pun intended, a small-caliber bullet could blast through a man's skull and knock his brain out the back, where said brain would then land intact on the floor. *Maybe it fell out when he was already on the floor?* I theorized, but that didn't account for the lack of a bullet hole in the glob.

That jellied mass presented a further problem, as our kits had no means to clean it up with. We were in danger of appearing unprofessional in our bunny suits, our white gloves, and our clear plastic goggles, which I'd removed because my breath made them fog up. Brain in the eye or not, I couldn't see with the goggles on.

Finally I remembered seeing a broom by the door leading from the kitchen to the garage and, more importantly, the dustpan with it. Discreetly and using goony hand movements I'd doubtlessly picked up from watching some over-the-top Special Ops program on TV, I gestured to the puddle, then to the dustpan, and finally made a scooping motion that was undetected by our police presence.

Dirk, comprehending (probably because he had watched the same goony program), grabbed the dustpan and, using it like a small shovel, scooped into the mass, separating it from the rest of the blood. It quivered on the lip of the victim's dustpan as I held the garbage bag open.

The jelly brain-mass had a mind of its own, though, and proved to be wilier than the dustpan or Dirk. Slipping back off the metal scoop and onto the floor, it splatted but remained mostly intact. The wet sound it made splashing into the blood almost got to me as I struggled to maintain both my composure and grip on the bag. Dirk scooped again, and this time got it, dropping it and the dustpan into the safe confines of the bag.

The rest of the blood came up easily off the floor, and I was down on my knees cleaning by the stove when I found them—the man's glasses. They were large and thick, identical to the owlish ones belonging to the man in the picture that I'd noticed. A long chunk of dark hair was entwined around the glasses and stuck in the metal connecting rod for the nose grips.

When he fired, his eyeglasses must have flown off his head, taking a bit of hair and some blood with them. I held them up to the policeman.

"I don't think he needs them," I said.

The officer shrugged. The glasses also went into the Hefty bag.

When we were finished, Dirk gave the officers a copy of the invoice and asked how they had heard of us. The older officer responded that they'd worked with us before, a few years back, and really liked our company. Before I could say anything, Dirk responded, "I thought you guys looked familiar."

The whole job had taken us an hour and a half and was the easiest $250 I had ever made.

That night, though, I had a cigar and a glass of Maker's Mark bourbon while contemplating the evening's events. I knew religion fairly well, having been subjected to a particularly strict vein of it for eighteen years, and was familiar with where most churches stood on suicide. Few look upon it favorably. Most add a particular bend that makes it especially unpalatable. A lot of churches, though not the Mormon one, believe that suicide is a hell-worthy offense.

So this man, a minister, a person who earned his living educating others about right and wrong, risked what he believed was a hell-worthy offense to save face in front of his congregation. He must have been enduring a terrible shame. And that made me dislike organized religion all the more.

When you think about it, the Catholic Church's seven deadly sins are pretty much our most basic emotions turned against ourselves. It's only too natural to feel horny (lust), to want more than what you have (greed, envy, gluttony), or to feel angry or boastful about your accomplishments (wrath, pride). Or sometimes a little bit like saying, "Fuck it," and kicking back on the couch with a cigar and a glass of Maker's Mark (sloth).

All of these qualities are presented as things to be ashamed about or feel guilt for. And it was exactly that type of weight that led that minister to kill himself. Out of shame that he could not endure, he chose to make his wife a widow and, if he had kids, to make them fatherless.

Perhaps it could be said that he'd lost his way, that he'd fallen away from his so-called flock. Regardless, clearly the shame induced by the weight of religious judgment took him from a minor sin to what the church would undoubtedly consider a major, if not mortal, one.

His devotion to being the monitor of justice for his average church-goers was so great that he determined he deserved to "burn in hell for all eternity" rather than face telling them he himself had a momentarily faulty moral compass. That religion could wield such power over a person's life further convinced me it was something that should be monitored more closely.

• • •

The next morning, I received a phone call from Dirk. He was doing "sheriff work" that he couldn't get away from, but we had our first trauma scene. I would have to go alone.

A trauma scene differed from a crime scene in that the death involved was of an accidental nature. That is to say, no crime had been committed. Suicide is technically illegal in the United States, so those are still considered crime scenes. However, the bedroom floor where a heart-attack victim lay unattended and died would be a trauma scene.

Our latest was located in Stanton, which is in western NORCO, or North County. Some people in North Corona (part of Riverside, natch) claim they alone should be considered residents of NORCO (North Corona = NorCo), but to me that's like losers begging to be called deadbeats. Stanton's part of a tri-city suckfest of poverty that includes Westminster and Garden Grove, with affiliates in Cypress and Santa Ana. There's a heavy concentration of different cultures in the lower-income areas, and as a result, gangs are prevalent and crime activity is high.

I didn't know what to expect as I drove out there. I felt fairly confident about doing the work, since I'd taken a sort of supervisory stance on our first job. But man, it felt better to have a higher-up along as reassurance that the blame for a job done wrong wouldn't totally be on me.

I was supposed to call a certain number when I got to the trauma scene and speak with the mother of the victim. Instead, a brother showed up—a well-to-do, chubby fellow named Oliver. Though he was sad about his sister's death, he clearly didn't want to be there. He wasn't particularly close to his sister, but their mom wasn't in a good enough state to deal with her daughter's death, and apparently the girl's husband was even worse.

I was shocked to find out that the girl was married; the way Dirk had laid it out for me, a cute little girl had fallen down the stairs and died. I'd been prepping to deal with the emotional heavies that would go along with cleaning up a dead kid, and as Oliver let me in to the two-story house, I was relieved to find the girl had been an adult.

She'd tumbled down a long set of thinly carpeted stairs, landing hard on a stained-wood platform below, where she died. It had to have been a broken neck, I decided, as there were only two small spots of blood on two differing stairs and a small puddle on the wooden platform. The stairs ran down directly along the inside wall of the house, and the platform was a box step behind the front door.

"It was pretty upsetting," Oliver informed me. "Her husband came home from work last night and tried the front door. It was unlocked, but he couldn't get it open. He had to run around to the back sliding door to get in that way, and when he came through the living room, he found that it was his wife's dead body he'd been banging up against.

"He tracked some blood off the platform and maybe onto the carpeting, as well as into the bathroom, where it's on the sink and counter," Oliver told me.

Maybe? I thought. *How could he not know if it had gotten into the carpeting?* And then I really noticed the inside of the home.

The house was easily the dirtiest, if neat, house I had ever been in. There wasn't trash per se all over the floor, but every bookshelf and surface area was loaded with horrifically dusty merchandise from every mail-order catalog known to man…or woman.

NASCAR hadn't yet licensed the merchandise that these people wouldn't buy. Interspersed around Hummel children and plastic figure molds of Ford trucks pissing on Chevy trucks were Native American trinkets with metallic stickers identifying them proudly as "Made in Taiwan." In the spaces where books, magazines, or other tchotchkes weren't crammed, someone had halfheartedly started to amass a bottle-cap collection. The house was an ode to white-trash values. *A crime had been committed here after all…*I thought. *A crime against good taste.*

I'd have chalked it up to extreme collecting and moved on, but then I noticed the really dirty aspect of the house. The level to which animals had taken control of the residence would have made George Orwell shudder. The carpeting had started out as a light peach color, but it was now salt-and-pepper black with literally an inch-thick, intermingling thatch of cat and dog hair coating it, not to mention the floors and sofa. Due to the animals' constant movement on them, the stair mats had been pushed to the sides of the stairs, giving each step a sort of "Larry Fine" appearance.

Poop stains, both large and small, had been laid on poop stains that lay on poop stains that lay on older poop stains. I was fairly certain that if I dug down about four layers worth of poop, I would find fossils from the Miocene epoch embedded within. Newspapers covered the floor in areas, and the atmosphere was thick with the musky foulness of stale air mired in mold spores.

On the wall above the couch hung a large American Indian dream catcher. I wanted to joke that they should have tightened the netting on the dream catcher, but I didn't, more out of shock rather than respect.

I couldn't even find the spots on the floor that might have been blood. I looked over at Oliver questioningly. He was clearly embarrassed about the way his sister and her husband had been living and was still taken aback.

"I haven't been over here in years." He shook his head, repulsed. "This place was my parent's house…it never looked like this."

I checked out the bathroom and found the blood stains to be rather mild, though present on the floor as well as the faucet and counter. I went back to Oliver, feeling bad for him. He was still stammering and trying to make excuses for his family. I could relate—I had always disenfranchised myself when it came to my family's Mormon antics.

"We don't have much money," Oliver offered. "I have some cash… and my mom sent me over with a blank check, if that's okay…"

"How's two hundred dollars?" I asked, figuring for the amount of work that looked to be involved, it was more than fair. I would be out of there in twenty minutes, tops. *Ten bucks a minute sounds reasonable for my time*, I thought. I wouldn't even be there long enough to contract a pulmonary hemorrhage from all of the black mold.

Oliver was shocked that it would cost so little, and I was feeling more than a little magnanimous when I pulled my bunny suit on. *There's no reason I can't brighten people's day*, I reasoned. *Make them feel a little better about their misfortune and make a little money doing it.* It was a business model that anyone could be proud of.

I set my crate down outside and quickly scrubbed the bloodstains out of the two top stairs. I moved down to the bottom platform, where the stained slats of wood had been joined together over a block of concrete. I scrubbed at the stain, which was roughly the size of an average footprint, but it wouldn't go away. I scrubbed again, using more elbow grease, but to no avail.

I realized that it would take more work than I wanted it to, so I moved on, cleaning up the bathroom instead. From there, I worked backward, scrubbing at the stains on the carpeting while Oliver went to tend to the couple's two dogs.

My furniture-stripping brushes were no match for the coarse animal hair that littered the flooring, and as a result, I was scrubbing away at stains that weren't moving. Frustrated, I renewed my attack on them, but it was like burrowing through a coal mine with a dental pick, and the stains wouldn't budge.

Outside, I called Dirk, angry with the reluctant mess, stripping off my black gloves, and splashing my sweat onto the concrete sidewalk. He didn't have any answers for me, and I could detect from his voice that he didn't really give a damn. After all, he wasn't the one doing it.

I turned my attention back to the wooden platform with a renewed sense of determination. If nothing else, at least I would wipe that goddamned stain out.

Twenty furious minutes later, I realized that it wasn't the stain that wouldn't come up, it was *the blood*, bubbling up through the slats. She hadn't died of a broken neck down there on that wooden platform; she'd died of blood loss, and it was all leaking from beneath that platform like a gigantic pustule.

I pulled back the carpeting from the platform as best I could, what with a large bookshelf overloaded with Time Life readers, seashells, and broken trophies weighing the space down. Sure enough, the blood had leeched from the platform and into the insulation of the carpeting, not bothering to come to the surface and be visible but rather hiding, just waiting to fuck me over.

If I was going to do the job right, I was going to have to move the bookshelf, remove the carpeting, remove the bloodied strip of carpet tacking with its rusty, tetanus-infused sharp nails, scrub the concrete, and soak all the blood out of the flooring.

Maybe Oliver would let me off the hook? I dared to hope. He came in from the backyard, and I explained the situation to him. I could tell, as soon as I did, that the situation wasn't going to go my way.

He fumbled for the nicest way to tell me to "go fuck myself" and, unsurprisingly, found the words. With his help, I set in and unloaded the large bookcase. Its shelving creaked under the sudden absence of weight, yet it couldn't quite find its way back from being bowed and at the verge of collapse for so long.

We moved the crap (in the human sense) on top of the other crap (in the animal sense) and were still only barely able to slide the heavy bookshelf out of the way. It threatened to splinter into a million tiny pieces, which wouldn't have surprised me, given how the day had shaped up.

But as we moved it as far as we dared, I was able to use the safety razor to cut away the carpeting. It was a small basic blade, though, not suited at all for cutting carpet. Dulling all too quickly, the blade forced me to hack my way through the carpeting in a spite-filled performance. All the while, Oliver stared awkwardly at me, his goofy fat face reminding me that I needed to eat more healthily myself.

After I shredded the carpet away from the platform, removed the insulation, and dried the concrete flooring underneath, I borrowed a flat-head screwdriver from the couple's garage to pry up the tack strip, handling the thin wood and bunches of sharpened metal gingerly. I couldn't imagine that some tin-pot housewife from the suburbs and nourishing an animal fetish was riddled with AIDS, but I could believe that feces + rust + blood + dirt = something nearly as bad.

Five hours after I started, I had the rest of the blood soaked up and had made considerable progress on the bloodstains leading to the bathroom. The inside of my suit was filled with sweat, while the outside, formerly a sheer white, was a mixture of browns, yellows, reds, and blacks. It looked like a United Nations meeting.

On the front walk, I stripped off the suit, and there was an audible splash as my abundance of sweat hit the sidewalk. It reminded me of the sound that brainlike gelatin surprise had made on the previous job when it took a swan dive off the dustpan. I was further repulsed to discover that some of the animal hair had found its way inside my protective suit. I picked off what I could and searched in vain for its entry point.

Wiping my soaked and reddened face, I felt I'd give almost anything for a glass of water but, despite my desperation, wouldn't take one from that house.

Oliver was grateful, and paid with cash. He even laid an extra twenty-dollar bill on the top with the caveat that I didn't give it to my boss.

"That one's just for you," he winked.

The money didn't look like much in my hand, and when it came back to me in the form of a paycheck, it felt like even less.

Dirk had decided that since apparently we were going to be busy, it wasn't fair that part of his cut of the business went toward business expenses while I walked away with a clean and clear half of a half. So he decided that since I was more a vice president in the company than an independent contractor, I should get a third instead.

Five long hours of work in the sweltering heat of the near summer, working by myself, and I'd made roughly thirty dollars (not including my sweet tip, of course!) for cleaning up serious biohazard. Migrant workers did better than that. Minimum-wage, pimple-faced whiners pushing a button on a cash register made more than that.

Somehow, some way, I had to do something about that.

red riding in the hood

Today I didn't even have to use my AK; I gotta say, it was a good day.

—*Ice Cube*

I'VE NEARLY DIED TWICE IN my life that I can recollect. The first time was my own ignorant fault—I'd gone down to the local beach with my good buddies Matt and Billy, when I was fifteen or sixteen, to shoot guns. You probably couldn't shoot guns off at the local beach, but remember I was only fifteen or sixteen and blissfully unaware of technicalities such as being "tried as an adult for manslaughter."

We weren't shooting the guns at anything in particular, just firing off rounds into the nearby sand dunes to feel tough. Matt had scored the guns, a heavy revolver and a small jumpy pistol, for the day from his boss at work. Why on earth anybody loans guns to children is beyond me. Then again, this was Eureka, where Skoal sales are directly proportional to visiting hours at the battered-women's clinic.

I'd taken control of the revolver, not liking the way that the recoil on the smaller semi-automatic was slicing into the webbing between my thumb and index finger. The revolver felt good to me, true Old West style—a real cowboy's choice. My parents were staunchly against guns and had done a fine job of insulating me from the seductive charms of a loaded weapon in my youth but had damned me into a curiosity about them that would prove dangerously innocent when I finally got to interact with one as a teenager.

Having been taught a fear of guns, rather than a respect for them as a tool for making beer cans explode, I'd never learned about such modern contrivances as a "hair trigger." For those as oblivious as I was, a hair trigger can be achieved by cocking the hammer at the back of a gun, thus vastly cutting down on the amount of pressure required to fire said gun.

Of course, naïve me, upon seeing the trigger ratchet back with the cocking of the hammer, I was certain that I'd broken the boss's gun. And so I turned it toward me, scared shitless that I'd done something wrong and could somehow correct the issue by looking down the barrel. I will never forget the blast of warm wind that licked my skull as the bullet whizzed past, racing up into the wild blue yonder.

In the act of turning the gun toward myself, I had tapped my finger on the hair trigger. The gun went off, missing me by closer than my mom would ever want to know about. After that, I put the gun down and stayed away from its kind for a long, long time.

My second brush with death wasn't nearly as much my fault, and that made it so much more intense. I was out with Matt again; this time he and his girlfriend and I had rented a patio boat. I was an intelligent man now at eighteen, no longer the foolish lout who played with guns.

I'd called in sick to work that day so the three of us could spend a leisurely day zipping around a large lake a few hours northeast of Eureka. (Ironically, Matt had gotten me a job at the same fast-food restaurant where he worked, and my manager was the one who'd loaned Matt the guns so long ago.)

Matt enjoyed playing captain, and I was more than happy to let him, lackadaisically hanging my feet into the lake water as the powerful engine pushed the medium-size boat through the water. She was raised off the water on the port and starboard sides by twin steel pontoons, pointed like ancient torpedoes that kept the flat-panel boat deck off the water.

I was enjoying my time and as carefree as a boy ought to be in the halcyon days of summer when May winds cede regime to the sun's unwavering stare. In a typical moment of dumbassedness, I decided that it would be hilarious if I attempted to go to the front of the watercraft and spread my arms aloft, à la *Titanic*.

This whimsical pursuit works far better if you are on an ill-fated ocean liner and supported by the confident arms of Leonardo DiCaprio and not a 250-pound oaf at the stern of what is essentially a piece of carpeted plywood raised on pontoons that is blasting through the water at twenty-nine knots (roughly thirty-three miles per hour).

Matt, being the intrepid captain manning the wheel, noticed that my large ass was weighing down the front of the patio boat and we were, in fact, starting to take on water. He attempted to slow down, but as our inexperienced collective was quick to learn, there isn't a "slow down" on a patio boat, only a "stop."

The laws of thermodynamics being what they are, I of course continued at the present speed straight off the front of the ship and through the motherfucking air, arms still spread like some messianic jackass. I am a resilient swimmer. (Thankfully, my mother did not hold the same opinion about swim lessons that she held about guns.) So I was able to turn my folly into an efficient dive that, from a viewer's perspective, could almost have been considered graceful.

Now, this is the part that sucks. Left to my own devices, I would have surfaced cleanly, swum back to the boat, had a good laugh about it all, and maybe capped my day off noshing on a delicious peanut-butter sandwich heaped with strawberry jam. Instead, I encountered that wholly unpredictable foil, bad luck.

Matt, you see, was concerned that the now-slack boat might drift over me, and I would hit my head on the bottom and possibly drown. The road to hell is littered with good intentions, and eager to induce some good intent, Matt decided that the smartest course of action would be to drive the boat over me. I had disappeared beneath the surface, and he was hoping that I'd dived deep enough to avoid the undercarriage of the rented patio boat. I hadn't.

I surfaced, eager to share a laugh at my expense with my two friends just as the shadow of darkness that was the patio boat began its pass over me. The whup-whup splashing sounds of the churning propeller blades were omnipresent in the air space afforded me by the sleek gray pontoons lifting the flat-bottom boat off the water.

My screams lost to the roar of the engine, slicing toward me at 29 knots, I flailed in vain at the precision-smooth pontoon metal sides, my arms akimbo again, desperate. This time anything messianic didn't seem the least bit jackassed. I begged at the pontoons to let me crawl forward and escape what I could only register as imminent *death*.

The propeller, part in the water, part out, was spinning too fast for me to make out the individual blades powering the craft that was encapsulating me and was now too close to write off as an escapable nightmare. I would be shredded and emerge as one of those comically red stains in the otherwise serene, blue lake water.

With the same adrenaline coursing through my veins that allows mothers to lift cars off their endangered children, I pushed off from the bottom of the boat, praying to a God I didn't believe in that the effort would be enough to keep me submerged deep enough and long enough so that wicked steel propeller would pass over me and allow me to glimpse daylight again. It wasn't.

My head resurfaced, popping up corklike directly to the left of the passing blades, their razor edges fanning at the tip of my nose with unholy menace. My arms followed my head to the surface, and in a moment too instantaneous to process, my left arm was swept into the twisting thrust of the propeller.

A violent yank wrapped the length of my appendage around the propeller head and swept my beautiful arm up into the mechanical process. A second later, it spat me back out and left me in the boat's swirling wake. I was incredulous to be alive, but certain I was missing my left arm from the elbow down.

And yet when my shoulder extended from the water, there was my arm, intact and aloft. Matt, of course, took my raised hand to be a gesture of thanks for quick thinking on his part and gamely waved back.

A nice long slice ran the length of my arm, not deep enough to warrant immediate medical care but enough to cause me an awkward explanation when I returned to work the next day, bandage wrapped on my forearm and back from being "home sick."

The scar has since faded and is now mostly lost behind hirsute sprigs of dark hair that betray my Eastern European heritage, but the point was not lost on me. Even though we humans control the actions that lead us on our life paths, sometimes an outside influence smashes in and makes the decisions for us.

• • •

Dirk called me up a couple of weeks after my gig at the Animal House to let me know that once again we had business. But he wanted me to come down to Santa Ana, where he worked, to talk about it.

I had never been to the sheriff's department, or any police station, for that matter. So, as a kid from a small town with no inner-circle access or political connections, I was pretty hyped about my visit. I had visions of walking down a concrete row with prisoners eyeballing me, catcalling, and maybe even spitting on me.

But I'd be grim, resolved, and wouldn't let 'em see they got to me. *I've got my freedom, and they don't*, I'd think. Then, as we were leaving, I would grab my balls and flip them all the bird, letting them know that the whole time, they were the ones getting punked.

What a disappointment when Dirk asked me to meet him in the alley.

Our latest was a special case, a murder. A sixteen-year-old gang member had been riding in the passenger seat of his parents' car, driven by one of his cousins. A rival gang rolled up on them and opened fire. It was an assault from the front and side; the driver was wounded, and the kid in the passenger seat was blasted apart. Bad luck is a son of a bitch.

The car had been through all the steps: it was towed from the scene, forensics did their kit, the car was impounded, and then finally it was released to the parents. Now it was sitting in their driveway, bloodied, riddled with bullet holes, and in serious need of a cleanup. The parents were hoping to salvage it, since it was their sole means of transportation. There was just one problem—communicating this to me. They didn't speak a word of English, and I only knew cuss words in Spanish. I would need a translator.

When I was in high school in my twenty-seven-thousand-person town, there was a requirement that in order to graduate you had to take two years of a foreign language. The choices were French, German, and Spanish. The smart kids, recognizing the direction the world was heading, all took Spanish. The second smartest group of kids, wisely identifying that two business languages of international trade were English and French, chose French. The dumbasses all took German. Guess which one I took? *Ja, und ich sprechen sie Deutch nicht so gut, senf.* (Loose translation: Yes, and I don't speak German very good now, mustard.)

To help me with the language barrier, Dirk called in a favor from a coworker named Leslie, who would help translate the negotiations between me and the parents of the victim. She was a few years older than my twenty-six and only vaguely Latina-looking. But as long as she spoke Spanish, she could have been from the un-planet Pluto for all I cared.

I took Dirk's truck for the gig; the fear was that there would be a lot of stuff to get rid of from the scene and my little red Chevy Cavalier, with its broken trunk that hadn't been opened in three years, wouldn't quite cut it. My Cavalier was an embarrassing vehicle to roll up to a crime scene in anyway. I had long been teased for having a "girl's car" and had compensated for that by never washing it, so that it would at least appear masculine and grungy.

Of course, when you are a cleaner by trade and you arrive in a filthy vehicle, your clients tend to cast a wary eye at you. I relished the opportunity to take the truck when I could. Besides, the truck meant my not losing out on gas money that I otherwise wouldn't be compensated for.

Leslie drove a little hatchback. Though she was officially a police officer, she wore civilian clothes and did office work, like Dirk. While I was en route to Dirk's office, he had briefed her on the address and location. She knew the area well. I tagged along behind her, having to race to make lights that she blazed through on yellow.

I hoped she wasn't attempting to set me up for a traffic ticket as part of some scummy police sting. The sheriff's coroner for Orange County had just been charged with money laundering and bribery offenses, so it wasn't completely out of the realm of possibility. As she raced along, her car blended in with the weathered vehicles of Santa Ana—plain, simple cars that didn't have a lot of cash invested in them for extras like rust proofing.

Her car guided me down streets that got smaller and smaller, past houses that were situated closer and closer together, and finally she turned onto an impossibly narrow street where her tiny car sailed along. In the truck I had to creep slowly, cautious to not slam my side-view mirrors into the beat-down cars polluting both sides of the pockmarked asphalt strip.

Even I, an ignorant, small-town white kid, knew where I was. It was a place you didn't really believe existed when you grew up in a pleasant suburb, a place that for many in this country's urban areas was just another fact of life. I was in the hallowed stomping grounds of rap culture. I was in "the ghetto."

Obviously I was, and largely still am, an ignorant, sheltered individual from a place where people leave their doors unlocked at night and don't worry too much about their kids running around late at night. For those of you like me, "the ghetto" is that part of any given city where the poorest of the city's inhabitants congregate and call it home.

In Eureka our idea of a ghetto was the trailer park. We knew the idea of a ghetto, and that was what we could perceptibly link it to. But we were wrong, because a ghetto is something so much more than a hamlet of poor folk. "The ghetto" has shifted to being something more sinister, a place built largely on fear and mistrust. For many in this day and age, being from the ghetto is a thing of dangerous pride.

Ghetto culture has its own way of communicating, from the graffiti tags that look like scribbles to most of us, to the clothes, to the tattoos. There are signs all around, and if you don't decipher them correctly, you could find yourself in real trouble, innocent visitor or not.

Leslie parked her car in the driveway of a one-story, tan-colored house with a three-foot-high rock wall built around the property. On top of the rock wall, linked metal spikes jutted skyward, flecked with white paint to form a gate. Rust revealed itself through wherever the paint had chipped off.

I had no other place to park, and not knowing the appropriate rules of conduct for where I was, I was forced to stop the big truck in the middle of the street. I was frustrated that Dirk had once again sent me out alone to do the work that would net me a third of a half, whether he helped me or not. But he was a sheriff, and there wasn't a whole lot I could say to that. Foolishly, I hoped that someone would take offense to the truck being stopped there and firebomb it...while I was outside of it, anyway.

Making sure to lock the truck, I pushed the clicker on the key ring multiple times so that the alarm-activated beep would sound out as a warning to the ne'er-do-wells that my truck was definitely locked and off-limits.

I walked up the short driveway, noting a manually operated gate with equally sharp fixtures on it that could be rolled across the driveway and padlocked. The front windows of the house had bars on them, and if the family had anything of value, it was not in plain sight.

I passed the car on my way to meeting Leslie at the front door. The back window was gone, shot out, shattered, and lying across the backseat, and the front and back side windows were either rolled down or missing. The windshield on the gray Corolla was shattered but held intact by safety glass. Large holes were pinged out where the bullets had forced their way through and done major damage. I didn't stop to look inside, but I could tell the car was going to be bloody.

Leslie waited for me to arrive before she knocked, and I introduced myself to her a moment before I introduced myself to the family. The woman looked like somebody's mother, a tired, middle-aged Mexican lady with sadness as a permanent fixture in her eyes. Her husband, a middle-aged mustachioed gent smiling at me with yellow teeth, looked like my uncle's gardener. I greeted them, embarrassed by my whiteness, and spoke directly to them, but speaking slowly as if that would help them understand me. Leslie translated, her voice tight, and I could sense a vague irritation at my inability to communicate.

Walking back to the car and putting my tight, black gloves on, I felt the heat from the late afternoon sun beating down on me. Sweat soaked my black polo, which no longer had that fresh, new look.

I then laid out the basics for the family. I couldn't do anything about the windshield or the bullet holes that had cut into the frame, leaving sharp contorted gashes that I could fit my index finger through. I didn't know a thing about cutting into or removing car seats, so I told Leslie to convey to them that I would clean the seats as best I could and vacuum the glass out of the backseat. I felt fairly safe in charging them $435 for the cleanup. I felt bad, but I couldn't see fit to charge a couple less just because they were poor. I was straining to promote equality, after all.

I didn't need Leslie to translate that the number was a large one for them. The man sent his wife scurrying back into the house while he discussed the number with another man, maybe his brother, who had just joined us. Finally they agreed and signaled to Leslie to tell me. I nodded enthusiastically, grinning broadly as if they had just shown me to my room at their resort, forgetting that I was negotiating over their dead son's blood.

Once the contract had been written and signed for the agreed amount, Leslie informed me cheerfully that she was leaving. I would be alone, the large, stupid, white guy with the nice truck, unarmed in the ghetto.

Inhabitants from other houses had taken notice that something was happening at the house. I could see them poking their heads around bushes and off of porches as I steered the Silverado into the driveway to take Leslie's place. The father gestured to inform me that he could close the gate and lock my truck in, but I waved him off with a show-no-fear mentality. I had to show the other creatures that this beast was not afraid.

· · ·

I'd gained a fair bit of eye-widening bravado in my time as a bouncer at a thug club in Long Beach, the LBC (Long Beach, California, for those unfamiliar with rap music lore). It was as simple as being a big guy who needed money and showed up at a club that needed a bouncer. I was still at Beverages & More in those days, back before I knew what a crime scene cleaner was. As a desperate bid to pick up extra cash during the slow retail season, I signed on to work as one of five security guys in the bar on weekends—Thursday, Friday, and Saturday nights.

The place was called New York Bryan's, or NYB's, and the owner, Bryan, appropriately, was one of those "throw 'em in the trunk of a car" goombah types from Brooklyn. Fond of leather jackets and a St. Christopher necklace, Bryan was barely two years older than me and already owned his own nightclub. Some would say he was connected, but I didn't believe that.

I had never been a bouncer before; the closest I'd come was working door security at a Humboldt rave where techno dorks would give you weed in lieu of the entry fee, and the whole place was kind and high. NYB's was different. The clientele wasn't hippy-dippy, free-love, peace-craving music enthusiasts. Instead, these were flash-and-dash gangsters, small-money rollers who parked their Escalades and Benzes at the red-painted curbs out front, ignoring parking tickets to the point that the cops stopped giving them out. The rollers had money to burn, and Bryan had a bevy of girls they'd thumb bills at to keep the entourage supplied with drinks.

There were others, too, non-thug types who'd pop in. Long Beach was a melting pot, and we had a constantly evolving crew of regular customers. People you could count on to be there week after week, until one week they weren't, and you never saw them again.

Tourists strolled the multitude of bars on Pine Avenue, each with a different ambience to get drunk in. Way down the block heading south, you had the Irish bar pumping out the strains of the Dropkick Murphys and Irish classics. Across the street was the Middle Eastern–themed Aladdin's; next door was the late-night taco place; and diagonally, the cigar bar, Cohiba. There were lots more, both independents and dives—mainstream places like Hooters and one-offs like Club 21.

Depending on what was happening in town, you could guess what the majority clientele would be that week. Not long before I arrived, the band The Killers had played at a juke joint, The Vault, down the street and came into NYB's for the after-party. They drank up seven hundred dollars' worth of booze in the VIP section and tried to leave without paying. New York Bryan himself stopped the band at the door. They paid up.

My first night at the club, a Thursday, we already had a drunk making trouble at 9:00 p.m. The older white guy was soused and didn't want to leave. The bartender gave me the nod to have him removed. I approached the old guy and politely suggested that he'd had enough and that maybe he should find his way home. The old guy told me to fuck off, and I lightly put a hand on his shoulder, looking awkwardly to the bartender for guidance.

"No, no, no!" the bartender shouted, a pretty burly guy himself. "You're doing it all wrong!"

He came around the length of the oak bar and roughly grabbed the old man above his elbows. Lifting him, the bartender bull-rushed the drunk across the nearly empty dance floor and threw him out of the gated patio, where he landed hard on the street, collapsing into the gutter. I stared, shocked and awaiting some sort of retaliation. But the old man merely stood, waved us away angrily, and stumbled off into the night for his next belt of Blanton's.

"You do it like that," the bartender said gruffly. From that point on, I understood.

• • •

I was sitting in the driver's seat of the Corolla at an awkward angle, not wanting the blood that had accumulated on the right side of the seat to get onto my biohazard suit. I had used our wet-dry vac to suck up all the broken glass I could, but I was still haphazardly working around the car, collecting the horrific remnants inside. I found an old, withered french fry sharing space in the cup holder with a dollop of brain and a tooth on the front passenger floorboard. I think it was a bicuspid.

I had given up on trying to scrub the car seats clean. They oozed new blood whenever I put my brush on them, and I finally accepted the truth—they had to be cut out. This time, though, I wasn't going to do any extra work for free. The sun was fast disappearing behind a rise of dingy tenements, and if I wanted to be out of there with all *my* bicuspids intact, I had to take the proper steps.

I knocked on the door and brought the old man out, the smell of Mexican food floating out with him and making me hungry. I tried to convey to him that I needed to charge him extra to cut the seats out, using that same slow, choppy English that we fools think will work.

I could see he wasn't getting it when his daughter came home, pulling her car past the truck and up into the garage. Thankfully, she spoke enough English to broker a new deal that I kept down to an extra hundred dollars and he reluctantly accepted. He wanted me to save as much of the seats as I legally could, though, because he still had to drive the car. If I were him, I would've just started taking the bus.

As I started cutting away haphazardly at the fabric of the front seats, I glanced up to realize I had company. A *vato*, a Mexican gangster, bald-headed with a thick *cholo* mustache, was staring at me from behind square black sunglasses and grinning severely. His lightly built frame wore a wife-beater undershirt as an outer shirt and tan shorts with tall white socks tucked into dark slippers.

I nodded at him convivially, never breaking what I perceived to be eye contact and never saying a word, pleasant or otherwise. I kept on with my work but never took my eyes off him. He leaned closer into the car, smiling dangerously, daring me to say a word, but I didn't. I couldn't let him know he frightened me.

Finally he turned and walked away. A bit later, two other similarly attired young men approached, both of them wearing full white undershirts instead of wife beaters. Neither one possessed the fullness of mustache the first one had had. I gave them the same treatment, though they didn't dare come as close as the other had, and finally they, too, walked off.

I began to feel like a fool, like I had overstepped my boundaries and wandered into silly-white-man land. Surely they weren't trying to intimidate me; they were merely curious, the same as in any other culture or neighborhood. Surely they were just nosy neighbors, and I was an overzealous ignoramus.

As I was finishing bagging up what I had taken of the seat covers, leaving little more than wire frame and splotches of yellow, molded foam, the original gangster returned. This time he walked up to me, and from the corner of my eye I could see children inside the houses stopping to watch out front windows, just as apprehensive as I was. He stopped within a few inches of me, and though he was much shorter, I could tell that he knew he could take me in a fight. I held my breath, knowing that it was dry and bad.

He pushed his sunglasses up while looking at me and said in clear, clipped English, "You clean up in here, okay. But that blood out there, on the curb," and he pointed off somewhere down the street, evidently referring to a separate crime scene, "that blood stays."

Better men might have acted differently; I, on the other hand, nodded to him, finished up, collected a check from the house, and left the ghetto. I was mad at myself for being scared, but I didn't fool myself; I knew that I would one day have to come back. There would be other crime scenes in the Santa Ana ghetto; of that I was certain. I just hoped they wouldn't be anytime soon.

CHAPTER 7

drunken madcappery, goddamnit!

All you need to be happy in life is a hummingbird feeder and a pellet gun.

—*George Davis*

CRIME SCENE CLEANUP WAS THE last thing on my mind when I moved to Fullerton. I had come with a purpose: I wanted to get my bachelor's degree in advertising. But I chose Fullerton, instead of, say, Chicago or New York or one of the other great advertising hubs, because of a girl.

She worked at the porn shop with me, and she was beautiful. Blonde and smart with a couple of major talents (yes, I'm talking about tits here), she was well read and articulate. I was sure she was only working at the porn shop to conduct independent research on the sexual proclivities of the middle class or some high-minded experiment of a similar nature. She was too good for porno.

I was a loner, living in Santa Clarita with no friends at all, and it was only too easy to fall for her. The beautiful coed and the dirty drifter: it had all the makings of an adult movie plot. I had a bad habit of falling in love with just about every girl I met, though, and I was destined to have my heart broken.

She moved to Fullerton to major in English, and I hadn't had the temerity to ask her out on a normal, civilized date, what with the two of us working in porn. In my mind, people who came together through porn, be it on the retail side or the production side, couldn't possibly have healthy, lasting relationships. My warped sense of the world convinced me, though, that if we met in a different setting, we might be able to have something magical.

So when she enrolled down at CSUF, I secretly did the same. We would find each other in some sunlit hallway, both of us bending to retrieve a dropped notebook, our fingers would meet and then, finally, our eyes. The recognition would set in and then the realization that destiny had pushed us together (cough). It would be passionate and romantic, like something out of a Nicholas Sparks novel.

When I abruptly quit my job at the porn shop, she disappeared from my life, and I just trusted to kismet that I would run into her again in the fall in a different town, a different place, as a different person. Well, I never saw her again, so that completely fucking backfired.

Whether she didn't get accepted or she changed schools or she knew that I was secretly enrolling to follow her and have a chance at falling in love (which I always thought of as vaguely romantic, but *everyone* around me considered creepy), she never ended up at the campus. Or maybe she did, and we just had two completely different schedules.

Whatever happened, I was suddenly stuck in Fullerton, with only my younger brother Chris for support. And while becoming close with him was great, I needed something else.

On my first day at CSUF, I was in shy mode the entire time I walked around the campus, keeping my head down and terrified that someone might ask me something. I was twenty-two, only a few weeks from my next birthday.

My first class was a basic tutorial on media, for which I had parked on completely the wrong side of campus and had thus spent a considerable part of the morning huffing and puffing my fat ass across the grounds to reach. Finally I stumbled into the class and, looking around, saw that my shy self was already in trouble.

It was a large class and already quite full; there weren't any open seats in the back or toward the end aisles where I could slide in, take notes, and disappear once class was over. No, I would have to take a seat down in front, where the talkative kids sat. The ones who actually asked questions and had questions asked of them. I seriously considered shit-canning the class for the semester, but it was one of the major prerequisites for my advertising major. So, resolutely, I buckled down and took a seat.

I kicked myself the whole time. Typically my neuroses would have had me coordinating my schedule against a map of potential parking and arriving at the class far before anyone else to ensure the best possible seat for someone of my disposition. Instead I'd spent the previous evening drinking a thirty-block of Miller Lite cans with Chris and then skating around the apartment complex to show any cool fellow tenants that we newcomers were "with it."

The classroom seats themselves were problematic for me, as they were those swiveling computer chairs that are attached to the desk and not really built for fatties or lefties. I slid my sweaty self into the desk with one of those embarrassingly loud maneuvers that had the whole class staring at me.

In the act of wedging myself into a seat, I knew it was no use continuing in the vein of the quiet, shy Jeff, and so self-preservation necessitated that my other side take over.

"Hi," I said, nodding to the guy sitting to my left, a Jewish-looking hipster with a goatee. "And hello," I added to the girl sitting next to me, a dark-skinned beauty who had the makings of a model.

Throughout the class, the girl and I got to talking, first out of polite boredom and then with a genuine interest in one another's backgrounds. She was beautiful and smart and had a couple of major talents. (Here I'm talking about kickboxing and singing.) I was already forgetting the reason I'd moved to Fullerton in the first place.

The goateed Jewish guy, Anthony, butted in to invite the girl and me to a "Back to School" BBQ that his frat was throwing at the end of the week. I took a flyer, never expecting to use it for more than emergency toilet paper. This was the same attitude that would make crime scene cleaning so appealing to me down the road. As someone with social issues, I found myself only too at ease being left alone with the remnants of the dead. I could talk to them, and they wouldn't point out that I had man boobs.

That Friday evening, though, with Chris and me sitting around bored, the flyer came flashing back into my mind. Chris was immediately as skeptical as I was about someone wanting *a Klima* at their party, and both of us were only all too aware how it ended for Stephen King's Carrie when she took a chance on the popular kids.

So we took steps to arm ourselves, me toting a pair of brass knuckles, and Chris his Walther PP-7 replica James Bond pellet gun. We googled the location of the party and set out grimly, expecting the worst. I knew it would be worse if wild, chatty extrovert Jeff had been invited to the party and introvert, fumbling nervous Jeff showed up, so I did my damnedest to summon the wild guy.

The dichotomy of my personalities was such that I had absolutely zero skills when it came to consoling the family members of my future clients. Either I was entirely too chatty, extending well-worn platitudes about "making the best of the time they had with the victim," or stammering to explain the technical aspects of my job that prohibited the relatives from just doing the work themselves.

Chris and I were concerned upon entering the party at the frat house, which looked more like someone's shitty, dirty house with a shitty, dirty backyard. It definitely wasn't what 1980s college movies had led me to believe about frat houses. I had offered to bring beer, but Anthony had maintained rather gravely that beer was not necessary.

"Kegs," I thought excitedly, impressed, and yet when we walked into the party, no kegs were to be seen. Instead it was an eclectic mix of normal-looking guys and girls hanging out drinking soda pop. Immediately, Chris and I realized that it was far more terrifying than being ambushed by popular jerks; *we were at a religious party.*

I was quickly assured that it was not, in fact, a religious party. Rather it was rush week, a two-week-long, alcohol-free series of events that were themed toward getting you to join a particular fraternity. Apparently the boys of Sigma Nu were recruiting me. Because Chris didn't attend CSUF, he couldn't join, but they said he was welcome to stay and eat burgers and hang out all he wanted. That was just fine with Chris.

The frat boys, whether I was being effervescent or not, completely kissed my and the other recruits' figurative asses. Their girls flirted with us, "the bros" all wanted to talk to us, and everybody was offering to get me more food and drink. I felt like a real member of society, someone who genuinely didn't have to worry about what other people thought. Even without kegs, it was nervously intoxicating.

While the other guys were a bit more normal and fratlike, Chris and I spent the majority of our time talking to a nerdy, chubby guy with atrocious teeth. He was completely obsessed with filming a shot-for-shot remake of *Back to the Future* entirely with Legos. My notion of fraternities was changing rapidly.

"Well," Chris said on the ride home, "if that guy can get into a frat, I don't think you'll have a problem."

I still didn't know if I was going to rush; it seemed like a major commitment for someone who was typically afraid of commitment. I'd at least told them that I would come to their next event, though. Something counter to my normal existence was exactly what I was seeking, but I was determined to take baby steps toward breaking out of my shell. Joining a fraternity seemed like a move in that direction.

• • •

Upon showing up at their next shindig, Anthony and two others took me aside and asked if I wanted to be one of them. Unhesitatingly, I said yes, my mouth having thrown the notion of baby steps right out the window. I didn't know if I could afford it; I didn't know if awkward ol' me would survive, but I refused to let my life be ruled by my fearful side. Crazy Jeff was taking back the reins, and he was determined to let the good times roll.

Over the next two weeks, I watched others join what would become my pledge class. I figured I was a pretty good judge of first impressions, so admittedly I was afraid of a few of the frat's choices. There was big Dan, a massively buff wrestler who dressed cool and partied with all the chicks who would never party with me. Carey, a young Asian kid; Jorge, a young Mexican kid; Ryan, a deaf guy; a black guy (Dave); and a couple of other odds and ends would come to constitute the class with the Greek letter designation of Beta Theta.

At twenty-two, I was the oldest of the bunch, and I felt like it. Particularly ostracizing was the fact that I was older than all but two of the active chapter. I'd committed, though, and quitting would have been more embarrassing than staying in, so I pressed on.

The night they initiated us as pledges into the Sigma Nu fraternity was also the night of my twenty-third birthday. I had become so excited about joining the fraternal ranks that I canceled the party my family was having for me up north in order to stand in a black button-down shirt, tie, slacks, and a blindfold to endure a sobering initiation procedure that lasted well into the night.

After that night, the kindness from the actives came to an abrupt end, and a little role reversal began. We became their slaves, forced to do their bidding and be subservient to them in almost every way. It wasn't anything like the horror stories that I'd heard about fraternities, where pledge classes were made to do the elephant walk (each guy grabs the dick of the guy ahead of him and they march in procession), the limp biscuit (pledges circle jerk onto a KFC biscuit, last guy to cum eats the biscuit), or even the dangerous stuff that had resulted in the deaths of pledges at other houses (mass consumption of alcohol, water, and so on), but it was still brutally hard work. For every bad thing, there were two good ones, though, and that kept us pledges coming around.

We were to be the last chapter to see the Sigma Nu house in its "glory," before the onset of black mold on the walls of the ramshackle building necessitated Sigma Nu's move out of the suburbs and onto Frat Row.

The house we moved into there was more like four condos mashed together. It had been trashed by its previous occupants, a frat that had been kicked off campus before my time, but it was so much more in line with what I thought a frat house should look like. If I was going to be a frat boy and have the frat boy experience, I wanted a goddamn proper frat house. Otherwise the fraternity would just seem like a bunch of friends that I paid for. The house on Frat Row gave us legitimacy and new lifeblood. If I was worried about having a proper frat experience, though, the rest of the row allayed my fears. Like in a Motley Crue video, scantily clad vixens trolled up and down the block looking for the best party while dudes manned BBQs on the front lawns of fellow houses. Empty alcohol jugs littered the span between the street and the front doors of frat houses, and a cacophony of sounds blared out from cracked windows held alive by arcing lines of duct tape. Most of the houses had switched to Plexiglas in their window frames, though, which was a telling sign all its own.

As I wandered the length of the street, scarcely able to believe my senses, a streaker passed by, greeting me with a cordial, casual hello. He was pursued by a gaggle of his frat mates who were taunting him for getting shut out while playing Madden on Xbox. Farther down the block, people were throwing rocks at passing cars, and four men were on a rooftop trying to slingshot water balloons onto the soccer field.

Many of the fraternities had attracted an untamed element seeking a wild lifestyle, and the myriad apartment houses running adjacent to Frat Row were teeming with uninhibited and unruly hedonists. Someone at another frat house even got shot (not fatally) the week we moved in.

It was truly the last vestiges of the Old West, and I had arrived smack-dab in the middle of it. Standing there in the midst of pulsing stereos, beneath trees littered with dangling sneakers, surrounded by scores of drunken party seekers, I knew that I was about to embark on a very different existence. Ricky Moses would have been proud.

I realized quickly that Sigma Nu was different from the rest. Whereas other fraternities on the row had a singular "look" to them—the Pi Kapps were the white, asshole jocks; the Phi Sigs were the stoners; Delta Chi, where Kevin Costner had once been a member, was all Mexican wannabe thugs now; the Sig Eps were all homosexuals or metrosexuals.

But Sigma Nu, I realized, was the catchall fraternity, the melting pot. We had everyone from gay guys to black guys to jocks to stoners, and yes, a whole bunch of nerds. We were the Animal House fraternity; while the other frats were eagerly participating in spirit events, shit like which house could cheer the loudest, Sigma Nus hung out on their couch drinking beers. I liked that; to me that was as it should have been. Sure the other frats gave us shit, but we didn't care. Mostly.

I had a different fraternal experience than most of my class. Being older, I was not expected to kiss as much ass as my younger pledge bros, and the actives were always looking to be entertained by one of my ribald porn-shop adventure stories. Looking back, I can think of no greater preparation for my life in crime scene cleaning.

Between scrubbing up vomit from those too drunk to clean themselves and seeing unwashed dishes lie unclaimed in the sink while festering with spores and single-cell life, I'd become immune to the wretchedness of humanity. All too frequently, people would miss the toilet—both numbers one and two, and you either accepted that as a facet of frat living or you got the hell out of there. But I couldn't leave…I had friends.

As the semester wore on, I cared more and more about the guys in my pledge class. I didn't think it was possible for me to consider a bunch of younger strangers my band of brothers, but Jesus, they must have put something in the water. We went on a "pledge retreat" where we spent two nights in the woods camping.

The first night it was only the pledges and Anthony, the active member in charge of our pledge class. We spent the evening around a fire, freezing our balls off high in the late-fall mountain woods, just completely shooting the shit and being honest about our biggest secrets. Some of the guys were very truthful, breaking down into tears while telling about their family issues or the challenges in life that they had to overcome.

Big Dan the wrestler surprised me with the revelation that the rest of his family were dwarves. I didn't know if I really believed him, considering he was a big, buff wrestler, but he said it in the "circle of truth" (that's my name for it; I swear to God they never called it that!), and I had to accept his word. When the pledge class asked me to lay some truth about myself on them, I chose instead to use humor as a defense mechanism. If I made 'em all laugh, they'd forget they asked me a serious question. Brotherhood or not, I wasn't ready for that level of commitment.

The next night all the actives came up and surprised us, bringing a shit ton of alcohol and giving all us "newbs" nicknames. No longer were we Jeff, Ryan, Carey, Nick, Dave, Chris, Neil, Jorge, Dan, Kevin, Justin, and Adam. We were forever in the annals of fratdom to be called: Beast (I'm a big, hairy motherfucker), 9-Ball (Ryan, the deaf kid, shot pool), and Binary (Carey, the Asian, was a computer guy).

Then there were Hippo Banger (Nick was a Jungle Cruise guide at Disneyland), Deluxe (Dave looked exactly like that character in the old Coke commercials), Shaggy (he looked like Shaggy from *Scooby Doo*), Bubbles (who knows? Neil was given his nickname by a gay guy), and Burrito (or some Mexican name).

Finally, there were Donkey Kong (Dan was a big, ape-looking, buff-ass wrestler), Spacey (Kevin was an airhead), Batboy (Justin looked like Christian Bale), and Deuce (Adam played poker). They weren't the cleverest of nicknames, but we had busted our asses to earn them. After we got our nicknames, the whole group got royally plastered. Someone even shit in his sleeping bag. I was home.

Coming back from the retreat, I was riding with 9-Ball and Donkey Kong when the brakes on 9-Ball's Pontiac went out coming down a mountain. I had just drifted off to some much-needed hangover sleep when I felt a hard jerk, and suddenly we were facing oncoming traffic.

We all screamed, and 9-Ball jerked the wheel again, carrying us over to the side of the road, where he used the emergency brake to screech us to a stop. Shaken and stirred, we called for a tow truck to take us down the mountain. Donkey Kong offered to have his brother come pick us up, and since we were several hours away from home and several hours from having new brakes installed on the Pontiac, we agreed.

Forty-five minutes later, the smallest car I'd ever seen came squealing into the parking lot, and the hardest, least friendly looking dwarf I'd ever seen in my life exited the driver's seat. He cussed out the lot of us, especially Donkey Kong, about inconveniencing him. Then he told us, especially Donkey Kong, how proud he was of us for joining the right fraternity. His name was Ernie, and he was a Sigma Nu from Fresno. Of course, out there they called him Napoleon.

"Don't call me a midget," Ernie warned as he drove us, cramped in his tiny car, back to his parents' house. "That's like calling a black guy a nigger." Nobody had called him a midget or a nigger, so continued silence seemed like a good plan.

We arrived at Donkey Kong's house only to find that his father was even smaller than Ernie, and their mom was smaller than all of them. *Donkey Kong wasn't lying.*

I had never been around dwarves before, and it was a truly unique feeling to be hanging out in their presence. Consider it the ignorant side of me, but I was actually shocked to see that they lived just like us normal folks, their house even being normal-size, but they had to use stepladders to get everything down from the cupboards. This was before the glut of exploitative dwarf shows on The Learning Channel, mind you.

When feeding time came around, I was served tiny chicken wings, mini pizza slices, and other hors d'oeuvres that were small in my hands but looked like a full-size meal in theirs. The experience was mental overload for an ignorant son of a bitch like me, and I have since decided that if I could only replay one memory over and over again in my head for an eternity, that would be it.

As the pledge period progressed, the actives became harder and harder on us about knowing the history of the fraternity and the importance of the symbols associated with our local and national chapters. We learned them, but not like we should have, apparently, and we paid for it.

One night the actives called us before them in suits and made us take a written test. I had instilled myself as the class clown from the get-go, and as a beloved member of the pledge class, I didn't take the test seriously. Any answer I didn't know became a joke answer. Once again I figured if I couldn't be honest, I'd make 'em laugh.

After the test, we were summoned back before them and retested verbally, each of the actives ripping us down for not knowing the answers. I, in particular, took a good amount of screaming and anger, and though I kept a stiff lip and endured the abuse, I felt like I'd been bitten by a beloved childhood pet. It was humiliating to be spurned by the guys you called friends. They called that night Candidate Review, C.R. for short. I realized that if I was going to get in, it was going to be honesty that got me there.

One of the pledges, "Batboy," took the abuse particularly hard, harder than the rest of us, and I had to sit with him in his van while rain poured down around us and the thunder boomed and he cried. For an hour and a half I endured his tears, his threats that he was going to murder the lot of them, and how he had done similar things like that before. I finally got Batboy calmed down, and with his assurances that he wouldn't murder anyone in the next few days, I went home. The evening had given me much to think about.

The next day at our pledge meeting we did a head count, and Batboy was missing. I hoped I wasn't going to somehow end up as an accessory to him murdering someone. He finally walked in halfway through our meeting, dressed all in black with mirrored black sunglasses obscuring his eyes, and dropped his pledge pin on the table. He was through, he said, and couldn't be talked out of it.

When he walked out, I felt an intense anger surge through me that I had never felt before. We were justifiably angry, me especially. Justin, or Batboy, and all the rest of them had made me feel something I hadn't felt in a very long time, a genuine kinship with my fellow man.

I bit back the tears as long as I could, and I was ashamed to be so publicly vulnerable, but fraternity life had stirred a light of humanity in me. I could hold it all in no longer, and I bared my naked soul as the tears tumbled down. I had lost a brother.

We had made it through most of our candidacy process as a unified front, defying the actives' expectations of our togetherness, and then there was a gaping hole and it wasn't the same. The others had an equally hard time with it. Deuce dropped next, and then Deluxe after him. Each one's loss a sickening blow to the beautiful experience I was having. We had been through the wringers together and were so close to becoming actives ourselves, and yet we were dropping like rotten apples from the tree. I couldn't quit, though; Sigma Nu had broken open something in me, and I craved the honesty and comfort that came from a brotherhood.

For me, the hardest loss for Beta Theta came during our I-week, a week when we all camped out at the frat house studying for our National Test. It was the final barrier between us and being able to wear the badges of pride that were the Greek letters "ΣN." Put through a battery of mental, physical, and emotional exercises, we were sleep-deprived and struggling to keep our GPAs afloat.

The night before the National Test, we were sent out on a late-night mission to T.P. a sorority house, which was clearly symbolism for...well, the hell with it. It was supposed to be fun. We drove over in two cars, feeling tired and wanting it all to be over with so we could go back to sleep.

We were just getting into the thick of hurling roll after roll of toilet paper over the roof and through the trees when the house lights suddenly burst on. Instantly we fled, each guy taking off in a separate direction, the brotherhood collective yielding to an "every man for himself" mentality.

I was in no mood or shape to run all the way across campus back to the frat house, so I decided to take my chances and head back to the cars instead. Along the way I teamed up with Spacey, who had the same thought I did. Spacey was an airhead, but he was good people and I could relate to him, as long as we talked about girls or skateboarding.

Back at the cars, we were surprised to find it had all been a setup. The girls had known we were coming, and they were in the act of dusting our cars with baby powder, Silly String, and eggs. Spacey and I, not ones to take shit from sorority girls, engaged them in a smash-ingly good baby powder, Silly String, eggs, and water fight, all of us getting good and messy.

I wasn't someone who was comfortable around girls entirely, so the fight was a good chance for me to flirt and interact. I made the most of it, but somehow, some way, something went wrong. One of the girls ran quickly into the house, flanked by two others, and Spacey stood there sheepishly. Another girl suggested we leave.

Together, Spacey and I took a long, wet, and dirty walk back to the fraternity house. Apparently he had grappled with one of the other girls in a manner that the girls had evidently deemed "inappropriate." Spacey didn't really think so, but he had been cited by the active frat members before for inappropriate actions toward girls at parties, so this didn't look good.

Spacey was already on thin ice, and we both knew that Sigma Nu was serious about how the sororities viewed its members. Spacey asked me what I thought he should do, and I looked at my brother, covered in flour and Silly String, and I said, "Quit." He did, packing up and leaving that night, saving the actives the trouble of ousting him. I didn't go back to sleep that night.

When I took my National Test, I knew I had passed it. I had settled in after C.R. and become an all-star. I was ready. I knew I had what it took to be a frat boy and to believe in the nobility and dedication that had been entrenched in me since my initiation. I had succeeded. I'd broken down my security barriers and opened up to my brothers as they had opened up to me. I was worthy of their trust. As such, I was no longer to be considered a boy in the fraternal manner; I was a gentleman, a knight in the Legion of Honor.

When I was inducted into the fraternity that evening and given a sweatshirt emblazoned with the letters of Sigma Nu, I felt the pride that came with being a trusted gentleman. And I wasn't alone. I had done it with those who had survived, the men, pledges no more, who I embraced as brothers. We were active members of a fraternal organization. At long last, we knew what it was to be men of respect and honor. Then we got shit-face drunk and ate gummy worms out of a stripper's pussy.

they're droppin' like flies

Person 1: What's the difference between toilet paper and a shower curtain?
Person 2: I don't know...
Person 1: Here's the guy!

I'VE BECOME AN EXPERT ON poop. It isn't by choice, mind you, but goddamned if poop doesn't show up almost every time someone dies. The sphincter muscle goes slack on a corpse, and bam! Poop slides out, leaving the body in a sad sort of poop cocoon. Maybe that's a bit extreme, but how often have you seen the phrase "poop cocoon" in print? This book is all about firsts.

Fecal matter is broken down into seven different types on the Bristol Stool Chart, which is a fantastically descriptive medical grading of human excrement. Types 1 and 2 are those dry, constipated lumps that are either in small pieces or a long, bulging pickle shape. Types 6 and 7 are more on the diarrhea side of things. Type 6 is that torn, shredded-edged shape with a soft consistency, while Type 7 is purely liquid. Types 3 through 5 are the healthier, more normal poops that leave the bowels like a rocket sled on rails. I most often deal with Type 6. It is the "death poop," or as I referred to it in the field, the "alcoholic's choice."

Poop can range in colors, which you'd know, depending on whether you've ever hopped off the bowl to take a look, that or you are frequent recipient of the "Cleveland Steamer" or "Hot Plate." (If you don't know, don't ask.) If you're like me, you've had to scrub poop from beside toilet bowls on a regular basis.

Poop can range in color from black to white (white comes from drinking barium, a thick liquid that's used for x-rays of the digestive system). But, depending on what you eat or drink, poop can also be blue or, if you've eaten a lot of vegetables, green. It sometimes is yellow, which happens with nasty diseases or an overabundance of bilirubin. (Bilirubin is red blood cells that have broken down in the liver and end up in the small intestine as an orangish color. In the intestine, bilirubin mixes with stomach bile to form that nice, healthy brown color that most good little boys and girls who eat all their dinner have.)

The bitch about poop is that when some people are near death, their mind retreats to a place of bitterness and simplicity, an almost infantile state of being. Poop becomes less a by-product of digestion and more like a crayon.

I actually first noticed this trend before I started in crime scene cleanup. A girl who hung out with the fraternity, perfectly pleasant in all respects, became known as a "frat slut." It wasn't her fault entirely. She just became so used to spending time with all the frat boys that they became her biosphere, and she banged the lot of them. Not all, mind you, I add with some bitterness, but an impressive number by guy standards. By girl standards, she was ostracized from the group and so became depressed. I'm sure we could get into a whole psychoanalysis of this girl's psyche, but our topic here is poop, and so her emotional problems, as far as you and I are concerned, aren't the issue here.

One night, after the fraternity had sent her home due to her predilection to drink and then become braying and abrasive, she decided to kill herself. Whether she really wanted to die or simply was making a grandiose call for attention remains unclear. What's important is that after she'd slit her wrists in the bathtub, she'd also defecated and then used the poop and the blood to write not-so-cryptic messages of hate on the walls of her apartment.

I know this because I had never seen a suicide attempt before, and I broke into her apartment through a window to check out the aftermath. A little creepy perhaps, but I'm also the same guy who near-stalked a girl to Fullerton and who cleans up dead people for a living, so let's dispense with the shock.

The next time I saw ca-ca as wall art wasn't when I viewed the permanent collection at the Museum of Contemporary Art but rather at a small, pleasant house in Claremont. It was our fifth gig in nearly as many months. We'd been referred to the homeowner by the Claremont Police Department. Pleased with the work we'd done for them on the minister's suicide, the police had dropped our names to the victim's relative.

This was interesting for two reasons: first, we'd only gotten the minister gig because the two Claremont cops mistakenly thought we were another company they'd had a positive experience with in the past, and second, because those same officers had gotten their asses chewed out as a result of us. Apparently the Claremont Police Department wasn't too happy about one of their officers signing off on the nine-hundred-dollar cleaning fee we'd hit them with.

The police department refused to pay, and Dirk had to call them to point out that their representative had signed the contract. Eventually they paid, but I heard it was not pleasant for the involved parties. Still, we'd once more been recommended, and I was all too happy to show up on the doorstep of a one-story, light-colored house for a little dark work. Dirk had once again begged off, citing that he had to attend to his real job.

I was to meet the owner of the house at the site, but she was running late, which gave me time to wander around the neighborhood. It was one of those pristine places with nice parks and a homeowners' association that regulated the number of trees you could plant in your front yard. I had a real hatred of homeowners' associations for exactly that sort of reason, but I had to admit the area looked nice.

The owner, frantic after her long drive home from work, was apologizing even as she pulled up. The house was a mess, she said. The forensic team had been out there for the past several days on the speculation that the incident had been murder. They'd finally ruled the matter a suicide, but not before coating the house in a dingy black dusting of graphite.

(As *CSI* enthusiasts doubtlessly know, graphite powder is a dark, fine powder that's sprayed across doorjambs, knobs, walls, telephones, remote controls, and any other surface the suspected perpetrator might have contacted while inside the house murdering. The powder sticks to the oil exuded from the fingertips in the shape of fingerprints. It is also a tremendous pain to get off the walls, but I didn't know this at the time.)

I was excited because I had consulted my father, whom I considered a very sage man, on the matter of my frustrating financial woes. I was now working regularly by crime scene standards, but I still wasn't making any money. My buddies, working as bank tellers and waiters, were out-earning me, and they didn't have to contend with gang members threatening them or strange brains in their eye sockets. To top it off, I was having trouble making money off people's heartbreak and trauma, and I didn't think I had it in me to be a dirtbag.

My father empathized with my position. In his younger years he'd done construction projects for acquaintances and had had difficulty charging them an amount that would make the project worth his time. He'd compensated for this by creating a simple equation: take the number that he wanted to charge them and double it. My father, being very intelligent, said I would be surprised how well this would work.

I walked around the lady's house that day, surveying the wreckage and calculating a number in my head. It was easy to see why the police had thought it was a murder. Bloodstains streaked throughout the house into numerous rooms, and a bistro set in the kitchen had been upended and destroyed. That, coupled with the copious amounts of graphite powder, made for a very unsettling scene.

The worst of it was in the bathroom, where the rampage had both started and ended. An abundance of poop, smeared across the white walls of the shower, was what finally convinced the forensics team that it was suicide.

Rather than crafting messages, as my friend the frat slut had done, this chap had chosen to make a series of squiggles and overlapping lines of putrid, dark-brown funk. I didn't know it at the time, but that dark-brown color was indicative that the victim had been constipated, but evidently not so constipated that he couldn't make a nasty mess for me to deal with.

The shower curtain had been pushed aside, and I had an unfettered view of the man's mashed dark stool lying down by the drain. It was small and hard-looking, with divots forced into one side where his fingers had gripped the thing. I was fascinated to see that he had wielded the scat not like a pencil, resting it on his middle finger and the webbing between his thumb and index finger (I'm a lefty, apparently we hold the pencil differently), but rather like a knife, using his whole hand.

It was a blunt instrument to him rather than a tool of finesse; one could appreciate the evident fury in his motions. Anger had caused him to revert back to a primitive level where his mind couldn't formulate the necessary words to express what he felt about abandoning life. We, the living, were left only with a bizarre set of symbols that even Robert Langdon would have been clueless to decipher.

The departed had been the homeowner's uncle. He had lived there with his sister, the homeowner's mother, for some time, but his sister had wanted him out. It was her home, and he was crashing the place, cramping her old-lady style. Finally he had pissed his sister off so badly that she'd gone away to stay with a friend, refusing to come back until he'd moved out. Sometime during the week between when she'd left home and the daughter had come by to check on the situation, the man had slashed his wrists in the bathtub.

Apparently, though, the length of time it took him to die was not what he'd expected, and he'd left the relatively easy cleaning environment of the bathroom to wander across the off-white carpet of the living room before sitting for a spell in a light-colored chair there. Then he'd moved into a second bathroom, where he spent some time checking himself out in the large mirror over the sink.

After that he just went fucking nuts. I tracked his bloodstains into the sister's bedroom, where he'd violently torn through her clothes hanging in a closet before running into the kitchen to wreak havoc on the aforementioned bistro set. Probably feeling faint due to blood loss, he finally managed to find his way back into the original bathroom, lie back in the tub, crap into his hand, and got busy with the wall.

Figuring out what to charge the homeowner was a nerve-wracking experience. I was determined to try my dad's strategy, but I was terrified of the word "no." If she said no, I knew I wouldn't be able to back down and suggest a cheaper price. I'd never been a haggler; I didn't understand the delicate art of ripping people off back then. If a salesperson told me the price of something and I declined it, and then he tried to reel me in by quoting a cheaper price, I would have been tempted to shit in my pants with anger (and then possibly throw them at the guy). It just didn't seem to be good business to me if a salesman could offer me a lower price initially and didn't.

So I resolved to charge the woman $1,535, take it or leave it. The $1,535 was double what I thought the job was worth, and it also seemed like a real number. I figured if I quoted her $1,500, she probably would be suspicious. As if that was some number I just tossed out...Then she might start trying to haggle and lowball me, and I would end up doing the job for peanuts. But $1,535, that was mysterious. That made it seem like there was some complicated pricing system, the details of which would be unpleasant to hear.

As soon as I dropped the number like a bomb into the midst of the conversation, not at all as confident in saying it as I would have liked, we both froze. In the silence that followed, I was ready to apologize, to cry out that I wasn't some huckster, some charlatan, some demon out to fleece her dry. I was thinking about quoting her a cheaper price, something many hundred dollars cheaper than the number I had found the audacity to utter aloud, but she spoke first.

"I'll get my checkbook."

I started in the bathroom. Grimacing, I gripped the poop, my gloved fingers slipping just above the grooves. My fingers are bigger than his, I thought, as I chucked the thing into the depths of my trash bag. I hit the walls next, using plenty of industrial paper towels and several furniture-stripping brushes to massage the ample brown smears from the grout lines.

When I was finished, the bathroom was immaculate, a glowing white testament to the power of Simple Green, paper towels, and elbow grease. While the homeowner made phone calls from the kitchen about how horrible the whole affair was, I moved on to the living room.

"All finished in the bathroom?" the lady asked me, walking out of the kitchen.

"Oh yeah," I beamed. "That place is glowing."

Whether she didn't believe me or was simply curious to see what my definition of "glowing" meant, she marched into the bathroom.

The tub beamed her reflection back at her from the scrubbed fiberglass and porcelain shell. I wanted her to drop to her knees and weep at the majesty that was my cleaning job. I wasn't a neat and tidy person in regular life, but crime scenes brought out the Mop & Glo in me. All business, however, the woman pulled the shower curtain across the length of the tub with none of the gusto or showmanship of a magician. Suddenly, it was my turn to weep.

The accordion-like folds of the white plastic sheet revealed a Rorschach test of unimaginable horror and carnage. Whatever the man hadn't done to himself in the rest of the house, he had saved for himself here. An exuberant thrust of blood sprayed viciously outward and then collected in the folds of the curtain like raindrops in a spider's web.

A squeak eked from my throat as the woman turned to me, one eyebrow thrust violently upward. I grinned the grin of he who eats shit for a living and splayed my hands outward, suggesting that ole Jeff Klima knew it was there the whole time.

"I planned on taking that last," I said, along with a silent prayer that those words alone might be enough.

She let me slide on the shower curtain, though we both knew she knew that I was lying. Her arched eyebrow had told me as much. The rest of my time there was spent in a frenetic silence with an emphasis on being thorough.

I had shown up in my dirty Cavalier with its faded Hawaiian-print seat covers, the antithesis to a logical crime scene vehicle. I called my ride the "Red Rocket," not because she was fast or sleek, but because my little red car certainly resembled a dog's penis. And if nothing else, I was sure I looked like a dick driving it.

As I loaded the last of the biohazard bags into the front seat of the Rocket, which bore no placards or other evidence of a legit cleaning operation, the homeowner came outside, checkbook in hand, and scribbled the payment out for me with the attitude of someone who knew she had just been taken for a ride.

I was grateful for the check but ashamed for not having charged her less. The heat lamp that was her merciless stare had long since wilted the confidence in me. I drove home, bags full of blood and shit brimming next to me, wondering how not to be such a pussy.

• • •

Because crime scenes seem to happen in patterns, we soon had a call for another gig. This one came courtesy of a lesbian whose mother had killed herself in a bathtub. It was an evening job, so Dirk didn't have a good excuse not to tag along.

The job hailed from Panorama City, a north Los Angeles County locale that was anything but panoramic. I'd made the mistake of going there once while shopping for a hat. Panorama City is to Skid Row as phlegm is to smoker's cough. It was our third job in Los Angeles, and this one had come our way as a result of some girl's finger randomly poking down on "The Trauma List."

The Trauma List is a leaflet police officers carry with them that lists all of the property remediation companies in California. Considering that there are a lot of property remediation companies in California and that the list rarely gets renewed, there was a good chance of someone choosing a company that was no longer in business.

We, Orange County Crime Scene Cleaners, were located at miserable spot number 252 on the list. That put us somewhere far down on page 4. Not a great place for a company to be when random choice dictated much of your client base. More difficult was that the list also contained companies that didn't clean up crime scenes at all but instead specialized in such facets of property remediation as mold removal and water-damage repair. The odds of us being found amid the likes of such noncompetition competition were terrible.

The list had been generated on a "first come, first served" basis, and Schmitty, with all his years in the industry, had a much more desirable listing at number 4. But since we were his guys for all of Southern California, when that chick's finger popped down at the number 4 slot, it might as well have found us all the way at the end.

We arrived in the early evening on a street full of dead trees. The houses were all ancient bungalows, small places built out of wood that had been more or less scraped together by the winner of some early twentieth-century bidding war. I knew the insides of the homes wouldn't look much better.

We pulled into the driveway to find a deep-green Volvo station wagon waiting for us; a rainbow lightning bolt decal was emblazoned across its back window.

The butch half of the lesbian couple (her mother being the one who had checked out) nodded to us gruffly. I nodded back, and Dirk gave me the go-ahead to negotiate—probably not because he'd been impressed by my acumen in screwing over our last customer, but because he was intimidated by dealing with hard-looking lesbians.

The more masculine lesbian was a tough one, the kind of person who would punch a tree when she was angry. It took her awhile to get calmed down enough to talk with us, apparently because there was some guilt over the fact that the body had sat stewing in its bathwater for over a week, unnoticed.

The couple had just driven from San Francisco (natch) to deal with the situation, and their emotions were still quite fresh. And here I was trying to affix a price tag to her mother's death. The "he" stalked off to deal with her hang-ups, pursued by her partner, and I was left with the goofy Dirk, who wore a cow's expression of placidity. After all, he wasn't the one who had angered the lesbians.

Finding the front door unlocked, we entered the house to an immediately obvious smell. A fly smacked against my cheek and I spat, swinging my hands anxiously. I had no urge to repeat the horror of my first job.

The bungalow was steeped in inky blackness. The day had been a warm one, and dry air hung heavy with a stench that I will forever recognize as the breakdown of unattended human flesh. It was musty and ripe, as if someone had opened a cellar door at the same moment they farted. Oh, and did I mention that this person seemed to have been living off meat sandwiches for about a year when they did it?

It's an odor unlike anything else you will ever smell. Even the stench of a rotting animal doesn't quite have the same noxious thickness to it. The scent of decomposing flesh sticks to you, clinging to your clothes and filling in the open spots in your pores. Even in the heat, I regretted not wearing my bunny suit to investigate.

We moved toward the bathroom, and the buzzing of flies intensified. Our flashlights, seeking out obstacles in the dark, occasionally captured the blur of a passing housefly instead. Out of my peripheral vision, I could just discern the outline of an overloaded hanging sticky trap. Dirk was ahead of me and fumbled around for the bathroom light fixture.

A streak of blood, the width of a wooden ruler, had dried to the back of the porcelain bath, extending down the outside rim. It was easy to recognize as the position her arm had lain in as it bled out. The flies were clogged three deep on the screen of the small window high above the tub, and they looked more eager to leave the scene than I was.

Insect carcasses littered the floor, extending out into the hallway. Far larger and far more ominous than those were the presence of several odd shapes on the bathroom floor. Tan patches, not at all matching the rest of the tile pattern and about the size of a two-dimensional flank steak, were sealed to the smooth squares of the tiled floor.

I got down on my hands and knees to inspect them. I had cleaned up some crime scenes in my day, and yet for the life of me, I couldn't recognize what I was seeing. I thrust my face down low, my nose almost connecting with one of the odd shapes.

"Fuck," I gasped, straightening up quickly, suddenly understanding.

A person, for all the different smells we give off, is really no different when dead than the average piece of meat. If you soak a dead person long enough, say in a bathtub full of once hot water, he or she, too, will fall off the bone.

The thin patches plastered to the ground were wide strips of the dead woman's skin that, saturated with water, had fallen off her corpse when the paramedics removed her from the bathtub. On the floor, under the heat of day in a house resembling a pressure cooker, the water had evaporated and the flesh had sealed, airtight, to the old tile. It looked as if someone had skinned a basketball and each piece had come off in large, smooth hunks.

It got worse. Paramedics had evidently done the work of pulling the drain plug for us, as it was hanging from its chain off the far ledge of the tub. The water had largely dissipated, taking most of the small parts of what spilled from the woman down the narrow drain. A too-big wad of waterlogged flesh had stopped the process cold, though, and a good couple inches of fetid, murky liquid remained in the bottom of the tub.

Rimming the rest of the tub, showcasing for us where the water line had been, was a nice ring of human grease that had dried tight to the porcelain. I shook my head, knowing that had I stayed at Beverages & More, I would never have had to deal with this...but I also would never have gotten the opportunity to deal with it either.

We went back outside to lay some consolation on the lesbians while attempting to explain to them the extent of the cleaning that was necessary. Neither wanted to go inside the house to see firsthand, which was fine with us. If they didn't want to look, it came down to our word on how much the cleanup would cost.

On the way over, my boss and I had dared to dream that we again could charge $1,535, hoping that such a scenario was possible. It was, and more. Emboldened by their reluctance to enter the premises, I suggested to my boss that we up the price to $1,635! He almost shit himself at the prospect but then nodded in agreement. I went off to suit up, conveying the look of professionalism, while he, having not pissed off the bereaved, quoted our price.

The bunny suits were mostly a prop, Dirk had once informed me. We didn't really need them, except to guard against getting blood on our clothes.

"They're mostly for show," he would say, likening the cleaning of a crime scene to a performance art. "There aren't any diseases that can be caught from old blood."

Upset by the price Dirk had quoted, the "he" of the lesbians took off again, and I settled back against the truck, awaiting another long night. Finally her partner called her back and the negotiations were finalized, with Dirk agreeing to come down in price to around nine hundred dollars. It felt like a slap in the face to do the job for less, but money was money.

It was agreed that they would leave, we would clean, and they would come back when we were finished. It was a fair proposition, but first we had to reassure the "he" that our company was licensed and bonded by the state (I still don't know what that means!), and that we weren't there to steal anything. The idea that she even considered that notion horrified me, particularly because I had had a glance around and would be damned if there was anything worth taking. Last time I checked, my hard-on for thievery didn't extend to old *TV Guide*s or mason jars full of buttons.

As I messed with my crates back at the truck, I heard the sudden rustle of plant life behind me. Instantly I thought of all the horror films I'd ever seen, where some soulless behemoth leapt out of the bushes to twist some dickhead teenager's head completely the wrong way. Or maybe he would simply squeeze my head until my eyeballs popped out.

I turned quickly, expecting the worst, and instead saw the watchful eyes of the neighborhood, come to stare. Eerie and unsettling, all the neighbors and their children stood amid the foliage of front yards, watching silently. I smiled and nodded, but none of them responded. They were just curious, but their curiosity was born of fear, and they didn't dare make the bold strides forward to confront me. I found it very intimidating.

With Dirk manning the blood on the tub, I started on the floor, first using the scrub brush to work at the human jerky, and then finally resorting to flipping it around and using the tapered lip of its handle to scrape piece by gummy piece off the floor of the bathroom and hallway. Apparently the house hadn't been wide enough to get a stretcher through, so the paramedics had had to tote her pliant, slimy, grease-soaked corpse through the hallway, dropping flesh hunks as they went.

After several hours of intense cleaning, Dirk and I each sought out menial tasks, since neither wanted to be the one who inserted his hand to unclog the greasy drain. Finally I snapped, sensing a losing battle. Holding the black trash bag open, I reached into the foul water until my gloved fingers connected with something agonizingly squishy, for which I grabbed and yanked. The drain opened up with a broad sucking noise, and I disposed of the loose flesh into the bag, trying hard not to look as I tossed it in.

There was a medical laboratory smell to the piece, which was about the size of a marshmallow, and it made me think back to when I had to dissect a frog in high school. I could feel the wetness through the thin layer of my latex gloves, and the natural, oily grease found in skin made my gloves slick to the touch. And still, for the sake of the job, for the sake of not having to go back to working for minimum wage, for the sheer knowledge that I had held a piece of a human being that most would run screaming in horror from, I persevered.

child molesters don't last in prison

Can you fly, Bobby?

—*Clarence Bodiker,* Robocop

I'D PUT OFF DIRK'S PET project of soliciting the police departments for as long as I could. Every time he'd phone me regarding the solicitation of new business, I always had some compelling reason to delay the cold calling for just a few more days. The last thing that my fumbling, awkward side needed was to try to sell a half-cocked janitorial service to cynical authority types with guns. And then one morning, Dirk had an epiphany.

Even while on his job as a sheriff, Dirk still managed to dedicate large amounts of his time to helping our crime scene business grow. Dreaming up new gimmicks to increase our presence in the community, he'd finally hit upon the "million-dollar idea."

Being in the property and evidence division of the sheriff's department, Dirk was in a special position to make an "innocent" phone call. Dialing the police department for the city of Orange, a nice little suburbia adjacent to Anaheim, Dirk got hold of their fleet commander, a tough Old West cowboy type we'll call Glenn Johnson. Glenn was a no-bullshit kind of guy, so when Dirk called, claiming that the sheriff's department needed a line on a crime scene cleaning company, Glenn had just enough salt in his veins to take the bait.

Despite Dirk's claim to the contrary, Glenn was adamant that he'd never used a cleaning service to perform biohazard service on the patrol cars and jail cells, and that the officers of Orange had always done the work themselves. Dirk persisted, saying that he'd heard Glenn had used this new cleaning service, "Orange County Crime Scene Cleaners," and that he'd heard Glenn really liked them. Dirk was eager to call the company himself, but he wanted to make sure that Glenn really had, in fact, liked them.

Now, I don't know what stars aligned for this scheme, but again Glenn was interested. He, too, was sick of the officers exposing themselves to unnecessary risk. He didn't give a damn what the fat cats upstairs wanted and was eager to employ an outside service to clean the piss, shit, vomit, blood, and general whatnot out of the jail cells and police cruisers. And if Dirk had heard positive things about this "Orange County Crime Scene Cleaners" from somewhere within the law enforcement community, well, that was good enough for old Glenn. And lucky for Glenn, Dirk just happened to have their phone number handy.

Dirk, full of prankster merriment, then called to put me on notice that I could expect a call from Orange and to harangue me into employing a similar method on every other law enforcement agency in Southern California. He had done "his part" and delivered our first one; the rest were up to me.

Finally out of excuses, I picked up the phone. All I had to say was that I was looking for the "fleet commander" or person in charge of vehicle maintenance.

"The service will sell itself," Dirk said confidently. Once the other agencies found out that we worked with Orange, they would be chomping at the bit to work with us, too.

Dirk had previously supplied me with a list of phone numbers for all the various Southern California police departments. Of course, what he neglected to mention was that each phone number was the direct line to that department's chief of police.

Rather than some office phone that the sergeant in charge or, say, an operator could answer, only then to refer me around the police station, Dirk had supplied me with direct access to the top brass at each police station. And the top brass, by and large, hates phone calls from solicitors. Especially stammering, awkward ones calling under a pretense of urgency.

Chief after chief took me through the third degree, demanding to know what business an imbecile like me had calling his or her line and then possessing the audacity to ask him or her to transfer me out. Most, after I explained that I was attempting to make their biohazard issues easier on them, simply hung up the phone. The reedy squeak of my phone voice gave me away. Any man who talked like that on the phone couldn't do them or their agency a damn bit of good.

If I did manage to get passed along to an operator, she would then inform me that their police station didn't have any sort of "fleet commander" and that the best person to decide if they needed biohazard service for their cars was the chief. I quickly abandoned that method of attracting new business.

• • •

In the meantime, I had received a call for service out in Claremont once again. I made a mental note to have our business send those two officers a fruit basket. It was only when I reached the neighborhood in my Cavalier that I realized I was back at the shit-smearing-uncle house.

Confused, I rang the doorbell and hoped that no one else had died as a result of my cleaning job…say, by slipping on a wet tile floor and cracking their skull open. A wrinkled old lady answered and introduced herself timidly. She was the mother of the homeowner, sister to the dead man, and the catalyst for his rampage. She'd moved back in and had noticed something that apparently I had missed.

I was led into a bedroom that was occasionally used by a visiting granddaughter. There, unnoticed by the homeowner or myself on my initial visit, the uncle had gone into the granddaughter's bedroom and rifled through her white wicker dresser, probably looking for lacy panties that he could wear on his head. His deep-red blood stood out sharply against the twisted thatches of whitewashed wicker, and I was incredulous that the mess had been overlooked. It was also, according to Dirk, not my problem.

I had called him for guidance as to what to do for the old lady, and he pointed out to me that their check was already in the bank. We weren't in the charity business, he said. Since I had already gotten the homeowner to sign off on the work we'd completed, if they wanted us to do additional labor, they'd have to pay for it. Besides, Dirk reasoned, how did we know that it wasn't from a different crime scene? I had no choice but to charge them.

The blood had already found its way down into the spacing in the wicker, so cleaning it was going to be a pain in the fucking ass. We'd already charged the hell out of them, so two hundred dollars sounded like a more than reasonable number when you compared this job with the work we'd already done. Granny was born of Depression-era stock, though, and I could tell from the look on her face that two hundred dollars seemed like more money than anybody had ever paid for anything, ever.

For two hundred dollars, her look declared, she could have bought a house, two cars, a bushel of prunes, seven mules, four donkeys, a small airplane, and brunch at the finest café in town, not to mention cool lemonade and a hot slice of all-American apple pie heaped with vanilla ice cream for dessert. I was practically a con man, coming into her daughter's house and asking outright for that kind of money.

The moment she snapped "absolutely not," I knew I was fucked. But cleaning the dresser looked like a bastard amount of work, and knowing that Dirk was behind me on this gave me the confidence to stand firm. I felt bad for the lady and didn't want to screw either her or her daughter over. Money was money, though, and I was through with getting the shaft.

The old woman was a shrewd judge of character and could see by the look on my face that I wasn't budging either. Why, with two hundred dollars, I could pay 1/2000th of my student loans off. That or buy some primo weed and a slice of hot apple pie heaped with vanilla ice cream.

It was while I was daydreaming about weed and pie that she asked me to leave. My expression switched from ecstasy to extreme befuddlement. There was blood on the wicker dresser, for God's sake! Who was going to clean it up? Eisenhower? The dismissal flew directly in the face of my vow to perform my cleaning duties to the best of my abilities. I couldn't just leave with possibly infectious blood curdling on the granddaughter's dresser, no matter what Dirk claimed about old blood not being harmful. And yet the old lady wanted me gone.

Feeling ashamed of my greed, I offered to at least spray down the dresser with our germ-killing enzyme for free, hoping to convince her that I was good people after all and not out to rape her pocketbook. Her demeanor was as cold as that aforementioned lemonade as she allowed me to do that. But the moment I was finished, she was at the front door, holding it wide open so that it could hit my ass on the way out. Clutching my crate of cleaning supplies, I left, head down, feeling like a company man, bought and sold.

• • •

Shortly thereafter I got a call to go to Culver City to clean up after a murder. A young soldier at the National Guard armory there had had a problem with another guardsman and, in an attempt to resolve it, had taken a bat to the rival's skull. When the MPs discovered the killer, he was in the midst of trying to scrub up the gymnasium where the murder had occurred.

The military police had to mace him to the ground. As a result of this, Dirk excitedly informed me, I would need to use my expensive-as-hell, full-face gas mask. Mace, when it dries, crystallizes into a powder that lies dormant until you reactivate it with water, which was found in most of my cleaning supplies. To catch a face full of reactivated Mace would be a very bad day for me, Dirk warned.

I drove up to Culver City, thinking how the gas mask was yet another piece of equipment I wished I had some training in. The Red Rocket's engine wasn't enjoying the stop-and-go traffic on one of the country's busiest freeways, the 405. Culver City was near the heart of Los Angeles, and the armory was just up the road from the hallowed ground that was the Sony Studios production lot—hallowed grounds for a film nerd like me, anyway.

The guard at the armory was late, which I thought odd considering the stereotype about military precision. It also didn't help that I'd been suffering a case of "blue balls" all morning that threatened to send me behind the nearest shrub for a vigorous few minutes.

Finally my liaison arrived, just as I was starting to seek out a nearby park bathroom that I could get all George Michael in. The guard had a clipped mustache and a hard, stocky body that doubtlessly came from a lifetime of physical fitness routines. I'd bet he even did pushups before, during, and after sex.

I was led into the gymnasium, which had the floor markings to operate as a basketball court as well as a myriad of other indoor activities. In addition to the firm black boundary lines there was an impressive amount of blood splashed across the floor and up onto the walls. My contact was an all-business type, so I decided that I would impress him with my all-business knowledge of the crime scene business. In thrilling sermonlike analysis, with overtones of Sherlock Holmes, I laid out for him what exactly had happened, based on my previous knowledge of crime scenery.

He let me go on for a bit with my "clearly he hit him over here" and "the victim died over there" speech, complete with sweeping arm gestures reenacting the violence of the altercation, before telling me that based on what the suspect had confessed and what the police detectives had confirmed, my analysis was completely wrong. Embarrassed, I shut up and scribbled out a cost for my services.

"I'm late for my kid's soccer game," he said. "I'll probably call you out tomorrow to do the actual cleaning…" I left, nodding, and even pointed out a spot of blood that looked like it had been overlooked by the CSI techs. "I'll call," he said again, dismissively. He never called.

I'd begun to feel pretty down. First all the police stations in town had made me feel like the second biggest schmuck on the planet (even in my woeful state I had to figure there was some asshole out there who felt worse than I did); then I lost two accounts, one of which we should have just done to protect our reputation. Then, to show me up, Dirk had gone out and scored contracts with two more police stations in Southern California: Lake Forest and Corona police departments.

Granted, it was much easier for a police officer to call upon fellow police officers and work that angle, but that sort of logic had little effect on my psyche. I did, however, take a bit of satisfaction in the knowledge that there had been a catch for Dirk when signing up Lake Forest. He had to hire the niece of their chief of police.

I imagined the sort of girl who would have an interest in dead bodies. She'd be a Goth chick, with really frizzy, dark hair, lots of eye makeup, and the sort of tits that looked big because they were propped up by a belly that was barely contained in her faded Marilyn Manson concert T-shirt.

The chief maintained that she wanted to be a CSI technician after college, though, and working with a crime scene cleaning company would look impressive on her résumé. So then I began to imagine a frumpy, studious, intellectual girl, all brains and no looks. Thus you can probably imagine that I felt like a character in an '80s teen comedy when I pulled up at Dirk's house for our next gig only to see a wildly sexy blonde chick with a rockin' body and a hot ass waiting for me.

It was one of those moments in life when your car maneuvers the curve in the road like the whole thing is in slow-mo, "Oh Yeah" by Yello playing on the radio, and her standing in the middle of the street with a cowgirl hat on, chewing seductively on a piece of red licorice. Well, maybe that's not exactly how it all went down, but if you want to envision it differently, write your own damn book. In this book, we'll call her Misty. And it sure didn't help that Misty was cool as hell and openly bisexual.

I'd been dating Kerry for over a year at this point, but if I'd had any sort of ring on my finger when I saw Misty, I would have quickly slid it into my pocket. Not that it would have mattered any, since I didn't have anything going on that impressed her. I could see the disinterest in her eyes as she shook my hand. I might as well have been one of her grandpa's poker buddies for the complete lack of sparks between us. And yet I was a man...I had to try.

On the way to the job, I drove Dirk's truck hard, because that's what a motherfuckin' guy does when he's got nothing else. He performs the shit out of whatever piece of machinery he has at his disposal, be it car, truck, or riding lawnmower. Hell, it doesn't even have to be mechanical...I knew a guy who once threw a metal trash can to impress my sister. It didn't work, of course, but man, he threw the shit out of that trash can, both literally and figuratively. Did I mock him for it at the time? Yes. Would I have done the same thing for Misty? Someone give me a trash can.

I was only slightly embarrassed that I was using Dirk's truck. He'd been promising me that the business would supply me with a truck of my own as soon as it made a little cash, but we just weren't there yet. He once again had elected not to come on the job with us, despite it being an evening gig and him being the "evening guy." I was the "day guy," but because I didn't get paid if I didn't go on the job, I was also the "evening guy." Dirk got paid the same percentage no matter what, so it was a no-brainer for him to stay home and eat bonbons while I toiled. Only this time, I wasn't too annoyed.

Initially, I'd been pissed about Dirk bringing a new hire on board. The money situation was already tight, and even though a second person would have been incredibly useful on all the jobs I'd done up to that point, I'd managed. I couldn't bear to see my percentage sliced again to placate the police chief of some podunk South County watering hole.

Then, smiling slyly, Dirk confided in me that though she'd be doing equal work, he was only paying her twenty-five dollars an hour. That might seem like a lot, but the average crime scene required about four and a half hours of work. If you cut that in half, she'd be making around fifty bucks for risking her health. On the other hand, if I held tight to my father's formula, I would net several hundred. It was chauvinistic, it was mean, but it was math I could live with.

Our latest job turned out to be in one of the few nice pockets of North County—a house in the hills with a Cadillac Escalade in the driveway. Instantly, the presence of the fancy SUV made me tack another several hundred dollars onto the bill, regardless the scene. If they could afford an Escalade, they could afford paying a larger chunk of my rent. I pulled the truck into the driveway next to the Escalade and checked out of my peripheral vision to see if Misty thought it was a cool move. My result: inconclusive.

A black lady in medical scrubs answered my knock. She'd just got home from work and was still crying over the death of our latest meal ticket. When I found out the story, I cried, too.

She and her husband, both doctors, had taken in a wayward youth who'd run afoul of the gang lifestyle and all the trappings that accompanied it. They were attempting to set him on the right path, and everything had seemed to be going well until the previous day, when the police had shown up on the couple's doorstep with a warrant to search the house.

The kid was wanted in connection with an attempted murder. (Where the hell was our call on that one?) Obviously, he was not as well-adjusted as the two doctors had thought. Though he wasn't there, the police had to confirm for themselves the absence of the suspect, as well as perform a search of the home.

The lady informed the police that she had a dog out back, a Rottweiler named Happy that ran loose in the backyard. If they would give her a second, she said, she'd put Happy in his cage.

Happy was a very friendly dog (his name apparently not being ironic), and she didn't want Happy covering the officers in big, wet, drooling puppy kisses and getting in the way of what the police had to do. Happy was like that, and he was regarded fondly throughout the neighborhood for his legendary kind disposition toward children, the elderly, and even neighborhood cats.

The cops, guns drawn, told her to stay put and then proceeded around the side of the house checking for the youth. At the sound of the side gate opening, Happy came running, curiously excited, and the cops opened fire, pumping six bullets into the big, sweet dog. Dying, Happy managed to limp back away from them in terror, his eyes wide.

Unable to comprehend the brutality of man, Happy finally collapsed on the pockmarked concrete beside the family pool. His last, whimpered barks were doubtlessly to inform the officers that he forgave them. The suspect wasn't at the house after all, and the police didn't find anything incriminating in their search.

Misty and I followed the path of the dog's last steps, noting the blood's presence in the porous concrete and up onto a wooden door where Happy had tried to escape into the house after the impact of the first couple of bullets.

The rest of the backyard was predominantly a pool, spa, and a small glass shed that housed the filter equipment and pumps for the pool. Beyond that, the backyard descended down a steep, barren mountainside, leaving the couple an impressive view of the rest of the mountains.

Right from the outset, I was concerned about our ability to clean concrete. The little dips and pockmarks flecked across the surface were too small for us to reach the furniture-stripping brushes into, and the blood had already sat through the summer sun for a day, cooking to the ground.

For this reason, I wrote the (now legendary in the crime scene cleaner world) phrase: "Due to porous nature of affected surface, some residual staining may occur." This was to become our caveat and got us off the hook for numerous future jobs, but at the time, it was merely concern for our limitations.

I once again wrestled with the price tag. They had an Escalade in the driveway, but it was "only" a dog that had died. (Sorry, Happy!) The dog had as much blood as a human, but the blood probably wasn't chock-full of doggy AIDS. It was a large scene, what with the dog dragging itself a good distance to its death, but the lady was black and I didn't want to come off like a racist. (I know, I know.) Finally, I went with nine hundred dollars. It wasn't as much as I normally would have charged, but I was doing it for Happy.

I put Misty to work on the side door while I turned my efforts to the main bloodstain, which was about the size of a beach umbrella. There was much work to do before it got too dark to see, and our tools weren't doing shit against the concrete. Two and a half hours of sweaty work later, we were no closer to being finished than when we'd started.

Because something like a portable light for outdoor work had never occurred to Dirk and me, all too quickly Misty, with only partial moonlight to guide her, said she couldn't see the blood anymore. I wanted to keep working, hating the idea of having to drive all the way out there again the next day, but I also didn't want Misty to think I was a tyrant.

Frustrated, I knocked on the front door. I'd already told the client that we'd easily be finished that evening, but evidently I was wrong. She was gracious, though, and said it was okay to return and finish the next day. Nobody would be home, but we could let ourselves in through the side gate.

Realizing that Misty and I would be returning to a fabulous house in the hills with a pool and a spa while the homeowner would be absent, I started strategizing how to broach the subject of bringing swimming suits with us the next day.

I know, I know, most of you will be pointing out that I had a good and serious long-term girlfriend already, and one that I was lucky to have, but a fella can dream, can't he? I'm a fucking dirtbag; I admit it. And anyway, I never got the chance to try to insinuate the whole spa-sex thing, because Misty couldn't go. Like Dirk, she had a day job and was only available to work evenings and weekends. I would have to finish up all by myself. It was like the cruelest masturbation joke ever.

The next morning, I headed out bright and early, sans swimsuit and grumbling about being alone. I had brought along a power washer that one of my frat brothers owned. Dirk didn't think it was a good idea, but as I pointed out to him, he wasn't the one using it.

The neighborhood surrounding the victim's house was nice, if a little compact. Most of the cars were gone from the driveways, and I was happy to see that those who lived there worked and were not a bunch of Ritchie Rich types who just hung out all day basking in their self-confidence and banging chicks who looked like Misty.

Knowing there would be no heavy furniture, beds, or carpeting that I would have to take back with me, I didn't bother with Dirk's truck and instead chugged up the hill in the Red Rocket. She was the first car I'd ever owned and was getting on in years. The one-hundred-thousand-mile mark had long since come and gone, and she didn't suffer hills well, but we made it together. I patted her dashboard appreciatively when I clambered out.

The stains at the crime scene were even darker, as the additional dose of morning sunlight had reheated the stubborn blood into the gray concrete. I had just hooked up the sprayer, happy to find an intact hose, and was blasting the concrete with a high-intensity jet of water pressure when I felt the first rumble.

Maybe it was God punishing me for having bad thoughts about him several chapters earlier; maybe it was because I considered cheating on Kerry with Misty; or maybe because I had recently ingested a strawberry Danish washed down with a large Dr Pepper. But I knew, karma or not, that I had to shit my fucking brains out.

I decided to race back to the gas station where I'd bought the cursed breakfast items, but I'd gone only half a block before I knew I wouldn't make it back down the hill before I painted my underwear like a Jackson Pollock. Anxious beads of sweat were puckering along my neckline, and I knew that if I didn't do something soon, it was going to be a photo finish. Clenching my ass cheeks together, I could feel the diarrhea pounding like infidels at the gate.

I raced back to the crime scene, my upper canines biting into my lower lip, and glanced around for the presence of neighbors who might let me use their restroom. There were some, but I was fooling myself. In moments when a bad shit was imminent, you'd better believe I was shy and awkward Jeff.

I waddled into the backyard and yanked on the sliding patio door, praying that they'd forgotten to lock it. They hadn't. I considered climbing the back wall to their balcony, hoping that that door would be unlocked, but there just wasn't any more time. Crying aloud with desperation and shame, I made a beeline for the pool shed, grabbing my plastic garbage bag and a roll of industrial shop towels.

It was a small shed with floor-to-ceiling glass windows. The engine for the pool's suction pumps took up most of the space, leaving me little to no privacy. With not a moment to spare, I yanked my shorts down and crouched over the bag, praying that it didn't explode outward and coat the pool engine in liquid brown, Type 6 shit.

The sound of my dump was something akin to the racket you'd imagine a runaway freight train making if it jumped its tracks on a hillside covered in washing-machine parts and drum kits. The whole thing was a calamitous force of relentless blasting emanating from my colon as I made choking, relieved sobs, my naked, dirty ass squatting over a trash bag filled with dog blood.

It was then that I noticed one of the neighbors standing outside. He wasn't looking in my direction, thank God, but assuredly he'd heard the noise, because it had sounded like an airplane full of chili had just exploded. His property was slightly elevated, so his view into the backyard where the shed sat was perfect. If he'd turned his head a bit more, he would have seen a pathetic large man, bare bottom stained with feces, a look of pained shame plastered across his face.

Tears welled and I sniffled a little bit, anticipating my discovery. I tried in vain to crouch behind the pool engine and swore to myself that if I got through this, I would never even consider cheating on Kerry... or combining a strawberry Danish with Dr Pepper.

God or Kerry must have heard my cry, because the man's phone rang and he stepped back inside to answer it. Quickly I wiped, using an entire roll of industrial shop towels in the process.

In the clear, I stepped back out and resumed spraying the patio as if nothing had happened. I had been right to include the catchall about residual staining. The area of the patio where the blood had been was noticeably a darker shade of gray than the rest of the area. I chalked it up to the same effect that baby oil has on a tanning person and got the hell out of there.

The ride home was especially miserable, because my car's broken trunk meant that the putrid bag of blood and excrement would be riding shotgun with me. The blood I could handle; the smell of excavated sewage from my small intestine was something else entirely.

• • •

My next job, though, made my broken trunk a real issue.

An emergency situation had come up on a weekday, so Misty was once again unavailable. It was for the best, though. Being an attractive female, she might have been problematic at a medium-security prison.

Again I didn't know the details in advance, but feeling confident that the job wouldn't involve a bed, carpeting, or large furniture, I rolled out in the Red Rocket. I'd never been to a prison before, much less juvenile hall or any other detention area. It wasn't that I was so good; it was just that I was lucky never to have been caught. I was excited, though, as there was an aura of danger about the job. Melodramatic notions of being caught in a prison riot and having to shoot my way to freedom swelled as I drove out. Why let the fact that I didn't carry a gun get in the way of a perfectly good fantasy?

NORCO California Rehabilitation Center first opened as a luxury hotel in the late 1920s. During World War II it was converted into a naval hospital. After the war it was converted into a housing facility for narcotic addicts. In the 1980s they began taking on convicts as well. There are now roughly four thousand male and seven hundred female prisoners in residence there.

It is the only California corrections center that houses male and female prisoners with a shared exterior perimeter. Whatever I was to do there, I really wanted it to be on the women's side. If there were a prison riot, I'd crack a bottle of bubbly and let the good times roll. (That is, I would if I hadn't vowed mid-diarrhea that I would stay faithful to my wonderful girlfriend.)

I arrived at the prison on the fringes of Riverside, sweating profusely. The air conditioning in my car hadn't worked in years, and each summer seemed just a little bit worse than the one before. Hopefully, I wouldn't worry about the AC much longer, as Dirk maintained that I would soon have my very own work truck.

Driving up to the prison, with its eighteen-foot-high chain-link fences topped with sprawling rows of razor wire, I felt like one bad motherfucker. I grinned an evil grin and pretended that all the guards and razor wire were to keep the inmates safe from me.

An electronic gate at the entrance stayed shut as the guards considered my car. It didn't look like the usual vehicle that came crawling up to their delivery entrance. Feeling cool, I had my window down and some Chris Isaak belting out of my CD player. Fuck protocol, I was the Crime Scene Cleaner...too cool for school.

Finally two guards stepped out, hands on their weapons. A call was made to the control booth. As the enormous metal gate slid open, my car sidled forward, stopping ten yards later at another enormous chain barrier. The rumble of the first gate sounded behind me as it clanged closed. Guards moved to either side of my vehicle, and I quickly turned off the Chris Isaak. A third guard stepped out of the booth and up to my car. "You are?" he asked.

"I'm Jeff—from O.C. Crime Scene Cleaners…Apparently you have a scene for me?"

"Please step out of your car, sir."

I felt like I was on an episode of *Candid Camera* or one of those reality shows with the goal of making regular assholes look like stupid assholes.

"I'm here to clean a crime scene for you…" I persisted, not wanting to leave the sanctity of my car.

"Please step out of your car, sir. It's routine."

Grudgingly I exited the vehicle, imagining that if I had a gun like they did, maybe I would be the one coming up with the routines. The security guards checked the inside of my car for contraband or prisoners that I was apparently trying to sneak *into* the prison and then the backseat, glancing through my supply crates. I had several razor blades in there, but I felt like the guards were on a need-to-know basis.

"Pop your trunk, sir."

The question blindsided me completely, as never once had I considered that I might have to open my trunk for them. Suddenly I felt a million miles away from that confident son of a bitch with his Hawaiian seat covers.

"My trunk doesn't open," I said, feeling like I'd been caught committing a crime.

"We need to be able to search your trunk, sir."

"It's broken," I said with an awkward shrug, my cheeks crimson. I expected the guards to start shooting at any moment.

"Can we go in through the backseat?" the officer inquired, though it wasn't really a question at all.

I like to think that I'm not a messy person, but that's miles from the truth. Since using my car as a "crime scene vessel," I'd been especially prone to throwing water bottles and fast-food wrappers behind my seats, expecting my slobby ways never to come to light. And now, in front of these trained soldiers with their immaculate uniforms, I was to be unmasked.

I couldn't pass on doing their crime scene; if I tried to leave, there was a better-than-good chance they'd detain me and search my car anyway, just to see what I was hiding. Ever more frantic, I tried to remember the last time that I'd had any... *my friends* had had any drugs in my car. I thought it had been awhile, but what a way for it to be discovered, if that turned out not to be the truth.

With no other choice, I began the long process of removing the trash from my car so that they could investigate the trunk. The crates came out first and most easily, and then empty plastic bottles slipped out and clattered to the ground. And then more plastic bottles fell out, one even rolling beneath my car. I saw the guards notice it, and my shame grew.

Worse still, cheese residue from food wrappers had melted in the heat and attached to my seat backs, and I had to peel it off quickly, the loopy strands of dairy stretching long before the officers. After many uncomfortable minutes made worse by the desert sun, I was finally able to pull down the backseat so that a disgusted guard could climb in and shine his light across the span of darkness.

"It's clean," he announced, though I knew he was using that term loosely. I felt very naked in the gated enclosure.

"Feel free to put your supplies back in," the guard said. I quickly heaped all the water bottles and sticky wrappers onto my front passenger seat, resolving to clean them out when I got home. Back in the driver's seat, I awaited the opening of the gate. Then another guard came out of the control booth and spoke with the head officer.

"One more thing, sir," he waved me out of the car again, and I could tell that he was enjoying making me look like a dickhead. He pointed to my khaki knee-length shorts. "We can't have you wearing shorts inside the prison grounds...The prisoners wear shorts. Wouldn't want you to get mistaken for a prisoner and get shot," he added matter-of-factly, pointing to one of several guard towers.

The officer pulled a pair of humongous, gray elastic-waisted pants off the gate from a stack that looked like they stayed outdoors no matter what the elements. Sizing me up and then looking at the pants, he quickly rummaged for an even bigger pair. Beyond any point of dignity, I reached for the zipper on my shorts.

"No, no, just slide them on over your pants," he said quickly, embarrassed for me. I did so, struggling to get the bottoms over my bulky sneakers. The pants were hot and stiff, and they felt gross where they rubbed against my legs.

"Our delivery drivers know not to wear shorts," he said, as if that were some sort of explanation. Once more I waited for them to open the gate. "Williams will ride with you up to the scene," the officer added politely.

Williams, a fit black guy who looked like you expected a cop to look, stepped up from behind my car and tugged at the passenger door handle, which was locked. I leaned across, opening it for him, and then we both looked at the mound of refuse on my passenger seat. Exasperated, I swept it back to the floor, where it would doubtlessly remain for several more months.

Finally, with Williams securely on board, the officer gave the order to open the gate. We started to roll forward once more, but the guard, who was smirking by this point, flagged me down yet again.

"You forgot this," he added, handing the errant water bottle back through my window.

We rolled through the prison's winding pathways with Williams pointing out the various officer-related mishaps along the way…the night guard who'd fallen asleep at the wheel and crashed through a portion of the fence here; the infirmary nurse who'd fallen asleep at the wheel and crashed through a different portion of the fence there. While looking at the various sights, I almost crashed into the fence.

Finally we rolled up to the scene of the crime. Williams was eager to see the damage. Normally consigned to the delivery gate, this was a welcome change of scenery and source of excitement for him. I waited as he climbed out first, having been shamed into complying with protocol. A fire truck staffed with prisoners waited in the wings, and several official-looking vehicles were positioned around an expanse of yellow tape.

Not expecting anyone to stop me, I walked up to the tape. A mustachioed older guard quickly held his hand up before me, but without the glee that the gate guards had exhibited.

Behind him I could see that the ground was mottled with blood and hideously large chunks of flesh and brain. I looked at the drab tan building before me, stretching up five stories or more. Near the top, an impossibly small window section was missing a board. Apparently the prison didn't feel the need for bars on the windows of a bathroom five stories up and with a sheer drop.

"Was this a suicide?" I asked the mustachioed guard.

"Homicide, most likely," the guard said. "The other inmates tossed a Chester out the fifth-floor window."

"His name was Chester?" I asked.

"No," the guard corrected me good-naturedly. "Chester…molester," he said, clueing me in to the prison lingo. "They threw a child molester out the fifth-floor bathroom window. Child molesters don't last in prison."

I looked at the tiny window, so impossibly high up in the building, and then down at the mixed-gravel-and-concrete landing spot. Blood was concentrated at the point of impact, with smears of brain and face blasting outward from there. Chester had hit the pavement headfirst. Then his body had bounced, flipped over, and come to rest about four feet from where it had first hit, eventually bleeding out into a stack of long, metal roof shingles piled against the base of the building. I picked up a chunk of the brain with my gloved hand and looked at it, imagining that I saw the tiny image of a little, naked boy seared into one of the wrinkles, clear as day.

Snapping back to reality, I suited up and began to work. Lacking the proper tool to pick up hunks of brain from the ground, I had to reach down and toss them into the black bag by hand while throwing imploring looks to the horrified prisoners, as if I was somehow worse off than they were.

The prison employed some of the minor offenders as firemen for a dollar an hour, and as such, they were allowed to hang around unshackled, watching me work. I couldn't believe that any of them were "minor offenders," as the bald thugs stained with facial tattoos looked like the first ones I'd have to gun down if my prison-riot fantasy came to fruition.

"Do we need to sign anything?" the mustachioed guard interrupted, and I scrambled for my clipboard, filling in all the basics quickly. I handed the clipboard to the guard, who, in turn, handed it to Williams. Williams looked around for someone else to deal with it, because he didn't want the responsibility either. Finally, Mustache called for a senior officer on his walkie-talkie.

When they heard that I was going to charge thirteen hundred dollars to scrub up one of their comrades, the prisoners–volunteer firemen made cracks about how I was the one who should be in prison, and how they were all going to start crime scene cleaning businesses when they got out. *Great, more competition; exactly what we need*, I groused silently.

Eventually someone arrived who was willing to shoulder the responsibility of my bill and I was back at it, working fast with all the guards and prisoners standing around watching, expecting something more profound than the basic janitorial work I was performing. I added the child molester's thick eyeglasses to the bag of trash, as well as several hunks of skin-covered skull fragments with long, dirty, unwashed gray hair extending from them. His hair would have been shoulder length if the shoulders had still been attached.

I wished I had included a "residual staining" clause in that contract as well, because the sun-dried blood wasn't coming out of the concrete there either. Finally, dehydrated and frustrated, I stood.

"All right," I announced. "It's now considered 'treated waste.' You can go ahead and spray the area down with your fire hoses."

"What about that piece?" one of the onlookers asked, pointing to a surprisingly large piece of brain resting on the hood of a nearby prison van.

Nonchalantly, I plucked the piece off and threw it into the bag along with the rest. "It's fine," I concluded, lying. "Brains don't carry disease." I had no idea if that were true or not. "Just nobody eat off that hood," I joked, but none of the men laughed.

When I drove back through the gate, I had to give the guards back their now sweat-stained elastic pants. I struggled to pull them off, but my shoes were wet from the fire hose and had to be removed first to get the pants off. My socks were full of holes with my toes poking out through the top on one and my entire heel hanging out the back on the other. I guess I just needed one last embarrassment before I could finally get out of that place.

pray for death

Ah, summer, what power you have to make us suffer and like it.
—*Russell Baker*

WE FINALLY RECEIVED A PHONE call from Cowboy Glenn at Orange PD. Since he'd agreed to use us, we'd been holding our breath waiting for some contaminant to infect the back of an Orange patrol car. And the moment had finally arrived. I rolled down there in Dirk's truck, establishing us as a bona fide company with *a truck* and not just poseur crime scene cleaners with a shitty little red car.

Pulling up to their south entrance per their instructions, I waited for the police to open their electronic gate. And waited. And waited. I was about to give up and seek out the main office when an annoyed electronic voice crackled over an unseen intercom: "Pick up the phone!"

I spied a callbox obviously situated just outside my window. Feeling like a schmuck, I opened it and picked up the tan phone receiver located within.

"Dispatch," the voice answered, and I couldn't tell if it was the same one from the intercom.

"This is Jeff Klima…from Orange County Crime Scene Cleaners. I'm here to clean a car," I said eagerly, keeping my ear to the receiver.

"One moment," the voice chirped.

The metal gate crawled open before me, and I was admitted. Being allowed into the lion's den was an exhilarating experience, and I really felt like a vital part of the law enforcement family. An older man in civilian clothes met me at the top of the ramp and beckoned me down into the underground. I drove past all the ordinary cars and trucks that the average officer took to work every day and descended down into the fluorescent-lit abyss.

Inside the underground parking garage, rows of gleaming black-and-white police patrol cars sat in lined formation, awaiting use. The man beckoned my big truck into an unused parking space and waited where he was for me to climb down and go to him.

He was old and leathery, the kind of roughneck they'd cast as a gruff ranch hand in a western movie. He even wore blue jeans and a button-up shirt tucked into them, no-nonsense style. I was certain his steely eyes could look into my soul.

"You're the guy, huh?" he said, as if disappointed by what he saw.

I nodded, remembering Dirk's advice that I act like we did this sort of thing all the time.

"Answer me one question—why should we use you?" This was not a man who wasted words.

"We are a company built on pride. We make sure that we always do a great job..." I began, laying a line of PR bullshit that he wasn't having.

"Why don't we just do the work ourselves?" he interrupted.

I stood there, my mouth hanging slightly open. This was everything I hated about meeting strangers. I didn't have the answers he wanted, and I was afraid to say something that might make him angry. I noticed another man standing behind me in dress slacks. By their expressions, I could tell that neither man was going to let me off the hook.

"We...take the liability off you?" I finally guessed, my voice cracking under the pressure.

"Exactly," Glenn confirmed, nodding at the man in the suit. "They take care of our liability," he reiterated, his attention fully on the other man.

"And are you licensed and bonded by the state?" Glenn probed me further.

"Absolutely," I lied, still not sure what that meant.

"Good for me," Glenn spoke to the other man again.

"Me, too," the man said. Apparently Dirk had already discussed rates and everything with them over the phone. We were charging seventy-five dollars to clean a car and one hundred to clean a jail cell—no matter what the circumstances. If it was dust from a mosquito fart or if a lunatic had ripped off the top two layers of his skin and thrown them around the room, we got paid the same. Personally, I was hoping for a lot more of the former. The money was secondary; we were really hoping that by getting in good with them, we would get the call any time they had a real crime scene.

Cowboy Glenn and the other man left me to the car, a black-and-white Crown Victoria wrapped several times in yellow police tape and with a biohazard symbol smartly taped in the back window. As if that weren't enough, an orange traffic cone had been propped up on the trunk.

I unwrapped all the tape, throwing it into my black trash bag, and opened the door to the backseat. Shining my expensive flashlight across the hard, plastic bucketlike seat, I could see the snotty glob of blood that had been smeared across the seat position often referred to as "sitting bitch."

It was prisoner blood, something that gave me a chill. When a little old lady gets bored with life and blows her brains out, you say, "Gross," but you quickly deal with it. When a prisoner bleeds, three big letters come to your mind: HIV. I suited up fully, wishing now that my boss had sprung for clear plastic face shields like our competitors had.

In place of facial safety equipment, I opted to hold my breath, tilt my nostrils downward, and close my eyes as I used a white cloth rag to absorb the red splash of mucuslike consistency. When it was all gone, the blood-slicked towel having been thrown into a trash bag and that trash bag having been placed inside another trash bag, I cleaned the rest of the car.

I'd told Glenn to check back on me in fifteen minutes, but I was so intent on impressing him that when he showed up, I told him it would take another fifteen minutes. In that time, I detailed the whole backseat, shining the clear plastic window between the front seat and the back, polishing the glass on all the doors, and even shining up the black plastic floorboards. For a finishing touch, I sprayed a quick blast of our deodorizer, which had a rich, pleasant bubble-gum smell, just to knock out the odor of the chemicals.

I stood waiting proudly beside the car when Glenn showed up and gave him the flashlight tour. I illustrated how I had taken the time to extract each seatbelt to its fullest extension and scrubbed both sides, how I had polished the metal plate that protected the officers up front from backseat donkey kicks, and even vacuumed out the front half of the car, removing candy-bar wrappers that roamed beneath the driver's seat like tumbleweeds in the desert. Most importantly, the blood, and any trace of it, was gone.

Glenn nodded appreciatively and used his own pen to sign the contract I handed him. I put my own pen awkwardly back in my pocket, but it didn't matter; it was official. We had a contract with a police station, and that was guaranteed business. Dirk had claimed that we were professionals, Glenn had put us to the test, and I had passed it with flying colors. Despite my slovenly appearance, I had earned the old roughneck's respect.

I lost it about two minutes later when I tried to back the truck out of the narrow parking garage.

Dirk's truck was an "extended everything" behemoth, and before I'd met him I'd never piloted a truck in my life. I couldn't see what was behind the tailgate; I didn't know the numerous blind spots; and I wasn't used to sitting quite so high. So backing up wasn't done with a confident, smooth reverse into a casual pull-forward motion. To make matters worse, the parking garage had been built with narrow lanes that would perfectly accommodate normal-size police cruisers but didn't have much space for an oversize truck.

Under Glenn's astonished gaze, I tried to execute a thirty-point turn, creeping dangerously close each time to inserting a tail pipe through various patrol car windshields. My side-view mirrors were only good for seeing Glenn's disgusted face closer than it would normally appear. While I didn't hit any cars that day, I'd once more managed to smash the hell out of my dignity.

To my credit, we received a call from Orange a week later, summoning us back to clean another car. This time it really was

AIDS-contaminated blood. A note left on the front dashboard of the car confirmed that the officer had transported a bleeding prisoner who was HIV-positive. I took all the same steps as before, not really knowing, but hoping that I was doing it all correctly and that nobody would get sick as a result of my methods. I still didn't have any training about blood-borne pathogens.

• • •

If I'd had any idea that second Orange PD call would be my last crime scene call of any kind for two months, I might have saved my money better. Believing that the good times were here to stay, I went into summer with no savings and the full expectation of more work.

Each time I placed a fumbling, frantic phone call to my boss wondering why no one was calling us or no one was apparently dying, he told me that he didn't know. Surely people were kicking the bucket, but either their survivors didn't know we were out there, or nobody wanted to pay us to do the work. Each phone call would end with my boss and me repeating our mantra: "Pray for death."

The miserably hot summer days faded into miserably hot summer nights. Chris and I were living in the frat house with no air conditioning and a hole in the ceiling that somehow vented dry, blazing furnace air down on us from the attic. Out of desperation, we'd attempted to block the hole with a boogie board, but someone had long since stolen the board for a beach trip. Kerry, miserable about my situation and hating that I wasn't working, convinced me to take a part-time job back in my old vocation: bouncing.

My frat bro Donkey Kong had started working at Heroes, a sports bar in downtown Fullerton. They were in need of burly guys to maintain law and order. It was mostly a cadre of fit, aggressive wrestlers from various colleges in the area. They all talked about how much pussy they could pull down, and how much pussy they used to pull down while working there before management had ceased their mid-shift use of a loft space across the alley for "quickies." I was hired after the "good times" were over, and as such, the other bouncers didn't trust me. It probably didn't help that I wasn't interested in talking about their wrestling stories or listening to tales about the glory days of pussy-getting.

There weren't a lot of fights at Heroes, which suited me fine, but the other bouncers were frothing for trouble. Anyone who'd get too drunk and need to be escorted out would frequently get the five-man rush, bouncers grabbing him from all angles and forcing him violently out the door. It was silly and bad for business. Most clients could be talked out, even at their drunkest, saving everyone from a scene, but that wouldn't help any of the bouncers score pussy at the end of the night. If it weren't for the bouncers, there would probably never have been a fight at Heroes.

Though I was sick of bouncing, it was my only source of income and saved my life for several months. All my money was made on Thursday, Friday, and Saturday nights, leaving me four other nights hanging out at the frat house and getting the drunkest I'd ever been. We'd finally discovered beer pong, which was making its way around the frat circuit long before it ever branched out into regular parties.

Night after night we played merciless games, with everyone chipping in money for quantity beer over quality beer. The girls didn't like it, but that just left more for us. When we ran out of beer, we'd venture upstairs to drink cheap liquor, belt out Journey songs, and tell dick jokes. And my wild side and I were right in the midst of it, leading the late-night streaking runs.

Sometimes we'd go "taping," which involved laying a strip of duct tape sticky side up in the street. A car would run over it, and the tape would stick to the wheels and get tangled up in the wheel hub, flapping around and making the unaware driver think he had a flat tire.

We'd first learned of the game from a fellow frat bro, Phil. When he was several years younger, he'd played the game with his friends until a Domino's Pizza delivery driver ran over the tape. The driver stopped, and seeing the kids laughing at him, pulled out a knife and stabbed Phil in the arm. Domino's nicely compensated Phil's family as a result, and many years later we had a great way to alleviate boredom.

We were also fond of stealing things as a prank, be it a giant pretzel machine, bike racks from the school, street signs, or the letters off of sorority houses. For all our differences from the other fraternities on Frat Row, when it came to drinking, we led the pack.

It was the easily the best summer of my life, and for the time being, I didn't care if I ever saw a crime scene again. Then one night, one of my frat brothers got drunk and punched out a window (one of our few remaining non-Plexiglas ones), slicing open the vein in his wrist. The blood expelled from him in comical spurts like some bad horror-movie prop, and it went quickly enough that he began to feel faint.

I put a compress on his wrist to stop the bleeding and ordered someone to call an ambulance. Apparently my time spent with the Boy Scouts in my youth had counted for something. After they took him away, I looked down resignedly at the large red puddle pooled on the concrete at the bottom of the broken window and went to get my crates. Drunken summer blues or not, I was a man with a calling.

the murder bed

Ordinary riches can be stolen; real riches cannot. In your soul are infinitely precious things that cannot be taken from you.

—*Oscar Wilde*

BY SEPTEMBER, THE ENTIRE SUMMER had yielded us one call from a Jack in the Box restaurant, which I had missed because I was out of town at a family reunion. In the grand scope of things, I was glad I missed it, because it was a call for service at midnight from a location in San Diego, an hour-and-a-half drive that Dirk had to make alone.

It was his first solo crime scene, which was nice, but it also established a precedent between us. If I went alone, our half was split into thirds (the other half of course going to Schmitty); if he went alone, I didn't make any money at all. That revelation stung, considering all his talk that we were in it together. But, as he didn't have to tell me, it was his company.

I also didn't know that Orange PD had called for service until I was heading back from my trip. There was a series of increasingly agitated phone messages from a sergeant questioning the quality of our work and if we were, in fact, still in business. I called Dirk in disbelief, asking why the police department hadn't contacted him in my absence.

He casually informed me that he was also on vacation, having left a few days after me. Since Misty was temporarily unavailable for work, that left no one running the business. Dirk didn't seem to have a problem with that. In the meantime, I called the livid sergeant and apologized profusely.

When I got back into town, Dirk told me that he'd handled the Orange PD problem. His method of handling it was to call another crime scene company and have them do the work. Dirk said our competition seemed nice about it, and he refused to believe that they would try to steal our client. All I could do was shrug.

• • •

A call finally came in one day from an apartment complex in North County, breaking our long dry spell. We had a murder on our hands. I picked up the truck and drove over to the address, which was part of a row of dingy-looking tenements. I would have missed the apartment entirely if not for the horde of news crews reporting from the front gates of the complex.

I slowed the truck to a crawl, but with no signs on the truck proclaiming our business, I looked just like any other curious dick-head. The curb in front of the apartment was a mess of news vans and battered old cars, and the street wasn't wide enough for me to double-park, so I ended up having to drive several blocks down and park in a tow-away zone just to reach the complex.

I hoofed it past the news teams, now pissed that they were hogging up the parking, and refused to offer them any "expert analysis," not that any of the bastards asked.

I stormed into the office feeling irritated and bossy, not realizing that the office was also the superintendent's home. He was seated at a small desk by the front door, the TV in his living room blaring some Vietnamese infomercial. The super was talking to one of the complex's renters, a Mexican family, assuring them that it appeared to be an isolated and, therefore, personal murder. I tuned him out and watched the infomercial instead.

Finally he broke from his negotiations with the family and offered me a seat on his couch. The wife had been afraid that because she lived nearby, she would be next. The poor superintendent had probably been dealing with similar complaints from other tenants all day long.

"I'm sorry about that," the super said, and I turned, not realizing the family had gone. I'd been absorbed with the thought of buying a set of commemorative gold-plated dragon coins that the infomercial was selling.

The super was a burly white guy, kind of like old-time wrestler Captain Lou Albano, and he had big eyes that sparkled with compassion for the victim. "Poor kid," he kept saying throughout our conversation. She was a Vietnamese girl in her early twenties and living on her own. Sometime during the previous couple evenings, someone had entered her apartment and stabbed her to death in her bed. Her older sister had been the one to discover her.

Out of respect for the victim and her family, the super wanted to wait for the sister, Candy Tran, to authorize my entering of the apartment. Desperate to work, I obliged him. In the meantime, though, I was going to move my truck closer. Several of the news organizations had finally given up in the heat of the day and packed it in, so I was able to pull the truck up right in front of the large steel compound doors. The doors had an auto-lock feature, so I realized that whoever had killed her hadn't just been wandering by.

As I climbed from the truck, a whirling dervish in pink passed by me in the undeniable form of Candy Tran. She was a slender Vietnamese woman in her late thirties, with long black hair. I could imagine the theme music for the Wicked Witch of the West accompanying her, except that she was wearing a hot-pink tracksuit that made a whishing sound when she walked. I jogged up behind her as she confronted the super.

"Yooouu saaaiiiidd heee wasss heeerree!" she drawled.

"He is, behind you," the super indicated. She turned and abruptly stuck a hand out for me to shake.

"I amm Caaannddy Traaaannn," she said with a nod. Then she softened to give me a look that showcased her heartbreak. "Howww doo youuuu dooo whhhattt youuu dooo?"

I looked at the super for a moment as if she was putting me on. I'd interacted with Vietnamese people before, and even the ones with pronounced accents had never talked like this. He didn't seem affected by it, so I took her small hand and shook it delicately.

"I'm Jeff. I guess someone has to do it, huh?"

The super led us over to the apartment and unlocked the door, choosing to stay outside. "Poor girl," he muttered once more as he left.

Candy and I entered, and I caught the smell of decomp right away. She'd been in there for a few days all right. The living room set looked brand-new, with the exception of a TV set off to the side. It was a sixty-inch plasma, one of the boxy ones, and it looked great except for the giant hole that had been violently kicked through the center of the screen. Another TV, one that was smaller and much less expensive but still nice, sat in its place between two tower speakers on the entertainment center. With the exception of the rotting smell from the bedroom and the wrecked TV, the place was immaculate.

Candy Tran shook her head, choosing to stay in the living room while I headed into the single bedroom. "Soooo saaaad. Shhheeee a gooood giiirrlll, aaaannndd eyyyyeeee juuust booouuuggghhht herrr aallll thhheeessssseee stttuuuuuffff."

The bedroom, like the living room, was beautifully attired, with a large dresser matched to the two nightstands beside the bed. Candy's sister had evidently been sleeping on the right side of the bed when she'd bought it, as the mattress and its linens on that side were a mass of crimson. It was a shame, too, because the queen-size bed frame itself was a beautiful wooden job with a plush velour-covered headboard. My bed didn't have a frame, only a box spring and mattress set on the floor in the frat house.

Clearly the blood had saturated the mattress because the liquid puddled on top could find no place else to go. It was like the formation of a lake—once the soil below is sufficiently hydrated, the moisture begins to accumulate above it. I was seeing that very same effect on the mattress, which meant it had to go. It would also give me good reason to tack on some more cash to the bill.

I lifted the thick mattress and was further impressed to see that the blood had gone through the box spring as well. The victim had done a good job of bleeding. Finally I dropped to my knees, using my flashlight to check beneath the bed. The blood had soaked through there as well and was pooled neatly on the carpeting below, where curious flies were investigating its outer edges.

Whoever had done it had stabbed the hell out of her. That kind of violence was typical of something personal. Someone had either wanted to send a message or was very angry with the young Vietnamese girl.

I returned to the living room, where Candy was perched on the edge of an ornate golden couch, part of a matched set with a loveseat. "Whhhaaaat yoooouuuu thiiinnnnkkk, Jeeeeeepppphh?"

"Well," I said, still befuddled by the way she was talking, thinking that maybe she had had a stroke or something. "It isn't going to be cheap. I have to cut the mattress apart and then the box spring, take the bed apart, and cut out all the affected carpeting…"

"Howww muccchhh, Jeeeeephhh?"

"Twenty-three hundred dollars." The number almost made me gasp when I said it. I could buy a used car for that much, but the company needed money. This was our first job in months. I didn't think she'd go for it, but desperate times had called for desperate measures.

"Jeeeeppppphhhh, thhhaaaatttt eeeessss fiiinnneee. Whhhhennn caaannn yyyoooouuuu start?"

I nodded, smiling. "I'll get my stuff."

While Candy cleaned out the fridge in the front of the apartment, I set to work slicing into the bed. I used a normal box cutter for the work, a miserable tool because it kept getting stuck in the heavy threading that bound the outside of the mattress. I cut the inner coils with a pair of metal snips I had brought knowing there was a bed involved. It was dangerous work because the snipped coil springs with blood-covered jagged edges had the propensity to go flying off. Any one of them could have sliced through my gloves or pierced my skin with ease. The bedding and springs and linens all went into two types of bags, saturated and unsaturated.

The wooden bed frame indeed had suffered some of the assault. Part of the right side had sloppy splashes of blood trailing down the inside edge, and two of the slats supporting the mattress had been hit, one of them soaked. I removed the saturated slat and cleaned the other one, along with the side of the brown frame. It was still a nice piece of furniture, though, and I disassembled it carefully, figuring that someone somewhere could make use of it. It would be a shame to toss something so elegant.

The carpeting came up quickly, and with the concrete base floor in the cheap apartment, I was able to lay some enzyme on that and call it a day. By the time I dragged the mattress, now missing a large, square chunk out of the right side, out to the truck, the last of the reporters were long gone.

I threw the black bags in the back of the trunk. I hadn't designated which was which, because really it didn't matter. Rather than paying a biohazard disposal company to take the oozy bags away, Dirk would typically throw them all in whichever local landfill was closest. Or if it was still early enough in the day and he was still at work, I would do it. It was a big no-no to do that, so we had to be discreet.

I walked back into the apartment to collect the rest of my supplies and to say good-bye to Mrs. Candy Tran.

"Jeeeepphhh, wwwhhhhattt hhhaaapppeeen tooo bbaaaaagggsss?" she asked.

"We take them to a biohazard disposal station, where they are incinerated at a high temperature," I said, my stock answer, which was complete bullshit. I knew the bags were really all headed to the dump.

"Caaaannnn I haaaaavvvvvee yooouuuurrr caaarrrrd?"

I pulled out a business card and handed it over to her. She studied the business card as if it were a menu. She pocketed my card and smiled broadly at me. "Thhhaaannnkkk yooouuuu, Jeeeeppphh."

Fortunately for me, by the time I left the scene the dumps were closed for the day, and my boss would have to do a little work after all. I swapped the truck for the Red Rocket and went home.

• • •

That night, Kerry and I went out to dinner with some friends to celebrate my return to business. We had just been served at the restaurant when my phone rang. I didn't recognize the number, but that wasn't unusual, as Dirk had about eight different numbers that he would call me from, and it was too late in the evening to be bothered by bill collectors.

"This is Jeff," I answered, my standard greeting, now that my personal phone was also a business phone.

"Jeeeepppphhhh, hoooowwwww arrrrreeeee yooouuuu?" the familiar voice drawled.

"Hello, Candy...I'm fine," I said, silently apologizing to my dinner companions.

"Jeeeepppphhhhh, wooooouuullllllddd yooooouuuu waaaannnnnt sooooommmmmeee offff thhheee fuuuurrrrnnnnittttuuuureee I haaaaavvvvee? I haaaavvvveeee tooooo geeeettt riiiidddd offfff itttt."

I instantly thought of that bed frame. "Yeah, Candy. That would be great. I'll come by tomorrow, if that's okay?"

"Thaaaannnkkkk yooooouuuu, Jeeeepphhhh."

We went back to the frat house, where we all sat on the couches I had donated to the house when I had to move out of my apartment. They were ratty now, full of cigarette burns and slices from when frat morons had randomly decided to stick a knife or other sharp object into the fabric. One side of the bigger couch was even shredded by a crazed dog that had lived in the frat for a month. It was a shame, because Chris and I had been planning on taking the couches back when we finally escaped the frat house, but they were ruined.

At around 11:00 p.m., I was lighting up a cigar when my phone rang again. I answered without looking at the number, anticipating a frat bro calling about my interest in a game of beer pong.

"Hi, this is Jeff."

"Jeeeepppphhhhh, iiiittt's Cannndddddyy. Caaaannnnnndyyyyy Trrraaaannn."

"I remember you," I said rolling my eyes.

"I juuuussssstt waaaannntted tooo reeeemmmmiiiinnnddd yooouuu tooo brrriiiinnnngg a truuuuccckkkk toooommmmoooorrroooowww."

"I will, Candy."

"Thhhhhhaaaaannnnnnkkkk yoooouuuuu, Jeeeepppphhhh."

I suddenly regretted giving her my card.

The next morning, I woke Chris early and convinced him to go with me to pick up the bed frame. He was grumpy but excited to see what kind of furniture was being thrown away.

Dirk let us use his truck for the move. Chris and I drove over to Stanton, just shooting the shit and laughing. Since moving into the frat house, we hadn't been as close as we had been, the two of us working different schedules.

Candy was waiting out in front for us, this time wearing an electric blue tracksuit. She beckoned us to park in her sister's parking spot behind the building.

"Jeeeeeppppphhhh, whhhhhoooo issss thhhhhiiiiissss wiiiiithhhh yoooouuuu?" she asked by way of introduction.

"This is my brother, Chris," I said, and Chris shook her hand.

"Yoooouuuu boooootthhhh loooook sooooo sttttttrrrrroooonggg," she gushed.

When we got into the apartment, Candy spread her hands before her. "Taaaakkkkkeeee annnnyyyyytttttiiiiinnnng yoooooouuuu waaaannnnnt."

I tried to play it cool, but I was like the kid in the candy store (no pun intended). "I guess we'll take the tower speakers, the entertainment center, the TV…" I listed, indicating the smaller, working one. If they caught the creep who had kicked in the big plasma, which was allegedly the victim's violent boyfriend, I would kill him myself.

Chris also suggested a nice lamp and a throw rug that looked expensive. The couches were too nice to leave behind, so we agreed we'd take those as well. And, of course, I told her that I was certain I could find someone who could use that elegant bed frame.

Though it took us two trips to do it, we got everything from Stanton to the frat house in Fullerton, a thirty-minute trip each way. We were both exhausted by the end of packing up the final load and were all set to leave when Candy approached us.

"Jeeepppphhhh, I haaavvveee beeeen goooodd tooo yooouuu?"

"You've been very nice," I said, incredulous at our good fortune.

"Jeeeeepppppphhhh, coooooulllldddd yooouuu dooo soooommmeeeetttttinnnggg fooorrr meee?"

"What is it, Candy?"

She had to get rid of all of her sister's things and be out of the apartment ASAP, though the super claimed it wasn't his edict. Basically, as a way of getting free movers, she had culled us over to take what we wanted and then guilted us into taking everything else over to a Buddhist monastery, where she was donating it to the local monks. Chris and I couldn't figure out a way to politely refuse, and so we did what she asked. Besides, we'd never been to a Buddhist monastery before.

We had to drive back home, unload the stuff, and then drive back once more to do it. And in the frustration of now being Candy's pawn, I pulled the bed frame out of the back of the truck, feeling an odd tinge in my back. It was quick and painful, but the sharpness of the pain faded quickly. I had felt familiar tweaks before when schlepping kegs at BevMo and thought little of it.

It was nightfall by the time I dropped my boss's truck off at his house, and the multiple trips had cost me in gas. But I'd gotten a bed frame, entertainment center, huge speakers, TV, CD player, amplifier, couch, loveseat, lamp, and rug out of the deal. All in all, it was a pretty good day.

I wasn't prepared for the reaction at the frat house that night, though.

I had done a lot of nutty things in my life, like stealing a newspaper dispenser that I put in our frat bathroom so visitors could read my journalism editorials on the can. But my frat bros and their litany of guests couldn't believe that I'd come home from work with a bed that a girl had been murdered in. It was quickly dubbed the Murder Bed and became a mandatory stop on tours being given through the house.

Most bros accepted it as "Klima being Klima," but one guy in particular got really bad feelings about it and was certain the bed and all the possessions from the girl's house were cursed. That night, Kerry's hamster, which had been living at the frat for over a year, died. The brother gave us the evil eye.

• • •

The next day, my phone rang. This time I recognized the number.

"Hello, Candy," I answered, not excited.

"Jeeeepppppphhhhh, caaaannnn I asssssskkkk a favvvvvooorrrr offff youuuuu?"

"I'm pretty busy, Candy," I said, putting my new TV on mute.

"Ohhhh, Jeeeepppppphhhhh, I wiiiiilllll paaaayyyyyy yoooouuuu."

"What is it, Candy?"

"Jeeeeeppppppphhhhh…ittttt issss mmyyyyy siiiissssttttteeerrr. Shhhheee wiiiilllll beeee naakkkkkedddd innnn heeeeaaavvvven ifff I doooo nottt seeeeennnndddd herrrrr clllloooottthhhess."

"Wait, what?"

"Wiiillll yyyooooouuuu taaaakkkkkeee herrr clllottthhheesss annnndddd innnnccccinnneeeerrratttteeee theeeemmmm?"

"You want me to incinerate her clothes?"

"Yessss, Jeeeepppphhhh. Wiiiitttthhhhh thheeee baaagsss offff heeeer blllllooooddd."

It suddenly made sense what she wanted me to do.

"Oh, Candy, uh, the bags of biohazard have already been processed at the disposal station," I said, picturing them sitting beneath the decimated mattress at the landfill near Dirk's house.

"Pllleeeeeaaassssseee, Jeeeepppphhhh, shhhheeee iiisss naaaakkkkeeed in heeeaaavennn. Itttt issss myy cuuulllttttuuuurrreeee."

"Well, that disposal station charges three hundred dollars per load…" I said, grinning like a crook.

"Jeeepppphhhh, moooonnnneeeey issss noooo obbbbjjjjeeeect."

"All right then. I'm at a crime scene right now, but I'll be over later to pick up what you want me to take. Just make sure you have it bagged and ready to go."

"I wiiiilllll, Jeeeepppphhhh. Yoooouuuu arrrreeeee soooo strrrrroooonnng. Thhhhhannnnkkkk yooouuuuu."

I hung up the phone and turned the TV back on, loving my life.

That evening, I interrupted my date with Kerry to talk her into driving over to the apartment in Stanton. Kerry was repulsed by the idea but still drove me. I changed back into my work polo, now crunchy from sweat and a faded gray from so many washings.

Candy was waiting outside for us, wearing a violet tracksuit. Seven large trash bags full of shoes and handbags and clothes were piled up next to her. I thought about pressing my luck and telling her it would be three hundred dollars a bag, but that seemed a little mean even by my new standards.

She paid me, and I loaded up Kerry's backseat and trunk, with Kerry glaring daggers at me the whole time. I swore to Candy that I would burn them all and that her sister would be well-stocked in heaven and no longer naked. Candy handed me a check and I thanked her, offering her once more my condolences.

We drove back to the frat house. Refusing to be a part of it, Kerry went inside, leaving me to deal with a car full of contemporary clothing. Part of me wanted to try to sell it, but I could just imagine the phone calls I'd get if Candy saw people all over town wearing clothing and carrying purses that once belonged to her sister.

Instead, I threw all the bags into the dumpster of a rival fraternity. To keep my karma in line, I took a purse and a pair of white pumps from one of the bags and threw them into a metal barrel we used for burning trash when it got cold around the house. Someone would set a fire in the barrel someday, I figured, and at least the sister would have stylish shoes and a nice purse. That was how women would be dressed in my version of heaven, anyway.

I figured it was the last I'd heard of Candy Tran, but no. She called several days later to check on my progress, probably noting that I'd cashed the check.

"They got taken care of," I assured her. "They're headed to the same place the mattress and all her sheets went." It wasn't exactly lying…

CHAPTER 12

back, back, back...and it's gone!

Every human is the author of his own health or disease.

—*Buddha*

DIRK'S MOTIVATIONS WERE ALWAYS IN the right place with the business. He wanted to get a truck for me, one that I could take home so I wouldn't have to go see him every time I had a crime scene. He wanted company vacations, and he wanted health care. It was a new business, still finding its legs. It wasn't easy that 50 percent of what we were making was instantly being shipped up north to Schmitty.

Dirk had even gone so far as to scrap the splitting of the net profit into thirds. He knew I was struggling, and he also complained that the money coming in from his take was just extra money for his wife to spend. He didn't need that. So he eliminated the rule of thirds and began splitting the pot down the middle, half to me, half to him.

It was good of him; he had a full-time job as a cop, making decent cop money. His wife had worked for the same company for more than twenty years, so she was making good money, and the crime scene cash was extra for him. On the other hand, I was living and dying on the crime scene money. The supplemental income I made bouncing for a few hours on the weekends wasn't anything real, food money mostly.

I had "graduated" in May of '07 from CSUF, taking the walk with six of my frat brothers. I wasn't an official graduate yet; I still had one class left that I was supposed to take over the summer. But with the financial drought from the crime scene biz, I pushed back my graduation until fall so that I could get one last financial-aid check (which I then used to purchase an arcade game and a kegerator). But it also pushed my graduation date back to 2008.

It was frustrating, though. I could barnstorm through crime scenes and make what boiled down to more than one hundred dollars an hour, sometimes even more than two hundred. I was making what doctors made, and yet I was a college graduate still living in a frat house. If only the work had been consistent, even moderately consistent, I would have had a chance at a real living, maybe even buying myself a new car.

My credit was fucked up from months of inconsistency, and I didn't have clear goals for a promising future. Like a loser, I used to joke that I would get married and raise my kids while living in the frat house. Most of my cronies had come and gone over the years, either graduating or dropping out of school to focus on something "real." I had the crime scene business. It was what I clung to, pushing my potential for income on anyone who would listen.

I wasn't a loser yet. At parties, anyone who found out what I did for a living was eager for me to share stories, to tell them about the unknown, but Kerry wanted me to quit. From the first time she met Dirk, she had sensed his weakness. I had done my damnedest to pimp the business to her, regurgitating all the claptrap that he had filled me with, and then I took her to meet him one night.

Like a broken record, he'd repeated all the same nonsense to her, only this time it was less convincing and less assured. But I was *Jeff Klima*, and I was determined to show her that the business would be a success. One day, when we were spending my money on a house and going on fabulous trips to exotic locations that only someone with an income in excess of six figures could afford, she'd see, she and all the other naysayers.

We hadn't yet succeeded in getting a truck, vacations, or health care, but Dirk decided one day to take an active stand and slash Schmitty's cut from 50 percent to 15 percent. I thought it was right on, as we'd given Schmitty a lot of money over the year for not a lot of turnout. Sure, he let us use his name, and he referred business to us whenever he got a call from that area, and yes, he hooked us up with his corporate accounts, like the Jack in the Box that Dirk had worked in San Diego. But all that was more like a "15 percent partner" than a "50 percent partner."

Dirk had often said that Schmitty was a bastard and full of hot air. He was always threatening to put Schmitty in his place, and I was always confident that he wouldn't. So I was surprised when he one day announced to me that he had talked with Schmitty and had gotten him to agree to a 25 percent take. It was much better than I would have thought Dirk capable of.

● ● ●

The dull pain in my lower back had resurfaced and was now constant but tolerable, more of an irritation than anything. I was able to mostly ignore it. Whenever I found myself slouching, I would arch backward and feel things pop back into place. I could handle doing that for the rest of my life, I thought.

I was relieved that Dirk had paid me outright on the Candy Tran job. The work check, plus what Candy had paid me for "burning" her sister's clothes, made for a nice increase in my finances. I promised Chris lunch if he would tag along for a trip to the bank to cash the check and go grocery shopping. He agreed, as his job at Home Depot wasn't yielding him the kind of hours he needed and he'd been living off ramen and microwavable popcorn.

We'd had a good laugh around the frat at Candy Tran and her murdered sister's expense, telling and retelling the story of how a Vietnamese broad was wandering around heaven with no clothes on, and I was well paid for it.

While I was at the bank, though, karma decided to kick in and have a laugh of its own. I reached for the bank pen to endorse my check and accidentally dropped it on the floor. I bent over quickly to pick it up and suddenly, feeling a sharp pop in my lower back, collapsed in pain.

Chris stood idly by as I attempted to lift myself back up, finally settling for crawling over to a row of seats by the entrance. I sat for a bit in blinding pain, desperate not to call attention to myself. I was scared. Not having health insurance, I knew that what was on the check wasn't near enough to cover an ambulance ride to the hospital, much less any kind of stay there.

Grinding my teeth together to the point that I thought they might explode under the pressure, I had Chris get the car and I hobbled out the door bent in half. He drove me home, and I made the agonizing trip upstairs to my room, where I lay on the newly assembled Murder Bed for the rest of the day.

The next morning, I awoke with the same nagging sensation in my back, but at least I could stand, if not completely straight. I convinced myself that I had to take it easy, but that night I was playing beer pong and puffing on a cigar like I didn't have a care in the world.

Several weeks went by before we had another call for a crime scene, and I was beyond ready. While I hadn't exactly taken it easy like I promised myself I would, my back hadn't worsened beyond that constant dull pain. The latest call was for a Motel 6, though, and I'd be working it alone.

A Motel 6 was pretty much the worst gig in the crime scene pantheon. We did them because Schmitty had the contract for them, but there was no real money involved. Correction: there was money involved, but the flat-rate chump change I earned for a Motel 6 corporate gig seemed like a waste when I could be earning eleven hundred dollars for four hours of reasonably easy work elsewhere.

We didn't set the bidding price for corporate gigs; rather, there was an established set of rates that Schmitty would charge. We never knew what the money was going to be like, but we could always count on it being low. Dirk's theory was that Schmitty didn't like us lowering his fee rate, and as such, he stuck it to us on the Motel 6 gigs.

No matter what we did or how long we were there, I could expect the same flat fee of $250. That might seem like a good chunk of change, but when you're scrubbing up a murder scene that starts in a bed and ends behind the toilet and involved the victim spraying blood on all the walls, carpeting, and ceiling, $250 seems like charity.

Motel 6 gigs were sometimes our salvation, though, so I was

thankful for them. But there was a lot of work involved in cutting apart a mattress and box spring, bagging the pieces, removing what was left from the room, cleaning the walls, pulling all the furniture out, and then cutting out all the carpeting and insulation...especially when you're alone.

My back hurt, but I had been dealing with it for so long with no medication that I just accepted it as the norm for a lower-class working stiff with no health insurance in America. I made it through most of the grunt work—lifting, bending, and pulling—and had the mattress and box spring loaded in the back of the boss's truck. It was only when I was yanking out the last of the carpeting that I could tell something was wrong.

I had been bent over and pulling, and when I went to stand fully erect, I found I couldn't. Every time I tried to force it, I felt a searing pain that burned across the span of my back like a flash fire. I dropped the carpeting and, with tears springing to my eyes, leaned back against the wall behind me.

Stubborn pride wouldn't let me quit. Gritting my teeth, I leaned backward until my butt and my shoulders were flush against a wall I had cleansed of blood minutes earlier, and then I walked my legs backward until I was upright.

The pain was complete now, encompassing the entirety of my back, and had the bed still been in the room, blood or not, I would have flopped down on it and sobbed. I felt like my spine was a roller-coaster car gearing up to be launched through my asshole. But my pride persisted, and I squatted with my knees to lift the carpeting.

Moving slowly and deliberately, I was able to work the carpeting out the door of the motel and over into the truck. Then I had the not-so-simple process of moving all the furniture back into the small room, which ended up taking another hour. Finally I was able to close the motel-room door for good, climb back into the truck, and drive over to the office, where I dropped off the electronic key card and collected a signature on the invoice, which Dirk would then ship off to Schmitty.

But I had made it; I was home free. I would be able to drop off the truck to Dirk, let him worry about taking the stuff to the dump, take my car, and head for home. After that, it would be a bag of ice on my back and bed rest until the next crime scene came up, hopefully a month away.

But it never works like that in the crime scene business.

Before I could call Dirk and let him know I was headed in his direction, he called me. "We've got another one," he said enthusiastically.

Stubborn pride or not, I was hurting. "I don't think I'll be able to do it...I threw my back out today."

"Do you think you can hold out for one more? Please...I'm not out of work yet, and I already told this guy you'd meet him. It's across the county, and I don't want to keep him waiting...please?"

I shook my head no but said, "Yes." Being on the phone, he only caught the "yes" part.

The apartment in question was clear out in the boondocks of Orange, and it was dark by the time I got there. It was especially irritating because Dirk was only fifteen minutes from being off work anyway, and had he asked the guy to wait, it wouldn't have been an issue. But that was Dirk, always afraid of missing out on the bigger, better deal.

Twenty minutes later the client arrived, and I was furious. Dirk could have met the asshole right on time and didn't need me at all. He still hadn't arrived himself, of course. I climbed out of the truck walking with the awkward, limping gait of Frankenstein's monster. The client, a long-haired, ex-hippie-looking motherfucker, didn't seem to notice.

"Hey, man, it's great that you could come out," he said enthusiastically.

"No problem." I said with a wince, and slowly followed him along the winding path to the victim's apartment, carrying my red crate full of supplies.

"Man, Roger was a saint, man...a saint. And he will be missed, man."

"Who's Roger?"

"Roger is like...Roger was like, my friend, man...just a beautiful human being, right? Well...I guess he was pretty unhappy in life...he had some darkness, you know? He killed himself."

I followed the guy into Roger's apartment, wincing instantly at the familiar smell.

"Roger's been here awhile, huh?"

"Yeah, apparently, man. He used a pillow to muffle the sound of the gunshot, and I guess nobody heard."

Roger's apartment was like stepping into a record store on Haight-Ashbury at the height of the 1970s. Posters of The Who, Led Zeppelin, and Strawberry Alarm Clock littered the walls while stacks of records filled up most of the free space.

The place would have reeked of patchouli if not for the over-whelming stench of death emanating from the bathroom. I shuffled toward the scent, and each step was electrified agony. The crate was heavy, made heavier by the addition of my Hudson sprayer full of the enzyme solution. There was nowhere to put it down without my crying out in pain, so I held it limply in my hands.

Roger had clearly been a considerate person in life, for in death he had prepared himself accordingly. Some assholes just don't give a damn and go flinging their guts all around the place. But not Roger. He had laid out a series of blankets on the floor to rest on, with a pillow to support the back of his head and another pillow beside it to catch the spray. And just in case blood and brain matter came out the front, he had laid a towel across his face.

"Man, Roger was a hell of a guy. He played the drums, did you know that?"

"How would I know that?" I retorted, not caring.

"One time, for his birthday...Hey, check this out," he said, realizing I wasn't really paying attention. "One time, for his birthday, I took him to this club, because Stan Millbauck was playing guitar, right? Stan goddamn Millbauck! Well, I knew the owner of the club, so I got there early and asked Stan if it was okay that Roger came up on stage and jammed with him for a song. And Stan said okay! So I took Roger there, and he had just a great night. It was his fortieth birthday, man."

The guy's story sounded like he wanted me to think *he* was a hell of a guy, not Roger, but I simply said, "Wow."

Needing to assess the amount of damage to the wooden flooring underneath the blankets and pillows, I squatted down once more slowly and maneuvered my crate off to the side. The coroner who'd taken

Roger's body must have replaced the gray towel, as it was stretched over most of the pillow, obscuring it.

"Man, Roger really liked music, man," the guy babbled in the background.

"Would you shut the fuck up?" I wanted to say but didn't.

I yanked the towel off quickly, as one might remove a Band-Aid, and despite my back, moved quickly upward. The grease of Roger's head as he melted had provided a wonderful source of nutrition for the hundreds of squirming maggots that were filling the indentation in the pillow.

"Oh, my God, those things are evil," the client said from behind me, repulsed.

I dropped the towel in disgust, and several maggots dropped from their perch on it, hitting the floor like so many gummy bears. Their pale white skin looked like they themselves were the dead, with small tapered bodies that squiggled and moved out of sync with those on the towel.

I didn't know why I was so repulsed. The maggots were really just like me; they were there to clean up the dead, get what they could off the victim, and then leave, moving on to the next meal ticket. I was a maggot, feeding off the dead.

"Hey, man, don't let them get away!"

I looked over to see several of them crawling across the floor and slowly put out a large, black sneakered foot to squash them.

Bending slightly at the knees once more, I pulled my clipboard from the crate and reached inside it for a pen and a fresh invoice.

"Hey, man, is it all right if we do this tomorrow?"

I looked at him, incredulous. "What?"

"My old lady is already hassling me about being out here tonight. I gotta meet her for dinner…are you available tomorrow?"

"Sure, sure," I said, putting the pen back in the clipboard. Really, I was grateful to be off the hook for the evening. If my back were anything like it had been the first time, in the morning it would be good for another couple of months. I slowly lowered myself down to pick up the crate.

"Hey, do you think we could kill all the maggots tonight, man? I'd feel bad if any of them got away."

I was wondering what had happened to the whole "love and peace toward all living creatures" sentiment, but I said, "Sure. " I then realized I'd left all my trash bags in the truck.

"Uh, you know what?" I corrected myself. "Actually, I'm not allowed to do any work without a contract in place," I said, lifting my crate and figuring that would scare him off.

"Oh, I'll sign the contract tonight, man," he grinned. "I'm not out to give you the high hat."

"I appreciate that," I said glaring at him. It all just needed to end. And where the fuck was Dirk?

I took the crate back, hobbled out to the truck, grabbed a bag, and returned to the apartment, angrily tossing the towel and pillow into the trash bag. I could see that Roger's body fluids had leached through the pillow and into the wood floor below. It would be a tough scrub.

• • •

I was out in the parking lot, saying good-bye to the client when Dirk showed up in my car.

"What's happening?" he asked nonchalantly when he got out.

"Where have you been?" I asked.

"I got delayed at work...you know how it goes." He shrugged. There appeared to be a smear of spaghetti sauce on his upper lip.

I shook my head, attempting to not freak out completely. In the end, I just wanted to get home.

"Where's he going?" Dirk pointed at the departing client.

"He's going home. He wants us to do the job tomorrow."

"Ooh, busy day."

"Why?"

"Well, I just talked with Mona Spears over at the Public Guardian's office. They deal with the estates of deceased people. She's got a gig for us tomorrow, and if we do good by them, they'll keep us busy for a long time."

"My back is fucked, boss."

"It's a crazy gig," he said, excitedly. "This old lady poisoned her son and then her cat and then herself. What's crazy is that the son was sitting in a chair by a window when he died, and for weeks people just thought he was a Halloween decoration as he sat there, rotting."

In spite of myself, I grinned. "That's pretty disgusting."

"Yeah, and the cat puked up a bunch before it died, so that should be nice."

"Sounds great," I agreed.

"Well, hey," he said, suddenly concerned for me. "Go home, get some rest, take it easy, and be over at my house bright and early, say 8:00 a.m."

I nodded and started to climb into my car, figuring I would leave my crate in the back of his truck for the next day.

"Hey," he said. "Take your crate with you in case we get a call from Orange tonight…"

I nodded slowly and retrieved my crate.

"Hey, thanks for handling all this tonight. I appreciate it," he said as I drove off.

The whole way home, I fought back tears, angry about the evening's events, about my pain, and my life at large. I felt like a loser.

• • •

Parking on Frat Row was always an issue, particularly at night, and that evening was no exception. Frat Row was on a small street surrounded by low-income apartments and housing. And most of the surrounding streets were either "No Parking" or "Permit Parking Only."

This left a square block of parking spaces for the hundreds of cars belonging to people in the frats, the apartments, and the houses. Not to mention all the cars of frequently visiting frat guys who didn't live on "the row"; the friends of people in the frats, houses, and apartments; and all the people who parked on Frat Row and walked the block to school in lieu of paying the $150 it cost per semester for a parking pass.

The school "graciously" allowed students without a parking pass to park their cars on school grounds, provided the cars were moved by 7:00 a.m., when the parking enforcement creeps made their first rounds, giving out forty-dollar tickets. People could park in the alley behind the frat house, but the city liked Frat Row almost as much as CSUF did, and they sent their own parking enforcement over there almost daily. Parking in the alley was a thirty-six-dollar ticket.

Other than those four blocks, there was nowhere to park in the surrounding two miles that didn't result in a ticket or a tow. And by the look of it, that evening was one of many party nights on "the row." On party nights, if you didn't have a parking spot by 8:00 p.m., you didn't have a parking spot at all, alleyway included.

Fortunately for me, after a half hour of searching, one of the dicks from Delta Chi moved his car from behind our alleyway, most likely in the pursuit of roofies. I risked it, parking my car behind the Sigma Nu house. My back feared a ticket a lot less than a two-mile walk.

Hobbling inside and up the stairs, stripping my shirt off as I went, I was grateful to see Kerry waiting in my room. She was spending the night, which was a rare treat because she hated the unbelievably filthy condition of the frat house. She'd come to drink, though, and was ready to party when I walked in, my face dripping with perspiration. I dropped onto the bed and immediately went into my sob story, attempting to cajole some sympathy out of her. It didn't work until she tried to get me to roll over and realized I couldn't. I was too pitiful for her to chastise.

The next morning, when my alarm went off at 7:00 a.m., I realized that something wasn't right. The pain that I had anticipated would diminish by morning had somehow intensified to a breaking point. Whereas previously it had only hurt to have pressure on my lower back, now every small movement or twitch was reason for an agonizing sob. I couldn't even get out of bed to take my morning leak.

I shook Kerry awake and confessed to her that I was in serious pain. It took a lot to coax an admission of weakness out of me, so she snapped awake and into panic mode. She demanded we call an ambulance, but I stopped her, citing the same reason as I gave you earlier. I continued trying to get out of bed, but gave up in frustration. I knew I was fucked. Defeated, I called Dirk and told him I wouldn't be joining him on the day's adventures. In the end, I knew Kerry was right. I had to go to a hospital.

In America going to a hospital without insurance is one of the lowest and most embarrassing things you can do. You certainly feel the doctors' friendliness decline after they see "NO INSURANCE" on your chart. Your waiting time for treatment increases; your quality of care diminishes; and male nurses have contests to see which of them can piss on you from farther away.

I didn't try to pass it off as a workplace injury; I couldn't do that to Dirk. Despite his goofiness, he'd still meant well by me and treated me fairly. (Jesus, listen to me; I sound like a battered wife.) If the company got hit with a nasty hospital bill, it would likely be the end of crime scene cleaning and I would wind up back in retail, college degree or not. In the end, I knew I would have to take on the burden and hope the hospital had a "mulligan policy." (For those of you who have insurance, the "mulligan policy" refers, much as it does in golf, to a freebie. Basically, the hospital realizes that you are a deadbeat and lets you off the hook for your care.)

The hospital ran a few quick tests to confirm that I was definitely in pain and then basically told me to take a hike. Sure, I was given the standard prescription for the generic version of codeine with no refills, but I knew the pills wouldn't make a dent in the pain. When I left the hospital, I still had no idea what was wrong with me.

Kerry was adamant that I didn't stand a chance of recovering in the frat house and insisted I stay at her parents' place, where she could take care of me, which I nervously agreed to. Back pain or not, it was her parents' house, and she was definitely still their little girl. I was some creepy, letch boyfriend living in a frat house past his expiration date with no health insurance, a busted back, and zero prospects for the future other than a dead-end job scooping up bits of child molesters and truckers (sometimes one and the same).

I stayed in Kerry's room for two weeks, occasionally coming downstairs to entertain Buffy, the family Boston terrier, and monopolize the TV. During those two weeks, I never took a shit once. Apparently generic codeine had that effect on people. It was just as well; I couldn't maneuver around to wipe, and besides, I was terrified that one of my fat-guy poops would clog their toilet. Bad back or not, there is just some shit you don't live down.

At the end of my two weeks, I could finally maneuver around well enough to deal with frat-house living. Chris had checked on me regularly and moved my car every Tuesday morning when the street sweeper came around at 9:00 a.m. sharp (thirty-two-dollar ticket), and a slew of other frat miscreants had dropped in to pay respects to their fallen brother. It really made me appreciate the majesty of fraternity and friendship, and the higher meaning of both. Of course, that might just have been the codeine talking.

When my pain meds finally ran out, I realized quickly the agonizing misery of life in a frat house. In the end, you're only as well liked as the good times you provide. And once you're an injured whiner, pent up in his room, stinking in his bed, you cease to be a source of good times.

My room was one of the two access points to "the taint," the congregational room of the frat house. As such, I was constantly being given the evil eye by newcomers as they'd pass by taking the house tour. It was a different era, and we were shopping for new recruits, so the place was a hotbed of new faces.

I would do my damnedest to give them a "what's up?" and thumbs up, "I'm a cool guy" sort of enthusiasm, but I came off more like some desperate and bedridden lonely weirdo. Even the Murder Bed ceased to be a reason for people to visit. Soon, the house tours were being given around my room. I could hear the younger bros taking their friends through the house, and they'd stop outside my door.

NEW GUY: What's through here? (The knob would turn.)

YOUNG BRO: There? Oh, nothing. It's where we keep the sewage pipes...Come on...Let's go back the way we came...(Knob stops turning.)

ME (Loudly): There's a man in here! A human being! I'm not something you can kick under a dresser! Can someone out there bring me a burrito from Rigoberto's?"

YOUNG BRO: (Silence.)

I spent the better part of the next three months like that, laid up in bed recovering. Sure I got up occasionally to pee and visit the brothers downstairs, even joining them in a few games of beer pong that doubtless slowed the recovery process.

To help me keep my finances afloat, Dirk gave me a check for six hundred dollars. It was a lot less than I would have made working those two crime scenes with him, but I greatly appreciated the effort. I would be back as soon as I could, I promised him. I wanted to do what it took to help the team.

CHAPTER 13

welcome to the dollhouse

When someone collects dolls, they are seeking to compensate for the imperfections they detect in their real children.

—Psychological analysis

MY FIRST JOB BACK CAME in early January. It was still in the middle of my three months of recovery, but Dirk had a new connection for the business, and he was eager to make it work.

Back when he had cleaned up the bodies of the old woman, her son, and their cat for the Public Guardian's office, Dirk had used his goofy innocence to strike up a friendship with the field agent, Mona Spears. (The Public Guardian is the county official responsible for dealing with the estate after a person has passed on and a legal next-of-kin has yet to be established.) Mona, in turn, had passed our name around to her colleagues, and they put us to the test.

My first assignment was for a short Mexican lady named June. She met me out at the victim's house one afternoon so that I could assess the damage to the property in terms of biohazard and write up an invoice to be sent out to the victim's brother, living in Florida.

If he agreed to our price, June and I would agree on a day, and I'd clean the scene under her supervision. She had to be on the property at all times when I was there, and she couldn't be on the property by herself. It was an intense series of checks and balances within the Public Guardian's office, and no one seemed to trust anyone else.

Needing money, I knew from the outset that I was going to jack up the bill. It wasn't as if the brother in Florida was going to see what it looked like anyway. He'd have to take my word for it.

I had picked up a cane in the initial stages of my recuperation, while filling my generic codeine prescription, and it turned out to be the lifesaver that got me through the whole back ordeal. Sure, it was a budget cane made for someone six inches shorter than me, but with my back the way it was, I couldn't walk fully erect anyhow.

June was forty-five minutes late to our appointment and full of apologies, but I was under strict orders from Dirk to win the P.G.'s office over, so I brushed it off with an easygoing chuckle.

Using my cane to lift off the stoop, I explained my injury to June, who took it all in stride. I assured her, as Dirk had assured me, that when I did the work, I would have an able-bodied staff member do all the heavy lifting.

The trauma scene that had occurred at the small, one-story, raised house was different from any I had done so far. I knew that instantly from my position on the porch, mainly because I had never detected the smell of decomposing flesh from outside the house before. It was going to be a bad one.

Stepping into the house was like entering one of those camper trailers that get towed behind a truck. The house was small, cramped, and poorly laid out. Immediately the spectral, unblinking orbs of a dozen dolls were upon me, silently watching, observing my every move. I moved out of their line of vision and, with my cane, hobbled toward the source of the smell. It was an awful odor, stinging the hairs in my nose, and I didn't want to open my mouth for fear of getting the taste inside.

June had outfitted herself with a respiratory mask to stave off the noxious fumes of the rotting dead. Part of my making a good impression on her and her office was forgoing the mask. Jeff Klima and the company he represented didn't have a problem with bad smells.

The little old lady had died in her bedroom, beside a large bed with a simple frame. Since my own bed-frame acquisition, I noticed other people's bed frames and rated theirs against mine. In this case, mine won.

It was an awkward scene because the lady had clearly been in the bed shortly before she had kicked the bucket, and at some point in her sweet-old-lady death spasms had tumbled to her right, dropping down onto her thick, green carpeting. The carpet material wasn't quite shag, but it was dense and plush and plenty ripe.

"She was in here for three months," June said from her position in the doorway. She didn't want to come any closer. "She just rotted away with her cat in here. The cat lived. It ran out when the police finally busted open the door."

"Three months?" I said, looking down at the amazingly in-depth outline of her body, crystallized perfectly in the fibers of the carpeting. Something looked off inside the outline, though, and I put on my black latex gloves to check it out.

Using the corner of the bed, I slowly lowered myself down onto the floor, keeping my back as stiff as possible and leaving nothing to chance. I was used to the greasy residue from a decomposing person leaving a haloed effect in their final resting place, as if the dead had attempted snow angels on their respective floors. But this was more filled in, more viscous than I had seen in a decomposition case.

June watched with an eerie sort of eagerness, and I knew that I had to act like a true professional and show no fear. I planted my hand down into the thick of the carpet, where her heart would have been, just to feel the difference. Imagine my repulsion when my fingers sank through the saturated carpeting and a chunky brown stew of melted guts slimed over the top of my hand, encasing it in a foul liquid nightmare.

Three months or not, the old woman was still very much a part of the room. I retracted my hand too quickly and felt compelled to man up in front of June. "Yeah, she's ripe," I confirmed from my crouched position. I could feel the coldness of her innards clinging fiercely to the glove with a Vaseline-like viscosity. Unable to escape the feeling of clammy corpse mulch through my skin, I ripped the glove off and stood as quickly as my back would allow.

"It's saturated," I nodded, as if there had been any doubt. "We'll definitely have to cut the carpeting out."

I spent the rest of the time helping June search for a will, which, given the sparseness and size of the tiny house, shouldn't have been a problem. Searching through her house, we discovered many more dolls, each porcelain and perfect, frozen for eternity with a penetrating gaze.

They actually freaked me out a bit, and I didn't know what had possessed her to start collecting the little devils in the first place. I had seen too many horror films at too young an age to even comprehend putting one of the creepy fuckers where I lived. We still hadn't found a will, though.

There was one door directly opposite the bedroom, which, unlike the rest of the house, was locked. The will hadn't been in any other room of the house, so June made an executive decision. "We need to break that door down."

I'd also seen enough adventure movies to jump at the chance to do some legal breaking and entering. Bad back and walking cane or not, I was determined to push through that door and into the room on the other side. Perhaps I'd even discover some long-chained-up offspring, so grotesquely deformed that the woman had made the ultimate choice to seal them up rather than let the cruel world put them on display. Or maybe it would be a manufacturing room for crystal meth. I was determined to find out.

I lowered my shoulder as I'd seen done in many a movie and ran forward, feeling surprisingly pain-free. I hit the door once and bounced back but kept the momentum going and hit it again. I was hoping that the door would burst inward, fragmenting into a thousand tiny shards as if it had been decimated by a barrel of dynamite, but the simple lock on the jamb gave long before the rest of it did. The entranceway extended inward, and my trajectory carried me into the darkness. June was quick to follow, reaching for a light switch.

I found myself surrounded by hundreds of perfectly angelic-looking monstrosities. Dolls, too many to count, lined five rows of glass shelves on every wall of the room, row upon row of them, like some macabre miniature army. Each one in the collection wore tailored clothes that represented an aspect of the thing's personality. The giant closet of hand-painted dolls had been locked away from view, too valuable to the old woman to leave accessible. If she had any children during her life-time, they could've never hoped to live up to their mother's ambitions.

I retreated from the room quickly, expecting unnatural move-ment from the hordes, and yanked the door closed as best I could, but I knew that it would be too late. The overpowering stench of the woman's remains had invaded the inner sanctum; the fetid particles would attach themselves to the dolls' whimsical costumes, and for the better part of their eternity, the dolls would wear their mother's dead essence like hideous cologne.

Without a will, June would have to make do with taking the impres-sive stack of small bills she had found in the old woman's makeshift office. When we had finally exited the house, I thought my job was done for the day and I wished her the best, promising to fax her office a copy of our invoices.

"Not so fast," June stopped me. "I'm not allowed to just take things from the house undocumented. I need you to be my witness while I note all this money."

For the next hour and a half I stood, shifting uncomfortably, watching her write the serial numbers of each dollar bill she had taken on a long ledger sheet. She didn't have a problem with how long it took; she was billing the estate at ninety dollars an hour. On the other hand, I would receive a flat fee from Dirk of twenty-five dollars for going out and making the assessment. It was only help to offset my gas costs. And I would receive that only if we didn't get the job.

Getting in touch with the Florida brother was an equally large pain in the ass, but Dirk wouldn't do the work without his signature on the invoice. Though the brother hemmed and hawed about it, he even-tually agreed to let us proceed for nineteen hundred dollars, which included removing all decomp and doing our best to deodorize the place. Wisely, I once again included my clause about "residual staining occurring on the porous surfaces."

Since Dirk was too wrapped up in work to concentrate on the daytime crime scene business himself, he turned to the next most logical source for a specialist in biohazard remediation to help me with the project: craigslist.

Of course, instead of contracting for a service technician with experience in handling hazardous material, Dirk, to save money, put out the call for a general-purpose handyman who would be paid twelve dollars an hour for his time. I couldn't wait to see what that would dredge up.

• • •

The day of the cleanup, my "handyman," Doug, was late. Of course, June was really late, as usual, so I had time to brief the guy before she arrived. I was less than relieved to find that Dirk had given him only the rawest details of the impending workday and that Doug, a broken-down, scummy-looking drifter sort with ugly yellow teeth, wasn't too comfortable with the idea of a "decomp smell." He also couldn't stand Mexicans, which he proudly informed me within two minutes of us meeting.

Since June was Mexican, I begged him to be a little sensitive on the issue and pleaded with him to act somewhat professional, as if he'd been with the company a long time and didn't have a problem with decomp.

"Okay, but no promises. I gotta real strong gag reflex, and if I hurl, I can't help that."

"That's fair," I reasoned. "It's a pretty strong smell...even she wears a mask...if you puke, she'll understand."

"Hey, what do Mexican firemen name their kids?"

"What?"

"José and Hose B!" He laughed as if it were hilarious. June pulled up in her Beamer, and I gave Doug a withering glance.

When she walked up, I stepped in front of Doug and said, "June, this is Doug. He's been with the company for a while now."

Doug reached around me to shake her hand and said in a pleasant voice, "Pleased to meet you, June." I relaxed only slightly.

When Doug stepped into the house, he scoffed. "Is this what it smells like? Hell, I could deal with this...I've smelled way worse in my day."

I quietly reminded him that of course he'd smelled worse; he'd been with the company for a while.

With the carpeting cut into sections and removed, I could fully appreciate the horror that the wooden floorboards beneath had become. Slick with creamy brown unidentifiable guts, the wood had actually puckered from the absorption of the house's owner. It was something that one would expect out of *The Amityville Horror*. Freaky dolls + owner being sucked into floorboards = creepy, talking house. With a crowbar and gloves, Doug pried out the affected boards, sending sharp, dry splinters across the room.

Almost as bad were the flies. Maggots had been lunching on the doll collector, but most of them had long since turned into flies and died, littering the floor, bed, and all furniture with a thick mat of insect husks. (Later, when Dirk opened the filter on the shop vacuum I took to the job site, the smell of dripping, soggy decomp and the thousands of dead flies overwhelmed him, and he elected to throw the vacuum away instead of dealing with it.)

As Doug worked, though, removing floor layer after floor layer, it became evident that he'd forgotten our talk outside.

"Yeah, the goddamned Mexicans, stealing everyone's jobs and sneaking into the country. You give me a flamethrower and an hour alone at the border, and I'll get some borders enforced."

I didn't know if he was talking about burning down the chaparral or actual Mexicans, but once he got going on the subject, it was impossible to quiet him. He quoted numerous statistics and conspiracy theories about Mexicans that all sounded made up to me. Doug was certain that he had an inside line on a Mexican plot to cede control of California back to Mexico via Los Angeles mayor Antonio Villaraigosa.

I shushed him when his racist ramblings became too blatant, but mostly I just let him go. It seemed that anti-Mexican babble kept him focused on his work, and I just wanted him to get through with it. Plus, June was off in some other room, still searching for the elusive will.

When we'd finished and Dirk's truck was overly full of hunks of wood flooring and bags of carpeting, June came in to survey our work. We had to cut down through all the levels of the house until we'd reached the dirt. Even then, there was still a layer of slime atop the moist, cool, dark soil under the house. I didn't have an answer for what to do about that, so I used a long strip of floorboard to scoop the obvious pieces out of view.

"Is it finished?" June asked, clearly wanting to be done for the day.

"It sure is," I confirmed, not knowing what else I could cut out or remove. I deployed several cans of deodorizer, which I left spraying as I sealed the room up. For good measure, I also dropped one into the darkness of the evil doll chamber.

June was intent on taking another small stack of money with her when she left, but I let Doug handle that as I went to sit in the truck. I'd overdone it once again on the amount of punishment I'd inflicted on my back and knew that it would just add to the amount of bed rest I'd need.

It wasn't until June's Beamer had turned the corner off the street that I reached into an envelope of cash Dirk had given me for the payroll. Doug had worked intensely for four hours, spewing slurs the whole way, but he had worked hard nonetheless, doing work that I could not.

Inside the envelope, Dirk had left me four twenties. Doug, having worked for four hours at twelve dollars an hour, was owed forty-eight dollars. My back spasms were sharp and jarring, and seeing no easy, quick way out of it, I rounded up and paid Doug sixty. He had done good work, and not only had he not pissed off June, but he hadn't puked.

Later, when Dirk found out that I'd given Doug extra cash, he did his damnedest not to rage at me over the twelve bucks, but he firmly reminded me I could have driven to a store to make change. I reminded him that he could have, too, and not left me with only big bills. We both walked away, and I had to remind myself repeatedly that no matter what, the job was still better than retail.

the sewer house

A house is made of walls and beams; a home is built with love and dreams.

—*William Arthur Ward, American author and educator*

THE PUBLIC GUARDIAN'S OFFICE MUST have been somewhat pleased with our work, because it got us invited to participate in the other side of their business: hoarder sanitation.

Dirk called one day asking if I would pick up a key from him and bring a camera. I figured it was finally the awkward moment where he was going to suggest that I get to know him better, a lot better (in the gay biblical sense, if you know what I'm hinting at). Fortunately, instead he sent me over to document one of these so-called hoarder houses so that he could formulate a bid for the county. If we got the gig, he said, it would be a nice little addition to our revenue stream. I didn't know exactly what a "hoarder house" was, but my understanding was that it would be a dirty house.

I picked up Chris along the way just to have someone to talk to. The house was out in Stanton, near where I'd just had a loony racist cut the floorboards out of the doll lady's house. While the area surrounding the neighborhood (Stanton) was shoddy and run down as expected, the neighborhood itself was not.

The homes, while not expensive-looking, were nice places where people kept their lawns uniformly trimmed and everything had a pleasant quality to it. Initially, Chris and I assumed that Dirk had given me an address for the wrong neighborhood...and then we saw it. At first glance it seemed unimpressive, with the exception of two ratty cars in the driveway. Aside from a little overgrowth on the front lawn and the need of a coat of paint, the house seemed boringly ordinary. But that was only at first glance.

If you looked harder, the oddities of the abode leapt out at you. To start with, both of the cars were completely filled with trash—and not just any trash, mind you, but really sinister old trash. Cupcake wrappers that featured the old package design of the Hostess company, newspaper bits that looked like they had gone through a hamster's digestive tract, and wadded balls of tissue paper were the immediately visible items, but inside the car's shell there was more, so much more. Only the driver's seat was visibly empty of trash. I snapped a picture.

Chris and I were shocked at the sheer volume of trash that had been wedged into the car, but that only served to prepare us for what was to come. The trash just inside the gate was a drum roll, a slow buildup of dirty baby diapers, cooking magazines from the 1980s, and random detritus rolling toward a crescendo. The closer to the front door we got, the higher the trash piled up, until it formed twin arches extending down from the sidewalls like fast-food-box ornamentation. I snapped another picture.

The front door was scuffed, as if someone had tried not very hard to force their way through. Clearly the person had never broken down a door in the name of service as I once had. I unlocked the door and pushed it open, only to be dazzled by my new definition of what a dirty house was.

• • •

I used to think I knew what a dirty house was. When Chris and I were growing up, our parents worked long hours. We were frequently home with our two other siblings to do as we pleased. And what apparently pleased us was living in filth. Apple cores would be pushed between seat cushions rather than walked out to the trash; pots and pans with clinging macaroni residue would be stuck behind furniture rather than set in the sink to be rinsed. Toilet paper used as tissues would be set on tables with the intention of them eventually reaching the garbage, but the paper would invariably find its way to the floor. The laundry pile created by six people in a busy household was enormous, and if left unchecked, it would spread out to every corner of the house, mixed in with jackets and dirty socks left on the floor.

My father would rage about the mess, but we were stubborn, lazy children who benefitted from a society turning away from physical punishment on the young. My mother, who'd grown up in a dysfunctional house, a hoarder house by today's standards, probably found the mess cathartic and was almost an ally in our messiness. Certainly she wanted to escape the dysfunction and wanted to have a clean home, but we didn't listen. We were raised to be creative dreamers, and as we saw it, our dreaming precluded us from keeping a tidy home. Eventually my parents got tired of hounding us to straighten up, and we hellions won our right to be filthy. (While the frat had prepared me for crime scene cleaning, growing up dirty prepared me for the frat.)

I remember the first moment that I was truly ashamed of the way my siblings and I were living. I was in high school and had just set a Dr Pepper can on the very top of the heap in the trash can. The pile was already mountainous, threatening to tumble over, and so I had used a Jengalike concentration to keep it from upsetting. My preciseness didn't really matter, because a layer of trash on the ground already surrounded the trash can. But I was resolved not to be the one to tumble the heap and had just succeeded in my efforts when there was a knock on the door.

I answered it to find an attractive older woman standing before me. She informed me that her car had broken down. This being the age before widespread cell-phone ownership, she asked if she could use our house phone to call her daughter. I allowed her in, and as I turned to hand her the cordless receiver in the kitchen, I could see that her eyes were not on me but on the abundance of trash and laundry scattered through the house. The coup de grace was the trash can, and I saw my Dr Pepper can with the sides I'd mashed in to make it sit like an angel atop a Christmas tree.

I suddenly felt the shame of my life's sloth like a lightning bolt. I didn't regret the woman's presence in the house, but the fact that I needed her there to figure it out for me. If I had any concern that I would slip back into a state of unclean living after she left, it disappeared when I found out that she had a daughter who attended Eureka High with me. A daughter who was pretty and more popular than me, and who would doubtlessly hear from her mother about the schoolmate who was kind enough to let her mother use the phone but who lived like a pig in his own filth. And the daughter would tell my classmates. It was almost as bad as if they'd found out I'd been raised Mormon.

I walked the halls in mortification for weeks, awaiting somebody's comment, but it never came. The necessary damage had been done, though, and I cleaned up the house big-time. Of course, my brothers and sister hadn't had the same epiphany, and they continued to make their messes, but I swore that I would never sink to that level again. And with the lapse of living at the frat house, I haven't.

Since most of my siblings have moved out and everyone has grown up, my parents' house also is now what my dad long wished for. Spotlessly clean and cheery, it looks like a grand collaboration between Norman Rockwell and Thomas Kinkade. My mom probably wouldn't mind if there were a bit more laundry around, though.

• • •

Because of my background, I thought I knew what a dirty house was, but that corner house beat my definition to shit. I'd been stopped from fully opening the front door by an unseen presence, so I knew it was either going to be a poltergeist or a very messy home. But even those expectations fell way short.

Wedging the door open wide enough to stick my arm and digital camera in, I began snapping pictures of the living room. The amount of trash visible through my forced opening in the door alluded to the condition of the rest of the house. An awesome mound, peaking and sloping into another pile, formed an unsettled mountain range of refuse that spanned the length of the home, with the summit of the tallest mountain easily extending over ten feet into the vaulted ceilings. Clearly, the living room wasn't filled with floor-to-ceiling trash only because the occupants had not been there long enough to accumulate the trash necessary to reach the eighteen-foot crossbar.

A multitude of spiders apparently had, though, because my digital photos revealed spider webs that could easily ensnare Frodo and all his pals. Spider webs extended from the ceiling down to the lowest levels of the trash, which in some places was only four feet off the ground. Walking around the back of the house, we found that the backyard and most of the remaining rooms were much worse.

Few things are as ironic to me as a pile of trash made from the containers of cleaning supplies, and I tried to convey that message to Dirk as I showed him one of the photographs I'd taken. It simply defied explanation, and I begged him to take a look at the house so that he could see that what I was relaying to him was true. But it didn't seem to matter, because he seriously considered fifty-five hundred dollars an acceptable bid for our services cleaning it all up.

I begged him to charge ten thousand or even twenty or thirty thousand dollars, but he stressed the importance of competitive bidding. He said we didn't have to take the cars and that they'd be gone by the time we started, so we could rule them out of the equation. By the way he figured it, we'd get a crew of ignorant people in there, pay them fourteen bucks an hour, get three giant dumpsters at five hundred a pop, work over a weekend, and the two of us would pocket around two thousand dollars each for our troubles. I wouldn't even have to work. With my back the way it was, I would only need to sit in a comfortable chair and supervise. I begged him once more to reconsider his numbers, which he finally did, raising the bid to sixty-five hundred. After all, we wanted to impress the county with our ability to do great work for cheap.

I didn't know anything about how the county via the Public Guardian's office conducted business in such affairs, but from the moment I walked around the house, I felt a connection, and I was confident the gig was ours. I knew that we were destined to intersect, that house and I, and so I wasn't surprised when a week later Dirk informed me that we'd won the bid.

Since he was still so involved with his sheriff duties, he informed me that once more I'd be doing the supervisory work alone. For that reason, I fought to have Doug on my excavation crew. If I was going to be out there for long hours watching people bust their ass, I wanted some hilariously uncomfortable racial tension to entertain me. Doug said he knew a guy who was a real hard worker, and to complement the mix, the oblivious Dirk threw in two Mexican guys.

I was frothing for the start date, anticipating the impending project to be *Raiders of the Lost Ark* meets *Do the Right Thing*. So my disappointment was palpable when Doug showed up with his buddy, a Filipino guy named Kool. Apparently Doug wasn't a complete racist. He was more of an "I hate foreigners less than I love money" racist, and begrudgingly, everyone got along just fine. Working in their favor was that the two Mexican laborers did not understand Doug well enough to be offended by his comments.

The dumpster Dirk ordered had arrived before any of us got there, and from the get-go I knew there would be a problem. While what the sanitation company referred to as a "forty-foot roll-off" was large, it was nowhere near what we would need dumpster-wise to put a dent in the trash.

"I think we're gonna need a bigger boat," I quipped to Dirk, but he didn't comprehend the reference. We had budgeted for three roll-offs, and one of them might have been enough to take care of what was in the backyard alone.

I would worry about that later, though. For the moment, I was keen on tackling the house. I had a comfortable director's chair set on the lawn under an E-Z Up canopy to keep the sun off me, but for the initial breakthrough I was determined to be in on the action.

Arming Kool, the smallest of the group, with a snow shovel and a pair of work gloves, the rest of us pushed on the front door, inching it open enough to slide him through. He had to stand at a hilarious incline on the sloping trash pile, careful not to sink into its boggy midst. Once inside, he used the snow shovel and his hands to scoop what trash he could away from the front door. Quickly I grew bored, though, and returned to the comfort of my chair, where I decided to employ a "Sorcerer's Apprentice" style of leadership.

It wasn't long before Doug brought out the first intact item: a surprisingly decent clock radio, unused and still in its original box. Not sure what to do, I consulted Dirk. He, too, was surprised at finding something of worth and commanded that the workers put all items of potential value off to the side. We'd consult the Public Guardian's office about the findings after the completion of the job.

Shortly thereafter, amid barrels full of trash, several more clock radios came out, also in original packaging. A blender was next, unused, and then another, cheaper clock radio. Then more kitchen items followed. The stack of valuable items was proportionately impressive to the trash removed.

We'd started the job promptly at 8:00 a.m., and by about 9:30 a.m. the first shark had arrived. She was an old lady who had the look of one of those *Bewitched* neighbor types with mounds of dyed hair, and she was being led around by a small dog on a large leash. She picked her dog up without realizing it was attempting to pee on the lawn and then dangled it aloft so that it could finish its business.

"Thank Jesus, you're cleaning out the Steward house," she said.

"The Steward house?" I inquired casually. I didn't know the back-story on the place, but I wanted to.

"Of course, most everyone around here calls it the Sewer House. Is it horrible inside?"

"It's worse than horrible," I confirmed to her immense delight. "What happened to it?"

"Oh, I don't know too much about it really. I've heard rumors. The guy used to beat his mother…She slept out in one of the cars. For two years she slept in a car, can you believe that?"

Over the course of the day, various well-wishers and gawkers alike came to give me their version of the story on the Sewer House. It seemed that a man and his wife owned several properties in the area and did fairly well for themselves. The two of them lived in the nefarious house in the 1980s with their son, a teenaged burnout and pill popper. When the husband died, the mother and son moved to another of their properties and rented the house out to a large family. The family kept the place nice and was liked by the community, but the owner's son wanted a place of his own.

His mother evicted the family and let the son move in. All night, the son would ride his bike around the neighborhood, threatening neighbors and making their kids uneasy. The mother and her son were both packrats, and by then the mother had made a mess of the house she was living in, so the county stepped in and kicked her out.

She and her son then moved large amounts of the trash from the one house into the corner house, adding trash to more trash. When the son filled up the bathroom with refuse, he eventually began pissing and shitting in bottles. When he got tired of doing that, he began to use one of the bedrooms as a toilet.

I had heard this from one of the county caseworkers as well, so I knew it to be the truth. And what was worse was that although we couldn't actually access the room yet, we knew which one it was.

The son didn't like living with his mother, so he beat her a lot. He was on crystal meth most of the time and had taken to threatening his neighbors with a pellet gun and then darting back into the mess of his house, crawling over the piles like a rat. The neighbors would call the police, but there wasn't much to be done about it.

The son made his mother live in the dirty station wagon, sleeping upright in the driver's seat. She was a big woman and developed bedsores all over her body, not to mention what the insects living in the filth must have done to her. One day the son beat his mother so badly that she had a black eye and was sitting on the sidewalk crying. A woman from a different neighborhood drove by, took pity on the mom, and drove her to the hospital. There, the old woman told the police about her son. They went to the house, called him outside, and arrested him.

That night, the mother told her savior that she had a large amount of money in a jar sitting inside the house. The neighbor woman went and retrieved the jar, which contained around fifty thousand dollars, and turned it over to the police. The police almost arrested her for doing it. Turns out you can't just break into people's houses to retrieve jars of money from their trash piles. Who knew?

When the county found out about the condition of the house, they seized it, intending to liquidate the assets, recoup their investments (us, among other costs), and put the remaining money into a care fund for the mother's well-being.

The son, finally released from jail, had an injunction against him to keep him from going back to the house. For the time being he was homeless, living on the street in a neighboring city.

By the time I called a halt on the first day, I knew that we were going to take a beating in the numbers part of the project. It was no surprise why we'd won the bid—we had no idea what we were doing and had underbid everyone else, probably by a lot. We'd already completely filled the dumpster, and we weren't even finished with the living room.

But by then the "loot" had also piled up handsomely. In addition to numerous pairs of new shoes (size 9), several more kitchen appliances, more clock radios, a brand-new black-and-white TV, and several stereos, we found a brand-new electric guitar, also in its original box and still wrapped in its packing material. When the men pulled that out of the house, I tried to look nonplussed. I had always wanted an electric guitar, and it would look great sitting next to my new bed frame.

My guys asked if they might be able to keep some of the stuff, and once more I deferred to Dirk. He suggested that they could take some of the smaller crap they'd amassed as long as the big-ticket good stuff went into our storage to hold for the Public Guardian's office. When the big-ticket items were delivered to Dirk's garage that night, the pile was short one electric guitar. Dirk was cool with that and asked if there was anything that he might've liked from the house. I told him I'd keep my eyes open.

That night, I laid in bed, strumming my guitar to the envy of my frat bros. Sure it wasn't as impressive without an amplifier to plug it into or any knowledge of how to play it, but for the first time in months, Jeff the old loser was noteworthy again.

My new acquisition was made all the sweeter the next day when my crew pulled out of the trash a new amplifier and a carrying case for the guitar, as well as a bag containing the brand-new picks, whammy bar, and an instruction manual on how to play an electric guitar. The Sewer House was like Christmas. Doug took all the shoes, and he and Kool fought over the lower-end kitchen stuff and clothes pulled out with the tags still on them.

• • •

While the house was certainly full of an incomprehensible amount of pure trash, feces, and spider webs, it also yielded a wealth of awesome toys. New high-end bike frames came out, two brand-new drum sets (I already owned a perfectly good one of those), several more stereos, and more TVs, not to mention all manner of electric tools. We kept what we thought the Public Guardian would want and gave the rest to the crew to take home. Everybody was coming out a winner except our business.

On the third day, we had used our allotted dumpster money and still were nowhere near finished. We also had only budgeted to pay the crew for three days of work, so anything more was going to start eating into our profit margins. The two Mexicans had to leave the project, as they'd been contracted elsewhere, and I had a two-person hole to fill in my crew. Enter Mark and Kim.

Mark was a frat bro of mine. He'd come in a couple years before me but was still a few years younger, and Kim was his girlfriend. They were an odd pair, but they wanted the work. Well, Kim wanted the work. She was a morbid sort and had eaten up all the stories I had told her about the Sewer House. She was begging to work on it, and when I needed two people, she and Mark jumped aboard.

It was a good and bad decision on my part. The good part was that Kim was so eager for my acceptance that she kept an eye on the crew, making sure that nothing shady was going on inside the house. The bad part was that she and Mark were more eager to explore the trash piles and gossip with the neighbors than work. Still, it was because of her that we found the cash.

I was sitting in my chair, stewing in my own loathing for the project, when Kim marched out with a bag full of wrinkly green money. Glancing into the bag, I was shocked to see that the majority of the money was twenties, but several fifties and hundred-dollar bills were in there as well. I could scarcely believe it. The money looked as if it had simply been forgotten and left in the bag for years.

Throughout the day, more money came out—more fifties, more hundreds, more twenties, and large bags of ones and fives. Out next was an impossibly heavy bowling bag without a ball in it but stocked full of coins. It was so weighty that the handle almost tore off when Kim walked out with it.

Once again I called Dirk, and his immediate suggestion was to put all the money into the cab of his truck and make sure none of the neighbors saw it...particularly not "the witch." The neighbor with the little dog had explained "the witch" to me over successive mornings. The witch was a woman who lived in the house directly across the street from the Sewer House and was the only one in the neighborhood who considered the son a friend. I was told I'd meet up with her eventually.

• • •

My first run-in with the witch came on our third day. I was sitting in my chair, keeping watch over the accumulating house treasures, when she came stalking up onto the lawn.

"What the hell do you think you're doing?" she cried, crazy and furious.

"We're working in conjunction with the county to remediate this property," I said, puffing up like a bullfrog. The bowling bag, which now contained all the loot, was sitting beside my chair. Discreetly, I pushed the flaps closed.

She wasn't deterred by my sense of presence. "I'm fine with what you're doing," she said, backing down only slightly. "But a lot of this stuff is mine," she said, heading for the stacks of stereos and other goods. Bending, she began to gather things at random from the pile and loading her arms.

"Drop it," I barked, well aware from the other neighbors that she might attempt something like that. She did, letting the merchandise tumble to the ground. She turned to face me, and I could see why the others called her a witch. Her dark hair was stringy and hung about her face like dying lengths of grass, and her skin was unnaturally wrinkled. She looked like she was an old lady, but there were patches in her thin face where she looked as if she was in her forties and all the drinking and smoking she'd likely done in her life had pickled her prematurely.

"You know, I'm friends with Gary, the son," she said with an edge to her voice that conveyed a threat. "He has a prepaid cell phone, and he calls me. Don't think he doesn't know what is going on."

"If he comes here, it's my understanding that he'll be arrested. So let's hope that he has the good sense not to. And if you keep threatening me, well…" I countered.

"I'm not threatening you," she cowed instantly, dropping the edge in her voice and adopting one of shocked surprise. "Personally, I say good for you guys. He needed to be evicted. You know there's all kinds of rotting meat in there? Just perfectly good steaks that he'd buy and leave out on the counter!"

After that she became my best pal, popping over throughout the day, always smoking a cigarette and trying her sneaky small talk to ascertain if I knew whether there was any money in the house.

"I heard there was, but some woman took it to the police," I'd say, shrugging.

"You knew about that, huh?" the witch said slyly, as if it were a trap, only to ask again hours later.

At the day's end, Dirk and I conferred and decided that we needed to just suck it up and start eating our costs. The Sewer House would be a learning lesson that we did for free. I wasn't happy about that decision whatsoever, as I had spent several days out there sitting around, which, when you have a bad back, is still hard work. Many more days and dumpsters would be necessary to complete the project, but that didn't seem to matter to Dirk. He wasn't the one out there doing it.

On the fourth day we finally broached the kitchen and the room that had been used as a toilet. First forty-odd three-liter bottles of piss, reduced to the flat, stale color of swamp water, were pulled from the house, the workers all carrying them extended from their bodies, repulsed. The feces content of the room had been reduced to a claylike consistency of dark black bricks.

Kool, wearing a painter's mask over his face, bravely dove into the midst of it, perhaps not comprehending what it was, and scooped it into a rolling trash can with his snow shovel. The others, too grossed out to even watch, concentrated on the kitchen and a large family room.

The witch had been right about the steaks, as large melted puddles of green liquid with familiar-looking T-bones in the middle had to be chipped off the counter. It was an interesting experience for the crew, because the level of trash in the kitchen was flush with the counters, and they had to stand on the Formica tops to push any of the trash down and out into the hallway.

The house was built like a swastika, with four arms extending outward from a fixed central hall. While all of the rooms had large, cumbersome beds, it was clear that none had been used, as they were all upended and used to brace up more trash. Clearly the son had favored sleeping in the trash, curled in the fetal position into one of the piles.

• • •

The finding of money, even money that they couldn't have, had re-energized the crew, and they eagerly tore into the remaining wreckage, searching through every nook and cranny. I tried to tell them to ignore the money and concentrate on getting the work done, but when Doug brought out an old fan still in its box and found nearly a thousand dollars stuffed along the inside edge, it made things tough.

The presence of rat poop sprinkled over the entirety of the house, and spiders that would dart deeper into piles as they were unearthed, made everyone extra cautious. No living rats were actually found, although several mummified skeletons, their tiny limbs splayed outward as they'd been crushed under the rubble, were taken out of the house and subsequently tossed into the dumpsters like rat Frisbees.

It was all quite a show, and the neighbors continued to stop by with their opinions and stories. A highlight came when the corpses of two medium-size dogs were found buried in the trash, sending a ripple of new speculation through the accumulated crowds. One dog, mostly bones, was found in the compacted piles of the fireplace; the other was midway up a peak in the family room and had a bit more meat still attached to it.

Nobody, least of all me, was interested in giving them a good Christian burial, and so they, too, went into the trash. Several neighbors confirmed that the son had had two German shepherds living with him for a while, but the neighbors had all stopped hearing them bark a few years back.

On the fourth day we had a new dumpster brought out once again, and more money was slashed from our profits, but the day would still yield some exciting finds. First the son's pellet gun was found, the one he'd used to become the scourge of the neighborhood, and it set off a frenzy with my workers. They were all certain that it was a real gun and told all the available neighbors that whenever a smoke break was called.

I finally had to point out that it was only a pellet gun, but still the hype was there and only added to the excitement when two real guns were found. The rifles were both covered in rusty patches that resembled an STD, and under Dirk's advisement we called the local police to pick them up. The arriving police laughed. They knew all about the Steward boy and the legacy of the house. Police presence on the street just made the spectacle grander, and with the presence of the erected E-Z Up shade, the Sewer House had taken on the appearance of a circus.

By the fifth day in the wreck, Dirk called me in for an emergency meeting. We were hoping to have all the trash excavated by the sixth day, but our cash supply had been tapped. We had no money and had resorted to paying the workers with the mulched bills pulled from the house. We didn't tell them that we were doing so, but it had to have been obvious, what with the stained, wrinkled bills devoid of all moisture and most of their color.

Each day I would make an envelope for each person and hand them their allotment of cash while keeping track of the money put out so we could replace it later. We'd brought Kim and Mark in at twelve an hour, and we'd keep Doug at fourteen dollars an hour if he could get Kool to accept twelve dollars an hour as well. It was all part of the little maneuvering we had done to keep us in the black. But by the fifth day we were in trouble.

We knew we needed another dumpster and at least a full workday out of each person. Dirk had already called the head guy at the Public Guardian's office and managed to squeeze an extra nine hundred dollars out of them with the promise that not only were we going to empty the house of trash, but we were going to make it spotlessly clean. I didn't like that idea, but at least it kept us from losing money on the deal for another day.

Of course, that also added a day in cleaning costs. My plan was to call a cleaning service in and let them worry about scrubbing down the walls and shining the counters, removing the cobwebs and cleaning the excavated bathrooms. I was sick of being out there, dealing with the sights, the smells, the neighbors (particularly the witch, who would hang out for hours on end, running commentary on every item removed from the house), and just the overall misery of staring at a house for eight hours a day.

I had moved my director's chair indoors and would sit, cane in hand, keeping tabs on my crew. This, of course, had the added negative of the neighbors creeping closer, walking free range into the house and exploring. I frequently had to kick them out for "insurance reasons," particularly the witch, who knew all about a hidden ceiling compartment that she herself was interested in checking into.

Such was her fascination with the possibilities of the ceiling compartment that Dirk actually came out on that sixth day to supervise the opening of said compartment. But, alas, like some *Geraldo* special, it was empty. Dirk saw the mostly excavated house in person and maintained that we would not be in need of a cleaning service.

By the end of the sixth day we knew there'd be a seventh day. We definitely couldn't afford a seventh roll-off dumpster, so Dirk instead rented a small, rolling bin like you'd find behind a restaurant. There wasn't that much trash left, and we hoped we could fit it all in.

On the seventh day the crew was as miserable as I was, but they were at least getting paid. Finally, though, we had achieved the basic goal of removing all the trash. I was sick of seeing the house and its scummy walls, and the persistent smell of the toilet room, which we'd actually had to remove all the tiles from, so stained were they with caked shit.

At the end of the day, Dirk mandated that I ask the workers to return again to help clean the house the next day at reduced wages. He didn't want to hire a cleaning crew, because he was certain he could get our guys back for cheaper. Not surprisingly, the crew collectively told me to go to hell. I didn't blame them.

So Dirk had returned to his old buddy craigslist and mentioned that he'd gotten a husband-and-wife team who were eager for work and would clean anything for ten dollars an hour each plus lunch. I wasn't too worried. The Sewer House, once devoid of trash, actually looked like an otherwise average empty house with dirty walls, cobwebs, and stained carpeting. Sure it wasn't clean, but it was miles away from how it had looked, and for once I was optimistic about its potential.

The morning that I met the "husband and wife" team, though, I knew I was in for a rough ride. The "husband and wife" were actually a boyfriend and a girlfriend in their early twenties, and the girl's appearance screamed "problem worker."

The two of them had a seedy look, exactly the sort of people who would take a one-time cleaning job on craigslist. Right from the get-go, the man, a recent ex-Marine, said that his girl was strung out because they'd been the victims of a "home-invasion robbery" the previous evening. The boyfriend, Dill, had left the house for about twenty minutes, and all their nice, expensive new stuff that they "totally had receipts for" was jacked, receipts and everything. The girl, who we'll call Pickle, hadn't gotten a good look at the masked men, except that "they were black."

Fortuitously for all, the couple had just purchased theft insurance on all of their new stuff. Unfortunately for them, they were having a rough morning, because the insurance company didn't want to pony up the dough, mainly because the cops didn't believe in the slightest that three black men in ski masks had just stolen all their electronic goods. So now there was talk of plans to sue the police department and the insurance company…that was about the time that the couple entered my life.

Gritting my teeth as I listened to the rants, I reminded myself to curse Dirk. I pulled a recently purchased collection of cleaning supplies out of the truck and handed them to the couple while I unlocked the house door. After letting them inside to go nuts on the place, I returned to the lawn to set up my director's chair.

No sooner had I sat down than Pickle came storming out of the house, got into the couple's car, and drove off, old brakes squealing as she went. I waited about forty minutes, honestly figuring that maybe she went to pee at a fast-food joint up the street or something. Finally, I went in and confronted Dill, who gave me a sob story about her wanting to get a charger cord for her cell phone so that she could call her mother.

"I can't pay her for the time she's gone," I said stiffly, feeling very much like some sort of plantation owner.

Dill was out on the lawn, jawing at me during his fifth smoke break of the morning, when Pickle came roaring back onto the street. Relieved, Dill went to talk to her. They argued for a few minutes, then kissed and made up, whereby she once again drove off. Dill came back to me.

"She's not going to work today," he said, shrugging casually.

My vision actually blurred with the intensity of my rage, but I wanted to keep cool and keep him going to not waste the day completely. Besides, he assured me that he could easily clean the entire house by himself by the end of the day.

"I did much harder work in Iraq," he reminded me.

At lunchtime he walked down the street and made a phone call, then came back to sit near me on the lawn. "Is it all right if we have Subway today?"

I had just learned of a Subway in the area, and after a week of eating pizzas and burgers, which we had supplied the crew with daily, I needed a fresh alternative. "Sure," I said. "If you keep working while I'm gone, I'll run out and pick it up."

"Do you have a pen handy?" he asked, and I retrieved my clipboard to write down his order. "I want a foot-long sub with turkey, lettuce, sprouts, vinegar, mustard, bell peppers, and ranch dressing," he ordered. "Make sure there aren't any tomatoes, onions, or pickles on the thing."

I suddenly felt like I was his lackey, but if that was what it took for me to escape the Sewer House, that was what I would do.

"Also I want a Diet Coke to drink," he added.

When I returned with the food and his Diet Coke, I shouldn't have been surprised to see that Pickle had returned and was sitting next to him on the lawn, neither of them working. When Pickle saw me, she took off running to the protective custody of her car while Dill stood up sheepishly. "She thinks you're angry at her," he admitted.

"Why would I be angry at her?" I said, really letting the sarcasm hang out there. Apparently he was oblivious to sarcasm, though.

"Oh, good," he answered reaching for his sandwich. "I told her that you were a nice guy." I shrugged, feeling proud of that for some stupid reason.

He then broke his sandwich into halves and set one down on the wrapper while taking a bite of the other one. I settled into my own sandwich, feeling happy about the fact that he thought I was a nice boss.

Dill then waved his girlfriend over while I was in mid-chew and pointed at me, giving her the thumbs up.

Slowly she came out of the car like an overly cautious squirrel and walked up on the lawn. Dill handed her the other half of the sandwich, which she quickly bit into, holding it protectively with both hands, squatting in a feral posture while she ate. If there had been food in my mouth, it would have tumbled out when my jaw dropped open. But I didn't say anything, because I was a "nice boss." I never felt like a bigger pussy in all my life.

After the meal, he burped and lit a cigarette while she returned to the car, not thanking me, and drove away once more.

"She's thinks you're nice, too," he said, though she hadn't said a single word during lunch to either of us. I could only shake my head and wait for the fuzzy visions of shapeless rage to abate.

He returned to work once more, and I called Dirk, asking him to come out and make sure the house was clean enough for what we had pledged to the Public Guardian's office.

When Dirk arrived at the end of the day, driving up in my Cavalier, Dill was full of excuses for the both of us about how the house was dirtier than anything he'd seen in Iraq after all. It still wasn't done, but it was passably clean in my opinion. Dirk, on the other hand, wasn't so impressed.

Though he didn't say more than two words to Dill, Dirk leaned close and gave me an earful. "Pay him, and get him the fuck out of here," Dirk concluded, his round eyes narrowed to slits.

"I can tell your boss doesn't like me," Dill said when I pulled him aside to pay him off. "You're a nice guy, but he's a dick," he said, raising his voice and looking in the direction of the house, where Dirk was investigating the work. I handed him his envelope. "Will you call me out to work for you again?" he asked earnestly, as if he actually thought I might.

"Sure, sure," I said, desperate to get the bastard out of my line of sight. He'd managed to make me feel like a chump enough that day.

"You're a good boss," he reiterated, though this time I didn't fall for the line. "That other guy really sucks. And besides that," he said, looking over at the Red Rocket, which Dirk had parked across the street, "he drives a really shitty car."

Pickle once again returned to pick him up, and they left my life, hopefully to go get shot in some convenience store robbery that I might later be lucky enough to clean up.

"Can we just be done with this thing?" I begged Dirk as he surveyed the house with disdain.

"No," he shook his head. "You're coming back tomorrow with chunties." "Chuntie" was slang for Mexican Americans who acted more Mexican than those born there. I knew that wasn't what he meant, but I couldn't be bothered to correct him.

• • •

The next morning, I drove out in Dirk's truck to the Home Depot near his house. I'd never hired illegal laborers before and wasn't eager to start. Driving over to their side of the parking lot caused a huge swarm of them to surround my truck, waving their hands to get my attention.

"I need someone who can speak English," I said to the crowd.

"I speak English," one of the men yelled. I pointed to him and two others, and they piled into the truck's king cab around me.

We drove down to the Sewer House, and it was just as I'd left it, horribly dismal-looking. The whole way down, I'd avoided making small talk with the guys, not wanting to incur some guilt about my own lofty position. But at the job site, I unlocked the house and turned to the English speaker.

"Will you make sure that the walls, counters, and bathrooms get wiped down extra clean?" I asked, speaking slowly. He stared at me blankly.

"Will you make sure the walls..." I began to repeat to him and then suddenly realized the problem. "Do you speak English?" I asked him again.

"I speak English," he said enthusiastically. It was the only English he knew.

Determined, I mimicked the motions of scrubbing and cleaning as I led them throughout the house and even donned gloves of my own to help get the work done faster.

The three of them put Dill to shame with their steady work pace, their silence, and their not needing a goddamned cigarette every twenty minutes. We all scrubbed tirelessly throughout the day, stopping only for burgers, which they scarfed down while working. At the end of the day, I once more called out Dirk to assess our work, finally feeling like we had done it.

"Nope, you're going to be out here one more day," he said upon taking a quick look around. "I told the Public Guardian's office that we'd clean this place spotlessly. You and your workers have failed to do that again."

At that point, retail business or not, I lost it on him. Feeling the sting of tears at the corner of my eyes, I was broken down, sore, and exhausted. My back was throbbing from the intense work, and he'd simply dismissed it. I cussed and yelled and told him where he could stick his job, because he was going to be one employee less, which was a serious issue, considering he really only had one.

Dirk considered that and asked me to calm down. I didn't want to calm down, but he apologized for marooning me out there as long as he had. He knew I was working hard, but he also knew how important the Public Guardian's office was to our success. With the patience of a father, he soothingly talked me down off my emotional ledge and promised that with one more day of hard work, we'd be finished. Once more we paid the workers off with dirty cash from the house.

On the last day, I returned to the parking lot at Home Depot for crew members. The other two hadn't shown up that day, but my non-English, English-speaking guy was there. Since he had knowledge of the job, I once again selected him. For good measure, I also chose a father and his teenage son. It was a bit unfair perhaps to the other workmen that this guy would get his family a double payday while they would bring home nothing, but I needed someone slender and tall who could clean out the grease traps above the stove. It proved to be a good choice on my part.

The team, myself included, busted ass once more, and finally by the day's end the house had achieved a new level of sparkle. With the exception of the heavily spotted carpeting that the P.G.'s office said we were off the hook for, the place looked like a model home.

Dirk came out once more and signed off on the place, freeing me from its curse. But there was still the situation of money.

We had spent a few grand of the money collected from the house on paying off the workers and the sanitation company. The bottom line, Dirk said, was that Public Guardian's office didn't know how much money we had actually taken from the house. It was all a matter of our accounting.

Dirk had broached the subject lightly, gauging my reaction, but it was a needless proposition. I was a huge advocate of the money serving as our recovery fund and the Public Guardian getting very little of it. I could just imagine it going into some file somewhere, unimportant to all parties concerned.

I don't know what he turned in to the Public Guardian's office, but when I got a paycheck that month, it was happily much bigger. Cash, an electric guitar, a trumpet, and some other odds and ends weren't a bad haul for all the work I had mostly watched get done. But I still knew we could do better.

CHAPTER 15

dodger red

Buy me some peanuts and Cracker Jack. I don't care if I ever get back.
—Jack Norworth, "Take Me Out to the Ball Game"

I DIDN'T GROW UP A sports fan. My father was allegedly a Dodger enthusiast when we lived in Los Angeles, and he went to ball games on a semi-regular basis. He even went to several games when the Dodgers won the Series in '81, the year I was born, and brought me back a World Champion Dodgers hat that my mom saved for me over the years. It was a side of my father that I never knew.

When we moved up to Eureka, land of no sports teams or major cities for at least six hours in any direction, he focused only on his magic and his acting. This was great for me, of course, growing up. Lots of kids had dads who were sports fans; I was the only kid in my grade that had a father who was a magician. It helped me make friends when he'd come in and perform for the school, getting me out of class to help him set up his act.

I had played Little League baseball and youth basketball for a year, each only to realize that I sucked. I wanted to give football a try, but its games were always on Sunday, and Sunday was "church day." I was a big, blocky kid by that point, and some full-contact sports could have made me develop some masculinity. Instead, I was immersed in the world of Doug Henning, David Copperfield, and knowing the difference between *The Tempest* and *Twelfth Night*.

It wasn't until high school that I realized what I'd missed with sports. Doug Henning and Shakespeare don't get you laid in high school; football gets you laid. Shakespeare can at least get you laid in college; Doug Henning will never get you laid. I had a very goofy existence in high school trying to talk sports with the other guys and failing miserably.

So I had lived a fairly sports-free life…until I started dating Kerry. Kerry's family was very into sports…super into sports, you might say. And so with that, I developed an affinity through immersion, going to hockey games and watching football all day religiously on Sundays and again on Monday nights. The Dodgers, the Lakers, the Ducks, NASCAR, drag racing, golf, bull riding, and any other sport that was on, we watched. And I grew to love it.

I still didn't know any of the players, most of the positions that they played, or why nobody in sports liked Bill Buckner, but I was right there every day, rooting for whatever sport was on. I loved the fighting in hockey and was mesmerized by a quarterback getting the ball on the opposing team's one-yard line and having two minutes to march ninety-nine yards upfield to win the game. I screamed my fucking head off when D-Fish sank a turnaround jumper for the Lakers with four-tenths of a second left on the clock to beat the Spurs.

Sports was humanity and power and testosterone-fueled superhumans sobbing at victory and defeat alike, so passionate for the game or even just for the bonus they would have gotten if they'd managed ten more yards. And we in the stands or at home, watching around the television, bonded or glared, loving and hating another human being because of the swing of a bat or the catch of a pass.

Nothing was as tense at Kerry's house as the day my Denver Broncos upended her and her father's Pittsburgh Steelers in the only game they played that season. There was nothing like the sheer majesty I felt when Kerry and I watched the Anaheim Ducks beat the Detroit Red Wings in the sixth game from box seats that we lucked into. That year the Ducks won the Stanley Cup, and there I was, a superfan by immersion, living and breathing with every play.

And so when I got the call from Dirk one day to roll out to Dodger Stadium, it was like a newfound dream come true.

• • •

Dirk "happened to have the day off," but I couldn't blame him for wanting to go. Everybody needed a good name-dropper crime scene in their repertoire. And by Southern California standards, Dodger Stadium was a hell of a good one.

I still had my walking cane, but I had taken to leaving it in the car merely as an incidental. I still wouldn't lift heavy objects, but Dirk was fine with that. I think he felt really bad that the company couldn't provide me with health insurance or workers' comp.

We cruised up the 5 freeway, him driving and me with my shades on, staring out into the expanse of LA. It had been a long time since we had rolled somewhere together, and I wasn't used to having the company. I hardly ever even listened to the radio, so I missed the silence when I would ride with Dirk, who chatted like a cabbie.

If he didn't have conversation in his life, I think Dirk would have exploded a long time ago. He was obsessed with my previous career in porn and fascinated by it all, with almost a child's awe. He was always asking questions about what porn stars were really like and what was the craziest thing anyone had ever bought. He was a big enthusiast of pornography and would've loved to work in the porn business, except his wife wouldn't let him. She was the dominating type and not in the kinky whips-and-leather way.

Dirk was also stuck on the song "Sexual Eruption" by Snoop Dogg. The lyrics had been changed to "Sensual Seduction" to make it more radio friendly. Dirk misheard it as "Sexual Seduction," though, and it had been adopted as his singing catchphrase to be spouted at any occasion.

JEFF: Man, this is crazy going to Dodger Stadium…

DIRK (singing): Sexual Seduction...

JEFF: I wonder what happened.

DIRK: We'll find out when we get there...We're supposed to talk to a Joe...or is it José?

JEFF: ...

DIRK: What was the craziest thing that ever happened to you while you were working in the porn shop?

JEFF: In the porn shop? Hmm, I don't know...I used to have this porn star that would come in, bring me weed, dry hump me...

DIRK: So you might say it was...(again, singing) Sexual Seduction...

The truck climbed Chavez Ravine to the waiting gates of the stadium's outer limits. After bandying with a guard who'd just turned away some random Dodger fans wishing to see the stadium and who took much convincing that we were legit, we were on our way as the truck crept through security and into the parking lot.

I expected to see a mob of reporters or major scene activity, or both, as we drove around the perimeter toward the first baseline, but it felt more like an abandoned city. Construction trailers dotted the land-scape, heavy machinery was set up for work, and yet there was no one around. We crept through the mess of trailers, the throaty growl of the Chevy truck announcing our presence in the early evening.

Two men in hard hats eventually stepped out to consider us, and we waved them over. "We're looking for Joe...or José?" Dirk asked of them when they reached the side of the truck. I expected him to tack on a "Sexual Seduction," but he didn't.

The men looked confused about both names. The one with a walkie-talkie asked into it, "Do we have a Joe or a José working on the crew?"

"No Joes, lots of Josés," came the response.

"We're from Crime Scene Cleaning," Dirk clarified.

"They say they're here to clean up the crime scene," Walkie-Talkie reported.

"Send them to Access Route 3...tell 'em to wait for a security crewman to escort them in. I'll send one over."

Arriving at Access Route 3, we were impressed to discover the cavernous mouth of a tunnel extending down into the bowels of the stadium. Tall, Dodger-blue metal doors protected the entrance, though one had been left hanging open and swinging slightly in a still-winter breeze.

There were no reporters or indeed any sign whatsoever that anything had gone down at Dodger Stadium. It was as if the park was keeping an extreme wrap on the situation. The beginning of the season was still two months off, so I'd ruled out fan or player death.

Fifteen minutes later, our security guard, an older Mexican gentleman in dress blues, arrived in a small security pickup truck. He was an overly friendly type who spoke English slowly and with a lot of effort, tacking on "my friends" to any sentence in which he addressed us.

Security Guard led us through the industrial cement hallways beneath the stadium, a location few ever get to see. There was no smell of beer, hot peanuts, or soft pretzels beneath the poured concrete innards of the historic park; rather, it was full of long, dark hallways, creepily antiseptic.

After a bit of walking that could have been achieved much faster by a quick zip on one of the idle motorized carts Security Guard wouldn't let us go near ("I don't want to lose my career, my friends..."), we stopped at Access Door 33. Bent metal doors, contorted by God knows what, were strapped closed by yellow caution tape. Across the hallway, we could hear the hum of electronics doing their thing. The three of us beneath the stadium were otherwise alone.

We ascended wooden planks set up for the construction that had been halted in the wake of the tragedy. The rickety boards, spanning gulches of concrete, groaned under my footfalls. I hopped from one to the next quickly, eager to avoid an accident myself.

It turned out to be a fall. We could easily surmise as much from the impact point upon the unpaved concrete of the stadium's base. The worker had dropped from a distance in excess of forty feet, falling quicker than he could shout and meeting a gruesome demise on the jagged roughness below. That same quivering mass of red present at the disgraced minister's home was present once again, although this time it had been mulched viciously by the impact.

Security Guard, though hesitant to leave us, was also clearly uneasy about being in the presence of some seriously bad juju. The temptation of the forbidden overwhelmed him finally, though, and he crept forward to take a look. The repulsion stretched across his face reminded me that most people weren't used to this sort of thing. I didn't see the scene as much more than one less rat in the race.

Finally having satiated his blood curiosity, Security Guard retreated out of the access tunnel, across the wooden plank bridge, and back out into the safety of the corridor. There, the soft glow of ceiling-mounted fluorescents offered sanctuary. Inside the cavern where we were, there was only the hard burn of a pointed work light and soft red guts.

The worker had fallen from his perch down into a sealed-off hollow cavern that comprised one of the load-bearing struts for the stadium. It was as if he'd fallen between the walls of a house, only the "walls" were comprised of thick, hardened concrete. Workers had had to drill through two feet of poured structure to access the splattered mess that had been their fellow employee. The excavation didn't make Dodger Stadium any less safe for the public, but it opened up a whole new mess of problems for us.

The newly exposed cavern measured roughly twenty-five feet across and at least sixty feet high with measured concrete steps etched into the ceiling. The steps were the underside of rising rows of bleachers alongside the first base line. They were the good seats, where the rich people sat. I whistled at the prospect of how far beneath Dodger Stadium I was.

We'd had to crawl over the chunky patches of blood and ripped skin to access the chamber, as the work crew had chiseled out the wall in exactly the place his body had fallen and hadn't factored in the need for a crime scene cleaner to move in and out of the space. Though the cavernous chamber was dark where our meal ticket had breathed his last, the glow of a construction light from the corridor revealed an outline of the sharp sloping rise of concrete that was the floor of the room. It wasn't so much a floor as it was the bottom of a pit. It was unpaved and rough, and had been poured by numerous cement trucks fifty years beforehand, their drivers oblivious to the damage the knobby concrete would do to a fellow worker's body half a century later.

I clicked on my flashlight, first to highlight the trauma we'd be dealing with, and then to play the beam across the room as I walked up the incline of the floor. The cavern wasn't airtight, because ragged and dark tunnels extended through the side walls of the subterranean cavern and into numerous other caverns probably similar to the one I was in. It was a creepy place, and I was eager to return to the safety of the blood and guts far below.

We'd already gotten the authorization of payment via a walkie-talkie to do the work. Considering it was Dodger Stadium, I would have done the job for free. Of course, since they didn't know that, a couple grand seemed perfectly fair.

The sheer amount of chunkiness and blood caused me to immediately forgo the sprayer. I was all for AIDS protection, but there was only so much a chemical could do against the sheer volume of a human's gummy liquid insides. Using cloth hand towel after cloth hand towel, I scrubbed at the ground, lifting the jellied mess into the trash bag, feeling it collapse from my hand's pressure the way a water balloon might.

Gnarled waves of unpaved concrete were exactly the sort of porous surface that I had always dreaded, the reason to employ my caveat in contracts, and as such, I resorted to using a crowbar and rubber mallet that Dirk had in his work crate to attempt to knock off the chunks of dyed rock base.

After several hours of chipping away at minuscule flecks, which went skittering off beneath the wooden plank bridge, Dirk voiced a bit of sensibility. "We should just paint over the fucker."

I quickly agreed, the magic of being in Dodger Stadium long gone from my heart.

"I'll go get some paint," he announced cheerfully, eager to be free of my halfhearted assault on giblets of reddened rock. This meant that he would have to take his truck and go in search of the nearest Home

Depot, leaving me in the barren pit, surrounded by poorly excavated chasms bathed in darkness and the weird stench of the air that occasionally emanated from them in short bursts like the breath of some overworked animal.

"Are you sure you don't want me to go?" I asked hopefully, raising the crowbar and mallet like some poster boy for Russian servitude.

"I'm sure," he said, leaving, the bouncing of the loose boards sounding his departure. I sat next to the mass of red ground beneath Dodger Stadium, able to only guess at the darkness of the night sky many ceilings above. My bunny suit, tied off at the waist, was a dirty crimson. I heard the muffled slam of one of the blue doors far, far down the corridor, and in that moment I knew what it was to be alone.

In the cavern of concrete, my cell phone registered no bars, and I cursed Verizon for not sending the "Can you hear me now?" guy into the dungeons of the stadium. And it was there, alone in the dark of night, with no cell-phone reception and only my vivid imagination, that I began to consider the notion of ghosts.

If someone had asked me at any other time on any other crime scene what I thought about the presence of the supernatural, I would have laughed in their face. I'd never felt a weird "cold presence" or a heaviness hanging over a crime scene that would suggest the presence of the supernatural. But there in that abyss…it was a bit like an atheist finding God in the face of impending doom.

Alone in the poorly lit arena, above the viscous splatter of a miserable soul, the sounds of non-life quickly began to intrude upon my sanity. A small rain of pebbles sprinkled down on me from the ledge far above, and I had to remind myself that it was wind knocking the loose bits down as it had done the whole time Dirk and I were bantering and scrubbing. It hadn't seemed nearly as sinister then, though.

Gripping the bloodied steel arm of the crowbar, I turned on my flashlight once more, flicking quickly through the ultraviolet settings that registered the uneven roof in a ghastly purple hue. I scaled the steep concrete as high as I dared, splaying the light across the expanse of silent night, wishing it captured a larger area in its beam. The added glow did little more than call attention to my presence, its rapid sweeping movements signifying to whatever hellish entity that might have been in there with me that I was exposed and vulnerable. I held the crowbar tighter, feeling the dense metal unyielding between my black-gloved fingers.

"Who's up there?" I called, attempting lighthearted banter with the darkness extending past the lip far above, from which our victim had dropped oh so suddenly.

No answer.

I looked farther up to where the concrete hill plateaued above me into further darkness, and the concentrated orb of my flashlight illuminated similarly ragged tunnels etched into the walls at the top of the room. Something could come at me in the cavern from myriad entry points, and I found myself cursing my father for screening *Alien* for me as a three-year-old.

"Can I get some more light in here?" I yelled again, wishing that the whispered air through the earthen tunnels was of human origin and that the human was friendly and capable of granting the odd request. It wasn't.

I crouched low on the side of the concrete slope, not daring to go back toward my work, where my ample back would be exposed to the dark of the nearby crawl space. Visions of flat red eyes haunted me and made me regret everything I had done in life that might have made me hell-worthy.

I didn't dare check my cell phone again, for it would displace my grasp on one of my two objects, the crowbar or the flashlight, and I was ill-equipped to suffer the disappointment of zero bars once again.

"I'm not scared," I announced loudly, my voice betraying me in the midst of the dark. "I'm not scared," I said aloud again, this time more to myself. My inner monologue asked me whom I thought I was fooling. It also assured me in no uncertain terms that I, too, would meet my untimely demise in these dark hollows.

The electronic snarl of some far-off compressor cut sharply through my bullshit and evoked the terror that I had been concealing poorly. Crowbar held aloft like the sword Excalibur, and the flashlight extended before me creating karate chop motions at the end of my pivoting arm, I ran for it. Ducking and slipping as I exited the hole, my bottom spotted red from odd concentrations of residue, I lumbered across the wooden planks, the wood creaking beneath me, and prayed there were no trolls below to snatch me into the terrifying unknown.

I leapt down to the platform, connecting with the battered doors, fearing the creatures that had ravaged them, and headed down the length of dim corridors to the safety of the night beyond. My bloody bunny suit whisk-whisked as the material swished against itself and I ran for my life. I hit the exterior doors fist first and blasted through them, emerging from the depths and into the smoky darkness of the Los Angeles night.

Dirk rolled up forty-five minutes later, casually munching a Big Mac, and found me still gripping the flashlight and bloody crowbar.

Those Big Macs brought me back to reality, and I graciously accepted one of my own. With me leading the way to show my fearlessness, breathing not a word of my experiences or lack thereof, I carried the cans of paint back to where the red mess was exactly as I had left it. In fact, the whole cavern now seemed exactly as it had before…harmless.

Not sure exactly how to go about painting over a human, I dumped the gallon can out atop the start of the puddle, its gloppy white thickness pouring out like batter onto a hot griddle. Shaking the last remnants from the can, I marveled at how the paint found its own way down the rocky face of the concrete, not quite washing over the blood trails.

Using a roller, I began to push the paint outward, thinning it, ensuring that it spread over all the traceable red. As the encapsulating white paint spread and coated the uneven surface, the red mixed with it to form sickly salmon pink patches in the whiteness of the rock.

I moved the roller around, pushing more paint over the heinous pink blotches, but that just freed up more spots, making the man's death seem all the more sickening.

"Damn it," Dirk swore. "That's all the paint I bought. Looks like you'll have to come out here tomorrow and lay a second coat."

• • •

When I returned once more to the ballpark's underground, I made sure it was during daylight hours. The second layer of paint didn't do much more to cover up where that guy impacted.

I'll bet that if you finagle your way into the labyrinth of corridors beneath the first baseline to the battered access door numbered 33 and make your way across the rickety plank bridge, you'll find the rough exposure where construction workers hammered their way through the wall to reach their splattered coworker's corpse. And in the entrance to the massive cave of uneven concrete beyond, you'll find a large splotch of white paint with sickly pink patches creeping through.

Just do yourself and your sanity a favor…and don't go at night.

CHAPTER 16

blood, blood, there's so much blood!

My father taught me to work; he did not teach me to love it.
—*Abraham Lincoln*

THERE WAS NOTHING LIKE AN abundance of work to make my lazy ass wish for less work. We had been rolling like crazy lately, as a seeming wave of death was overwhelming Orange County. All of the people who had managed to cling to their meaningless lives during the dry months had now decided to unburden themselves, one on top of another.

A month ago I had visited the Hotel Pepper Tree, a garish place in Anaheim with a South Beach, Miami, feel to it (though I have never visited South Beach, Miami). I had gone initially with the intention of collecting payment from the ancient and shaking brother of the doll lady. He had come in from South Beach and had made a beeline to a place of familiarity and comfort.

In that initial visit to the Hotel Pepper Tree, I had been struck by the tropical, pastel feel of the place, full of palm fronds and the sound of running water. It wasn't located in the most colorful part of Anaheim, the spectacle that was Disneyland, and so it stuck out in the dusty, drab surroundings like an oasis in Antarctica.

What had captured my attention about the place was not its sore-thumb exterior, though, but rather its decorating scheme. In this temple to the tropical, the decorating scheme was completely Arnold.

Evidently the owner of the place had been unwilling to completely shy away from his SoCal roots, and the twin corridors running the length of the building were adorned with a multitude of framed movie posters from the Governator's long career in Hollywood. It was Arnold Schwarzenegger's face glaring out at me from among the palm trees that I remarked upon later to anyone who would listen at the frat house. And then a month later, I was back.

Since my back still wasn't 100 percent normal, I brought Kim, from my work crew on the Sewer House, with me. She'd begged me to take her on a job, and though I had obliged on the Sewer House, she wanted more. Kim was attracted to the ghoulish side of life, the dark and dirty aspects of human nature, and as such, my job captivated her.

I had been unable to bring along Misty, the attractive woman who was actually employed by O.C. Crime Scene Cleaners, because she was too busy lately with school and her other job. Kim was attractive, too, though, and as she'd tellingly informed me at one point, she had her clit pierced.

Kim had been among the collective at the frat the day I had described the outlandish splendor of the Hotel Pepper Tree, and so it felt like a badge of honor that she could verify its gaudiness. We were there for a young man who had violently stabbed himself in his heart, cutting a hole in his Abercrombie & Fitch T-shirt and creating a trail of blood that ruined his Seven jeans.

From there the blood had found its way across the wide, polished brown tiles and into grout lines of the floor that were a little too deep and narrow to fit the head of the cleaning brush. The half of the room that the bed was on lay undisturbed, save a four-foot-long narrow patch of carpet lying adjacent to the affected streaks of tile. Kim was through the roof at the possibilities of cleaning up this dead guy; I was thinking about her clit ring and how the bed opposite the carnage was unstained. I tempered that thought, though, with the memories of my karmatic diarrhea on the dog job, and we got to work.

Kim was adorable bundling up in her bunny suit (one of Misty's). She was concerned about the possibility of disease, so she actually taped her gloves to the wrists of her suit with duct tape, something she'd evidently learned off a TV show, as it was never anything I had been trained in.

I cinched my suit off at my waist, so as not to ruin my shorts, and crouched down slowly till I was at face level with the tile. I wasn't worried about disease myself, feeling like an old pro now that I had been cleaning crime scenes for a full year. Besides, what sort of disease could I possibly get from the blood of an impeccably fashionable young man who'd come down to a kitschy and flamboyant hotel to kill himself in an overly dramatic manner?

The work itself seemed easy enough. I cleaned the blood off the tile with my paper towels, and Kim mirrored me every step of the way, busting her ass to show her value as a team member. She was working as a waitress and hating every minute of it. If there were any way she could get aboard with the crime scene cleaning and get out of her old occupation, she would do it. I knew the feeling.

Dirk was a bit of a pervert and would have been more than happy to go for it, and I myself couldn't imagine the downside of having two attractive girls working with us. We were paying both of them peanuts. Dirk and I split pay in half for all the jobs we did and now excluded Schmitty from all the ones he didn't immediately contract us for, while we paid the girls twenty-five dollars an hour for their work.

Kim said she wasn't in it for the money, but had she known I was making $250 or more an hour, she might have changed her mind. She was a good worker when there weren't neighbors around for her to gab with, and I did my part to make sure she kept on task. In the end, she seemed to fit right in with us as a member of our unit. Of course, we were a motley crew of slap-dicks, scumbags, and morons with little to no moral fiber, so maybe saying she fit right in wasn't exactly the best compliment.

• • •

One day, just as it was starting to get into the summer heat, we got a call from the Corona Police Department. Kim was waitressing and my back was feeling okay, so I took the call alone.

I rolled into their station with Dirk's words fresh in my mind. He was adamant that we do everything "right" to impress the cops, because that would entice them to recommend us to the private sector, where the real money was.

The Red Rocket and I were now a familiar sight at Orange PD; I'd grown accustomed to a casual friendliness from most of the cops. I would joke around with them, pissing and moaning about having to clean up piss and vomit and complaining how they had it easy. Whenever unfamiliar cops would approach me about my presence in their underground gate-access-only parking garage, I would respond innocently with statements like, "Isn't this where I go to register as a sex offender?" or "My brother's in there...I'm here to bust him out!" They'd panic for a moment, and then realization would set in and we'd share a laugh.

So when I arrived at Corona PD, it was understandable that I was expecting a similar level of professional courtesy. Instead, the office had me fill out paperwork explaining what my business was bothering them with, and then they left me to fuck off for thirty-five minutes in the lobby while they halfheartedly attempted to page the chucklehead who had contacted me in the first place.

Corona was a newer town on the fringe of the desert, and the residents had that "new town on the fringe of the desert" attitude to show for it, as if they were fucking Palm Springs or something. My rock-star mentality was beginning to get the better of me, and I stood up to announce that they could clean up their own cop car—I had better ways to waste a day. But the lady at the reception counter was even too busy for me to announce my intent, so I meekly returned to my seat.

Finally I was summoned into the police yard, where eight or so fleet vehicles awaited deployment. It was a miserable, cramped yard as far as police-yard facilities went. I'd clearly grown snooty, having become accustomed to the blissful shade of the Orange PD underground. In the desert of Corona, the sweltering sun cut straight through the morning haze and beamed like a spotlight on me, making my skin feel unbearably sticky.

My contact, Winston, led me over toward one of the black-and-whites, its fiberglass exterior cooking in the heat. Winston opened the back door, and the stale stench of death bull-rushed me. Blood has a metallic odor to it, and when it has been cooking in mass amounts in the trapped air of a police car's walled-in cage, you can taste it on the front of your tongue. I didn't have to lean in to see that the backseat was gruesome.

The molded fiberglass buckets of the backseat had large puddles of the red stuff, and in the heat the top layer was beginning to dry, forming a gelatinlike skin across the liquid pools underneath. Phlegmlike snatches of pulpy blood had been flung across the rest of the enclosure, staining seatbelts and the fabric overlay on the ceiling along with the frizzy wisps of carpeting laid along the back window. The twin steel bars that served as reinforcement for the Plexiglas window shield separating the good guys from the bad guys had caught the worst of it; one of them was drenched in a mess of red and black innards with a salsalike consistency. The guts extended out to the window shield, down to the floor, and up to the ceiling in a manner that spoke volumes about the level of violence that had taken place. It was as if a man had been caged up with a live chain saw too large for the enclosure.

"What happened in there?" I looked to Winston, wishing I had one of my assistants with me.

"Prisoner was drunk and didn't want to be arrested, so she beat her brains out on the metal support bar."

"She die?" I asked, amazed at her fortitude.

"What's it look like?" he retorted, and turned, leaving me to it.

It was far worse than any of the poop or vomit or HIV or hep C scenarios Orange PD had ever thrown at me. And because we were trying to shore up the all-important service contract with Corona PD, the job was being done for our "specialty police rate." I wanted to call Dirk out there just so he could see the sort of bullshit that he was sticking me with on a regular basis now, but he wouldn't bother to show.

I knew immediately that it would be in my best interest to suit up fully, because I was going to have to enter the car. With the wettest puddles of stewed guts splashed toward the middle of the ride and my back still not fully able to handle the contortions, I was going to have to climb into the thick of it and sit, my bunny suit absorbing the slimy patches behind me.

I geared up quickly and under the curious eyes of arriving cops who'd evidently never seen a crime scene cleaner before and were only just now learning about the vehicle's last occupant.

Most of the officers were less than thrilled to see an outsider in their clubhouse, and responded to my engaging smiles and polite "Howya doin's?" with an icy stare of mistrust. The ones who did talk were only there to engage in unfriendly mocking, telling me that I looked like the Stay Puft Marshmallow Man in my protective suit. They also mentioned my striking resemblance to that other obese, white-bodied entity of corporate gimmickry, the Michelin Man.

I smiled through it all as Dirk had implored me, bearing their insults from the back of the car, where I was surrounded by remains and the dense, sweltering desert air, heated immeasurably in the trapped confines of the backseat, scrubbing away. The more daring of the cops would wander up and leer down at me, reminiscent of the gangbangers from my first car job, guns at their hip, silently daring me to question them.

When the car was as clean as I could muster, I once more collected my things and got the hell out of there. Personality-wise, the cops didn't seem too much different from the thugs they arrested.

●　●　●

During what I later would come to realize was our heyday, it wasn't just crime scenes that were keeping me busy. The Public Guardian's office was proud of us for taking down the Sewer House with an efficiency that a government agency was probably unused to.

We'd actually had to rent a storage space to contain all the salvageable property we'd pulled from the mess—stuff like multiple drum sets, ornate lamps still in the box, and brand-new cooking gadgets. Along with salvaged jewelry and antique coins, it was a rather nice haul awaiting pickup by the county to do God knows what with. It was short by several thousand dollars and an electric guitar, but they didn't know that.

As a reward for our awesomeness, the county allowed us to bid on several more houses. Dirk sent me out with a camera to collect and document the homes in all their atrociousness for him to later compile into a bid. We were up against an unknown number of bidders for the work, if there was indeed anyone at all against us. For all I knew, the county had simply decided to say, "Fuck it. These are our guys."

I talked Chris into tagging along as he had done with me on the Sewer House; it had seemingly become a way of bonding for us to invade properties and assess the cost to remedy them. Dirk and I were granted a remarkable level of trust by the Public Guardian's office in that we were allowed to come by, pick up keys to properties vacated by death or insanity, and explore them at our leisure, unhampered by bureaucracy and county needling. As such, Chris and I would make days out of it, taking multiple sets of keys and hitting one property after another, exploring through the refuse like pirates, searching out money or loot that had been left behind by the owners.

In one house the mold was growing thick over the piles of kitty poop that had acclimated into small hills throughout the premises, and you had to be careful to not slip on the stacks of newspaper covering the floor, which would doubtlessly land you leg first in one of the ancient piles.

In another house that didn't seem too dirty at all, we emerged to find that our lower halves were thick with mites crawling up and down our naked legs. Removing our footwear, we spent the next few minutes slapping at and squashing the scrambling insects off our bodies.

At yet another house, we were attempting to open the garage door first when a rough-looking homeowner from nearby approached us cautiously. "Are you with the county?" he asked with all the suspicion of a self-important neighbor.

I nodded, figuring that it was close enough to the truth.

"I'm glad you're here," he admitted, his hard edge seeping away. "I hate looking at this house—it gives me the chills."

"Why's that?" Chris asked.

"Because the man who lived here was a child molester."

I had dealt with my fair share of those in the last year. "What makes you say that?" I probed.

"Weird sounds from the house…he was always taking kids there, but he lived alone…it was all weird. Everyone around here hated him.

The police never would do anything. Finally they found him dead in his living room; apparently the place was kind of a wreck." The neighbor neglected to mention how the man had met his demise.

"We'll see," I said with a nod, looking intently at the alleged predator's den. I figured that the ex-owner was just an eccentric uncle or something who caught a bad rap from the overzealous locals. We waited until the neighbor ran out of things to say and retreated, promising that we'd consider his offer to join him for a beer later.

Although each was far beyond the level of "messy," none of the houses we'd seen had been anywhere near as bad as the Sewer House. The suspected child molester's house came close, with garbage scattered in abundance throughout the place and with emphasis on kitchen trash. But where the Sewer House had gone well over six feet of trash in several places, some around the ten-foot mark, this place had its highs in the one-foot range, which was still a goddamned pigsty.

The molester's house had its own unique charms, though, what with boxes of conventional pornography stacked around the place and lurid magazines draped over the wreckage. There was even a large box of porno tapes occupying the space where the toilet should have been, as the porcelain toilet was taking up residence in the living room.

Most telling about the man's personal hobbies, though, and easily the most chilling, was an old, boxy video camera set on a steel tripod and angled downward, waiting to record the action on the master bedroom's king-size mattress. Surrounding it were stacks and stacks of unmarked videotapes, partially or fully recorded through, their content unmistakably toxic. Upon further inspection of the house, all available cabinets were filled with similar videocassettes, similarly recorded. It was enough probing for us.

Desperate to not get burned again on the contracting, Dirk, armed with my documentation and recommendations, bid the jobs above and beyond what it would take to do the work, eagerly scheming out ways for us to milk the county on labor and sanitation costs.

Since our transgressions at the Sewer House, Dirk had become fairly no-bones about his desires to make money any way possible. Of course we bid the jobs too high, and of course we didn't get them. We should have realized all county jobs had to include multiple bids. What Dirk took away from it, though, was that maybe, just maybe, the county guys did know what we had done on the Sewer House and they were denying us future work as a result. After that idea popped into his head, it was like talking with a conspiracy-theorist stoner. Paranoia abounded, and yet he was still after more money.

The county's goodwill toward independent property assessment came to an abrupt end shortly thereafter. In one of the only houses Dirk accompanied me to for the sake of bidding, a cozy little double-wide at a retirement community in San Juan Capistrano that we searched through (Chris was working at his job that day), $180,000 dollars was found in paper grocery bags under the sink.

Of course, Dirk and I didn't find the money; no, in typical "us" fashion, we overbid the assessment like crazy. The winner of the job, apparently a company of honest, good-hearted morons, found the cash and turned it over to the county. Some little old lady with no family members whatsoever was sitting on a gold mine of untraceable bills, and now it was all property of the government.

If it had been me who had found those grocery bags, neither Dirk, nor the county, nor you would have ever heard from me again. Not that I could live the rest of my life on $180,000, but I'm sure that kind of money buys a couple goddamn good years in Thailand. I can't believe we didn't look under the sink.

After the cash was discovered, the county mandated that all assessment visits to homes had to come under strict supervision of a county ward, and my and Chris's brotherly bonding trips went flushing down the drain. Most brothers might have continued to do bonding activities in spite of that, but most brothers probably have never heard the expression "As lazy as a Klima" (only slightly lesser known is "Don't trust a Klima with your wife's underwear drawer"). If there wasn't a possibility for making money, I doubt Chris and I could even muster up the energy for a staring contest.

• • •

Back in the familiar comforts of our regular business, crime scenes, Dirk and I were still trucking along nicely. We'd been out to several cleanups for little old lady alcoholics who had died in their homes.

Alcoholic deaths were always nasty because the people tended to shit themselves (a lot of Type 6s on the Bristol Stool Scale) in their death spasms and puke up stomach blood, which comes up greasy black with all the bile in it. Succumbing to last-stage alcoholism is apparently one of the worst ways to shuffle off the mortal coil, and judging by appearances, it certainly looked like it.

Old people posed another problem as well. When people advance in age, their balance gets unsteady, and they constantly need to put their hands out in hallways and against walls to keep themselves upright. This, coupled with dementia and senility, results in what we in the crime scene business call "train tracks." "Train tracks" are created by an old person's inability to fully wipe after using the restroom, and as such, their dirty fingertips, trailing down the wall, steadying the body, create long thin smears of contamination along midlevel surfaces. (This is why you should never touch the walls in an old person's house.)

Dead alcoholics would become a hallmark of this period, but another hallmark was the consistency of Motel 6 jobs. At Motel 6 after Motel 6 in Southern California, we were constantly getting the call out for some manner of craziness. Gunfights, murders, suicides, regular fights; in one extreme case, a man took a screwdriver to the eye (not self-inflicted).

It all became a part of the daily mill that had become my life. I believed that with the county at our backs and death in our sails, the good times were there to stay. I was frivolously spending the untaxed money I was making on lavish dinners and unnecessary toys, ignoring the debt of school loans and credit cards, leaving those bills for another day. (To save himself money, Dirk had me operating as an "independent contractor" instead of an employee.)

Yet, on another level, I was burned out on working and worried about the long-term effects of the job on my mental and physical health. I had begun to smell death everywhere, with a heightened awareness of the malodors of rotting blood and decomposition in supermarkets, on streets, and everywhere else. It was having a chilling effect on my psyche as I began to picture horrific crime scenes in the most common of places, knowing that something bad had likely occurred there at some point.

In parks, hotel rooms, and stores, I could visualize how the yellow police tape would be laid out, hanging off shelves and available surfaces; picture how the blood would look, depending on how long it would have the chance to sit; and where the brains, skull fragments, and various other bits and pieces would hit and come to rest. It was an unsettling time for me, and it culminated in a scene close to home.

Early one morning, Dirk rousted me with an aggravating phone call. The bleating plea of my phone had replaced the clang of an alarm clock as my least favorite noise. He had received a call out for an apartment complex in Fullerton with an address that seemed awfully familiar. It was for Sycamore Terrace, where Chris and I had lived happily until they stole my car and raised our rent. I drove down reluctantly, still exhausted from crime scenes the previous day and yet morbidly eager to revisit my old haunt.

The apartment complex looked newer and fresher somehow, as if they had decided to class up the joint the day after we moved out. I parked in the "prospective tenant" parking, which was fiercely off-limits to actual tenants, and wandered in. The curvaceous Latina manager who had chewed me out during the battle over the Red Rocket was manning the front desk when I walked in. She looked as good as ever.

I ambled up to her, feeling the weight of the bags under my eyes, and introduced myself namelessly as "the guy from O.C. Crime Scene Cleaners." She studied me for a second, finding something familiar in my face perhaps, and then let it go. She summoned a maintenance guy to take me to the scene. I recognized him as one of the thug employees who'd made me fear for my electronics equipment during my live-in time.

He led me down the familiar pathways that I remembered oh so well, past the laundry room I'd used, the pool and workout room I didn't use, past the billiards room I had used once. It was all unnerving as he marched me back, each fork in the path we took leading me closer to my apartment.

When I had first got the call, I had been elated that something could have happened in my old apartment…that the next tenant had been murdered or a washing machine had exploded, launching a thick bolt like a guided missile through the thin walls of the apartment and into the ocular cavity of some masturbating new tenant.

But as I drew nearer and nearer to the possibility that it might indeed be my old apartment, 1571, letter H, I hoped it wasn't. I was already having enough frustration with my current station in life, and I didn't want the added knowledge that I had ever been that vulnerable. That the guy who replaced me in my porn job was murdered was bad enough; to know I could have died in the safety of my comfortable apartment might have shattered me.

The maintenance thug stopped in the courtyard of my old apartment, with some stranger's furniture taking up residence on the patio that I'd called mine. My stomach dropped as he considered it, spinning around slowly, unsure which of the five or so apartments in the near vicinity was the one. I realized then that, after all, I wanted it to be mine.

Now knowing that it was indeed in the courtyard of apartments that I'd once called home, I realized that I had known all the neighboring tenants to some degree, from simple hellos to involved conversations to actually hanging out and drinking with them. The only tenant I didn't know in the area was the one currently taking roost in my old home. If anyone, I wished death on that person. At least I didn't know him.

Finally turning, the maintenance guy selected the downstairs apartment diagonal to mine. With an awakening jolt, I realized it was the Mexican family, the ones with the little kid who would sit on his plastic car and roll it noisily over the still-present cracks in the pathway. I could easily remember the grinning kid on his car, the mother nervously trailing after, embarrassed for the amount of noise her son was creating. It had been irritating then, but now that I feared that something had happened to the little guy or his shy mom, the noise seemed somewhat endearing.

As soon as the door was unlocked for me, I could see it had the potential to be "one of those days." Splashes of blood greeted me on the furniture, carpeting, and walls throughout the living room, and the trails seemed to continue through all major access points to the room.

I walked into the kitchen, following a thicker blood trail that made the leap from the living room carpet to the hard tile of the kitchen. The trail stopped—or, actually, started—at an open cutlery drawer containing numerous serrated-edged steak knives.

"What happened to the family that lived here?" I asked, my curiosity overwhelming my wish to stay anonymous.

"They weren't here when it happened," the bald thug responded casually, unaffected by the carnage around him. I figured he'd seen his share of shit on the street.

"What did happen?" I probed.

"There was an uncle living with them, and he became suicidal. They left him home alone, and he took a knife and he slashed both his wrists and cut his own throat.

"That would do it," I confirmed as if I were an authority on killing oneself. I followed the blood trail around the apartment as it criss-crossed over itself in numerous places. Evidently, after hacking open his neck and forearms, the uncle had run through the two-bedroom apartment flailing his arms wildly, attempting to dispatch all eight pints of blood in as broad an area as he could.

It was heartbreaking to survey, knowing that the family was not a rich one—the father worked as a handyman at an apartment complex not unlike Sycamore Terrace, and the mother worked nights some-where. They traded off on raising their young son.

The kid's bedroom had been converted so that he and the uncle could share the space, and the uncle, based on the amount of blood spilled, had spent some time in that bedroom, contemplating the kid's toys. The push car that the boy had noisily ridden around the complex, waking me up early in the morning after late nights at my bouncing job was in there, too, splashed with an unnatural red on its white body.

Pulse juice lay splayed across both beds in the room and the one in the master bedroom as well, where the despondent uncle had also taken the time to bleed into the wife's panty drawer.

From there, sensing that the end was coming, the man had snatched a crucifix off the wall and gone into the front bathroom, where he lay down in the tub to die. While there was an abundance of blood throughout the rest of the apartment and all its rooms, it was paltry compared to the damage he'd inflicted upon the walls and ceiling of the bathroom. Only in small patches could you discern the original paint color of the walls, and the tub, for all intents and purposes, was now permanently stained red. His body had ejected all the blood it had contained, leaving the man a pale, dry husk clutching tight to a crucifix. Though his body was gone, the crucifix remained in his place, the small Jesus coated in more blood than he himself had ever spilled.

I stepped outside to call Dirk and request his presence on the job.

"Can't tonight," he intoned in an awkward, quick voice he'd adopt whenever it seemed like he was telling a lie. "Taking the kid to Disneyland."

"I can't do this by myself," I pleaded with him, thinking of the sheer amount of furniture, mattresses, and carpeting that would have to be discarded, not to mention the repainting of the bathroom, which would never see those same walls clean again. I tried to convey the magnitude of the job that was before me, but my pleas fell on deaf ears.

"Call one of the girls to help you, but make sure you bid it low so we get the job," he suggested before hanging up.

"Did you used to live here?" the Latina manager asked when I walked back into the main office. I nodded, ashamed now for not mentioning it earlier. "I thought so," she concluded. "I never forget a face."

I wanted to make some further comment about how she fucked up my existence with her rent-raising ways, but instead I good-naturedly handed her my bid and told her to call if we got the job. There were two other companies arriving to compete for the business. I didn't know what their bids would be, but I felt confident the number I'd scribbled out for her would be more expensive…a lot more expensive. There was no way she'd be calling to offer us the gig. I was right, of course, and it earned me a nice, relaxing day off.

CHAPTER 17

cleaning up alcoholics is less fun than being an alcoholic

They speak of my drinking, but never think of my thirst.
—*Scottish proverb*

DEATH, LIKE THE MACARENA, IS a trend. Sure, everybody does it, but not everybody does it the same way…like the Macarena. As an expert in the death business—and to a certain extent, the Macarena business—I've seen many of the more common ways people have left the planet. But sometimes one way in particular suddenly becomes all the rage. The latest trend seemed to be the maggot-eaten leftovers stemming from unattended alcoholism.

The death rattle of an alcoholic is not a pleasant one for anybody concerned. For the family members, it is akin to watching someone slowly poison himself or herself; to the alcoholic it is a painful process of body parts ceasing to function and fluids and secretions being forced into other parts of the body. Upon death, a lot of black, bloody phlegm gets coughed up and surrounds the top half of the body, while feces, similar in appearance to the phlegm, tends to surround the lower half. For the crime scene cleaner, it's a smelly, messy way to earn a paycheck.

Our new best friends at the Public Guardian's office called us out to a scene for a fat, drunken wreck of a human being who died on his mattress and stayed there until the smell got the police involved. We were working with Mona Spears herself, our chief liaison from the P.G.'s office. She had the kind of big ass that looked like it was incorrectly bolted to her slightly smaller frame. Despite a hard-on for nicotine, she was friendly enough, though. Mona had helped secure us some past jobs, and everything between her and us was hunky-dory. So when she called us out to help with the fat man, we were quick to respond.

Dirk once again begged off on the work and sent me with Kim instead. Kim was eager because she'd broken her "death cherry" on the hipster at the Hotel Pepper Tree and was frothing for more guts. She wanted to know the pungent sting of decomposition, and I was eager to give it to her.

Kim's zeal for the dead was intoxicating, and I fantasized on more than one occasion about her and me out on some *Natural Born Killers* bender: Kim, me, a bottle of whiskey, shotguns, and her clit ring…just out for anything. I never told her about those fantasies, though. Those aren't the kind of things that you can tell just anyone. (Hi, Grandma!)

The dead man's aroma was hovering in the building of bi-level apartment cottages like a nimbus cloud, and I could smell him from the parking lot. It said a lot about the neighborhood that a smell that bad could go unnoticed for that long. Even Kim was rethinking her zest for the assignment when, as we got closer, she realized that the odor wasn't some neighbor scrambling bad eggs.

Upon opening the front door of the man's abode, Mona backed away quickly, choosing instead to take a smoke break on an adjacent stairwell. Kim requested a respirator mask before we proceeded, and being manly, I strode in quickly, wishing I weren't so manly.

The place was a home absent of furniture. He was a computer programmer in some capacity, what with his box-loads of parts and makeshift computing equipment spread across the floor. He couldn't have been that good a programmer, though, because I recognized most of the components as being older than I was, and his movie collection was all in VHS. The living room of the one-bedroom apartment looked the way it might if you had asked someone in the early 1980s to describe what a hacker's apartment would look like in twenty-five years.

Entering the source of the smell, the bedroom, it appeared that his nouveau, post-furniture, minimalist aesthetic extended in there as well. Save for one lumpy mattress, the middle of which was coated in the gelatinous, slimy green residue of a rotted fatso, the entire room existed at cockroach height. His computer, on which he conducted his day-to-day "operations of financial wizardry" no doubt, was set on the ground with the monitor residing in the middle of an empty pizza box, as if the pizza box were some sort of revolutionary new desk.

His eyeglasses had flopped to the ground in front of the bed, as if cast off during an orgasmic frenzy of pizza eating. His clothes were in the closet, at least, but they were bagged up in large garbage bags not unlike the ones I would use to haul away their owner.

Around his bed, in his closet, and on most of the available flooring in the bedroom stood testament to what this lonely man's life had amounted to: porno and scotch. The gaudy oversize box covers of the cheap porno were familiar stuff to me, stuff we'd kept at the porn shop under the sales-tag designation of "bizarre." Lots of movies featuring girls who had extra hairy genitals, pregnant women getting raped, and the calling card of every fat computer nerd, extreme bondage.

I could picture his Friday nights when he was sitting around sucking back belts off the dark-green plastic 1.75 liter bottles of Clan MacGregor's miserly scotch, stroking his doughy pecker, and wondering what life would be like if I…I mean he…were someone cooler.

I didn't even want to speculate what would be found on his computer in some file labeled "private," but in a scenario like the one that found our fat friend rotting away, I could assume that he was purchasing what the other dirtbag, the one with the video camera aimed at his bed, was filming.

Kim reacted much more vocally and harshly toward the dead man on the bed than she had to our cool guy in the hotel, which I found a bit shitty. It was so typical of pretty girls to write someone off because they died fat and smelly. I'll bet, stinky pervert or not, if he had shopped at a United Colors of Benetton, she would have found him more endurable. I reminded myself to pick up some Benetton clothes.

Taffy had scrounged up respirator masks for Kim and herself, and the two of them were dishing about our melted fella, gabbing away like a couple of Chatty Cathys. Kim had the innate ability to make friends with anyone, anywhere, over anything. While her work performance was shit because of it, she did good PR work for us with the locals, and she was easy enough on the eyes. She was worth every penny of twenty-five dollars an hour for both those attributes.

We got the apartment-complex manager to sign off on our work order, promising to make the smell go away, and got down to work. Kim went to work cleaning up the scotch bottles (which filled two and a half large trash bags) while I sanitized computer cords that snaked through the gut mulch on the bed, resembling interstate lines on a map.

Because the drunk's innards had pickled, one would have thought the smell of his rot would have dulled, but in fact the opposite was true. His aroma, the stink of his sweat secretions in the carpeting, the hunks of his flesh that had remained and changed color, the very essence of his nonexistence filled my mouth with a metallic bitterness, as if I had given a Duracell battery a blowjob.

What could be scooped off the stained mattress with cloth hand towels we took, and the rest of the queen-size mattress we folded in two as best we could, sliding trash bags over it like condoms. His rotting remains would end up at the dump, scattered in innocent-looking black bags along with his porno tapes and empty whiskey bottles. I think he would have liked it that way.

• • •

Dirk rolled with me on our next call, out to Huntington Beach, surf mecca of Southern California, for another rotted alcoholic. This one had collapsed in his kitchen, stewing away until a foul brown outline appeared in the flecked white floor tile and finally puddled under the stove. His outline, marked as if done by someone with Parkinson's disease, made it appear that his last motion on earth was the act of crooning Barbra Streisand ballads into his balled fist. Whether that was the reality or not was incidental; it made him more fun to clean up.

Dirk and I had the unpleasant task of meeting with both the dead man's mother and the owner of his apartment complex, a scumbag who looked like someone you'd guess was named Howard.

It was an especially bad situation because Howard, true to his scumbag roots, was interested in one thing—getting the dead man and all of his worldly shit out of Howard's apartment complex. The mother, on the other hand, was still freshly mourning the loss of her son. We had to separate Howard from the mom and work deals with them individually.

Howard would pay for the cleaning up of the dead man—only with the firm understanding that insurance would mostly compensate him later. The mother would pay for the removal of any and all property belonging to the victim, a forty-three-year-old man named Jasper.

The mother thanked us for our compassion during the dealings as she left, all the while glowering across the apartment complex's concrete driveway at Howard. Howard asked us for one of our embroidered polo work shirts to wear while he played golf.

Dirk and I began the work on a Saturday morning. It was the weekend and Misty was available, so she came along. Dirk was in his horny mood, so he peppered her with questions and innuendo about sex and her bisexuality, delighted by the fact that she didn't have a boyfriend, because she enjoyed sleeping around. Not that he or I stood a chance with her. I concentrated on my work to avoid getting wrapped up in the sexual harassment lawsuit I was sure was brewing.

Jasper's innards had soaked into the tile so completely that we had no choice but to remove the tiles. Using a long scraping tool with a thin, wide blade, we all took turns shucking at the stinky, brown tiles. Some of them chipped off neatly in patches while other, more affected tiles separated slowly and much more soggily, something akin to tearing a wet paper bag.

Once we were through the top flooring and down to the concrete, it became apparent that Jasper, like so many in death before him, had also melted into the concrete. He, too, would be painted over.

When Howard came to assess our work, he grimly pointed out that the carpeting hadn't been removed. We pointed out that the carpeting hadn't been affected. He pointed out that he would pay us whatever amount to remove the carpeting. Dirk and I agreed.

Howard also asked if we would say we were taking the countertops out, as well as the mounted vanity in the bathroom. Dirk pointed out that we wouldn't do that, as they weren't affected either. Howard pointed out that we could *say* they were affected and that it all needed to be removed along with the "affected carpeting."

Dirk said he didn't understand. I explained to Dirk that he was talking about insurance fraud. Howard needed us to bill him enough over his deductible to get the insurance company to pay for his deductible as well as eat the expense of new counters, flooring, and vanity for the apartment. In turn, his sons would do the work we allegedly did, and we would keep the cash. Except for the carpeting—Howard was adamant that we remove the carpeting. We said fine. Several thousand dollars later, Dirk and I were ripping out carpeting.

Dirk was a stubborn man, though, and refused to remove the floor insulation beneath the carpeting, assuring me that we were doing Howard a favor by leaving it. I will always agree to do less work, and so the insulation stayed.

The next morning, we were driving back out to the apartment complex in a rental moving truck, breezing by the sea on a sunny day with the windows down and the warm smell of colitas rising up through the air. Dirk was ruining the Zen calm of the morning by talking about porn and how it should have been his destiny to break into the porn business. On top of that, he was still obsessed with his Snoop Dogg song.

I was gazing out the window of the truck, happy about all the money I had made lately, when Dirk broke through my thoughts with the typical Dirk-style question of, "Have you ever seen a snuff film?"

I turned to look at him strangely; I had not, and I was uncertain where this conversation was heading.

"I liked that movie *8mm* with Nicolas Cage…it was gnarly."

I shrugged, not bothering to tell him that I thought the movie was a pretty good concept but done poorly. There was no point in pissing on his parade, and I looked back out the window. I figured he was asking because we had found Jasper's porno stash the day before in our cursory search of the apartment.

"I've seen a snuff film," he said, somewhat darkly for him.

I looked back at him, curious, as the existence of true snuff films is somewhat up for debate. A snuff film, for the pure of heart (If you're pure of heart what the fuck are you doing reading this trash? Get the fuck outta here...), is a videotaped murder, usually in somewhat of a sexual context. They were kind of an urban legend in the porno world, with the occasional customer at the porn shop asking about them or professing to "know a guy who knew a guy..." I was doubtful, so I pressed Dirk for the details.

"I wish I had never seen it," he began. "They told us that we could leave the room if we wanted before they showed it, but I wasn't gonna miss it," he said turning his head away from the road to look at me for long intervals, conveying his sincerity. The look he was giving me made me sit up and take listen.

"It was shown when I was in training at the sheriff's academy. There was this girl...she looked like she was fifteen or sixteen...lying on this bed naked. And then this boy comes into the frame, and he looks like he's probably thirteen. Anyways, someone off camera tells him to have sex with the girl...and he's young so he can't really get his dick all hard, but he kinda does...and he starts fucking the girl, really going at it... and she's moaning...and then, this hand holding a gun lowers into the frame and shoots the little boy in the back of the head.

"Well, the kid drops down dead on the girl, and she's all covered in blood and screaming, and then this naked guy wearing a mask comes into the frame and he moves the kid. And this naked guy is holding a knife and he has a huge dick. Well, he starts fucking the screaming girl while she's all covered in blood, and he holds the knife to her throat..."

Dirk looked back at the road while I stared at him, horrified and wishing that he hadn't told me about that, just as you probably wish I hadn't told you. But you, as I did, wanted to peek into that world and you've got to live with the vision that you got.

"The tape ends at that point, but they're pretty sure the man cut the girl's throat," Dirk finished grimly. I shook my head and looked back out the window at a sunny beach town that somehow now seemed a bit less sunny. Dirk instantly went back to being his unaffected self.

"Sexual Seduction..." he sang, without irony.

Dirk apparently wasn't done talking, because he wanted to impart more twisted knowledge.

"I've seen all kinds of sick videos at the sheriff's department," he said with a smile. "There was this one that this guy made...he set up a video camera to record himself so he could watch it later and... whatever...well, he was into autoerotic asphyxiation...that's where you like to choke yourself during sex..."

"I know what autoerotic asphyxiation is," I interrupted, thinking back to my own kinky youth and my lucky tan belt, Denise.

Dirk smiled a "Been there, done that" smile at me, and I smiled a "No, you haven't" smile back at him.

"Well, this guy got himself a rope," he continued, "and he strung it up in his garage and fashioned it into a noose. Then, naked, he got up on this ladder and slides a broomstick into his ass. Well, he's jerking off like crazy, and he slips off the ladder...well, the rope is too long and so he drops down, his feet not quite reaching the ground, but the broomstick goes up through him, turning him into a Popsicle..."

I shuddered at the reveal and thought warmly back to my lucky broom, Gretel.

"The last image on the videotape is the garage door opening, and the mom and kids coming home in their minivan to find him hanging there."

We thankfully reached our stop before he could lay any more human misery on me.

Misty was again busy that day (it was hard to believe that I had a coworker who actually worked less than Dirk), but Kim and Doug, our Mexican-hating contract hire, both showed up at the prospect of work. Kim went to task on the kitchen, chucking out Jasper's many empty vodka bottles. Being glass, they revealed that Jasper had been a classier drunk than the fat wastrel who'd preceded him.

Dirk and Doug took on the living room while I went to work on the back bedroom. I unloaded bookcases and a desktop under the watchful eyes of Jasper, who regarded me from the top of his tall dresser in a photo of himself decked out in an orange hunting vest. He wore eyeglasses and had a thin beard, giving him an "everyman" look.

It was mostly mindless work, unloading a lifetime of collected memories and possessions from a person's home. The lot of it seemed so meaningless and trivial to me, and yet to Jasper it probably was the stuff of dreams. But in addition to those nice, fluffy, cute dreams about puppies and wealth that we all have, Jasper evidently had some other dreams. Wet ones.

Upon our initial casual search of the house, we knew that Jasper kept porno on hand. What we didn't realize was how deep a rabbit hole his affinity for sex was. There has to be a link between alcoholism and a love of freaky pornography. I pulled open drawer after drawer of raw sex, now wearing gloves to protect my hands from his sexual proclivities. Jasper was evidently bisexual himself, because although most of his porno tapes featured women, the literature and toys he collected tended toward the man-on-man style of lovin'.

Picking up what appeared to be a prop life-size severed hand from a Halloween display, I noted two things: first, that it had a motor that made the fingers wiggle, and second, that the middle two fingers were covered in Vaseline and bits of poop.

"Why can't anyone normal die?" I lamented loudly. I threw the hand into the trash bag and continued digging.

At the bottom of the second of three large sex drawers, I found two lunch-sack-size brown paper bags. I glanced around quietly, ensuring my privacy, and hoped that I'd found money. If I had, it was quietly going home with me.

The bag contained not money but Polaroids, hundreds of them, all mashed into the bags. I reached into the midst of the stack and retrieved a handful, curious about their content.

After a quick glance through my newfound acquisitions, I summoned the others in the group to join me, secure in the knowledge that what I had was not of any financial value. Once the workers had assembled around me, I treated them to an eye-popping display of dicks. Short dicks, fat dicks, black dicks, brown dicks, shaved dicks, bushy dicks, all manner of dicks recorded on photo paper and crammed into a bag.

The carpeting of the bedroom was instantly recognizable as background in the photos, but otherwise it was a staggering variety of close-ups of dicks. The dicks weren't alone either (well, some were); the majority of the pictures showcased the athletic prowess of the urethra, as many of the dicks had been stretched open at the tip to accommodate other objects.

In some, penises were devouring action figures—their small toy heads absorbed down to their shoulders in the male organ. In other pictures, Hot Wheels toy cars were seen exiting the urethra as if it were the Hoosac Tunnel. Sometimes the objects were glass rods or metal Phillips-head screwdrivers, objects that I had thrown away earlier.

The other bag contained more of the same, with asses and anuses thrown in as well. Objects of various sizes and shapes had found their way into a multitude of assholes, including glass tubes containing small rodents. In one particularly nasty photo, an open-mouthed vase with a long, fat neck was jam-packed into a butt.

"You won't believe this," Kim gushed, seeing the photo. She disappeared into the kitchen and returned still gloveless, holding that very vase by the neck, the very neck that was mostly inserted into the chocolate starfish of a man's very hairy ass.

"It's the vase," she confirmed, excitedly disgusted. All doubt that it was, in fact, the vase was removed by the presence of a thin veneer of Vaseline fog that coated the majority of the vase's upper region.

"You do realize you're holding, without gloves, something that has been in a man's butt, don't you?" Dirk asked her, as incredulous as Doug and me.

"Ohmigod!" she shrieked, realizing. Fortunately, she had the good sense to toss the vase neatly into the full trash bag, where it sunk into the midst of other sexual craziness. The fact that I cannot detail the horror and revulsion that wrenched her normally attractive face into a grotesque mask highlights for me that I have no future as a writer. The horrified noises she made as she scrubbed at her hands beneath impossibly hot water were some that I will never forget, nor forget to laugh at.

"Don't touch the faucet," we cautioned her, teasing. "I think there was a picture of him fucking that, too."

Jasper's mom, per her deal with us, had rented a storage garage at a nearby facility that closed at 7:00 p.m. Dirk was adamant that we complete the excavation of the apartment and make it over to the facility that day, not wanting to incur the rental fees for one more day of moving-truck use.

Kim had exited the project shortly after washing her hands down to a couple layers of skin, and so it was up to Doug, Dirk, and me to finish cleaning house. We raced, taking what we wanted of the dead man's possessions and throwing the rest into the back of the moving truck, abandoning neatness in the face of a deadline.

At 6:35 p.m., having worked ten hours on the project and drenched in sweat, we finished. But the three of us didn't have time to collapse. Now that we'd filled the large truck with Jasper's crap, we had to take it to the storage facility and unload it.

We raced across town to the facility and made it inside the electronic gates with ten minutes to spare. Figuring that once we were inside the gates we had all the time in the world to unload the haul, we calmly set about rigging a system that would allow us to take stuff from the back of the truck to the second-floor garage.

But since 7:00 p.m. had come and gone, the doors inside the storage facility had auto-locked, and maneuvering through them and the elevator (which could only be controlled from the second floor after 7:00 p.m.) became something of a logic puzzle.

My exhaustion had clouded with anger and was not helped by my being outside alone when the caretakers of the property showed up. They were a middle-aged Mexican couple who spoke no English, but it was clear that they wanted us out. The facility closed at 7:00 p.m., and that meant everything.

"Five more minutes," I begged them, gesturing with my hands. The man nodded reasonably and they left. Twenty minutes later, they were back and we were still nowhere near finished.

Dirk joined me outside while Doug stayed inside to man the elevator and keep the electronic doors open. Dirk spoke a few halting words of Spanish, so he attempted to reason with them, himself as frustrated by the situation and as tired as I was. The couple and Dirk would not reach an agreement, it seemed, when the Mexican man suddenly stormed off with his wife in tow.

"I think he finally understands," Dirk said, bitter. "We're not going to keep this truck an extra day and finish tomorrow. Not happening."

We scrambled, though, to finish, a bit nervous about what the absence of the caretakers really meant. Finally, a little after 8:00 p.m., we were completely exhausted, soaking with perspiration, and all miserably angry about the long day, but at least the truck was empty. Dirk climbed into the cab, followed by Doug and then me, all of us squeezed onto the U-Haul's long bench seat.

Dirk was about to start the engine when the Mexican couple rounded the corner in line with the crotchetiest, most curmudgeonly looking old white man that I have ever seen. His pants were hiked up aggressively north of his belly button, and clomping toward us in Frankenstein-ish work boots, he looked as if we'd interrupted his Denny's senior meal.

"You," he said, pointing with an angry and crooked finger, doubtlessly riddled with arthritis. "You," he said again, pointing at the truck and at all of us inside as if it were all one big package. I climbed down from the truck, fuming, to confront the old-timer. Dirk followed my lead. Doug stayed put in the cab, seated "bitch."

"Sir, we thought that you just had to be *in* the facility before seven, not completely out of here," I tried to reason.

"No excuse," barked the man. "They told you to leave, and you lied to them."

I felt the blood rise on the sides of my neck, and I was reminded of the Sewer House and the miserable couple we'd contracted to help clean it.

"How could they tell us?" I snapped. "They don't speak any English!"

I imagined that Doug, inside the cab, was proud.

"You should have known. Now you're trespassing!" the old man said, returning my glare.

I stepped forward once more with the intention of pummeling the old bastard to the ground.

"What are you going to do?" He smirked the confident sneer of a man who has never been thrown a good beatdown. "Hit me? I'll call the police!"

I started to tell the old man that Dirk was a police officer, but Dirk shushed me, not wanting to bring that into the situation.

"Sir, we're sorry. It was all a misunderstanding..." Dirk attempted. "We're all done now. We're just going to leave."

"No," the old man said viciously. "You're not leaving now."

"You can't keep us here," I challenged, balling my fists up.

"What do you mean we're not leaving?" Dirk said evenly, still playing the diplomat.

"You've wasted an hour of my night...I'm wasting some of yours. I'm not opening the gates for at least an hour, maybe more. You're stuck here."

"You can't keep us here," Dirk uttered, his diplomacy shattered.

"Call the police," the old man taunted.

"Jeff, get in the truck," Dirk said hotly. "We're running the gates."

This was one of the coolest moments of my life. A childlike sense of wonder and joy blazed through me as I climbed back up into the cab of the truck, eager to cause mayhem, exhaustion forgotten.

"We're ramming the gates," I told Doug.

Dirk fired up the big truck's engine with a mighty roar, reversing hard away from the old coot, the wide-eyed Mexican couple, and all the stresses of the day. Backing down an alleyway, Dirk pointed the truck in the direction of the back gate, a broad one-piece affair that I imagined would shatter open with a nightmarishly sweet clang. That gate would know the full power of the *Crime Scene Cleaners*.

I was positively frothing with the possibility, and Doug seemed pretty amped as well. Far behind us, the old man and the caretakers watched our every move.

As we sidled back to blast through the hinged-metal span lying before us, we collectively noticed a small metal arm that stood to the side of the back entrance on our side, with the exit button for the gate. In a moment more anticlimactic than the one you are about to read, Dirk pushed the button.

The gate slid open sideways, creaking slowly as if it were an extension of the old man himself. My belief in life imitating action-movie dramatics was the only thing shattered that day.

"Good thing," Dirk reminded me, calmer. "We didn't buy insurance on the truck."

• • •

In a move that I have since come to regard as telltale Dirk, he called Howard the next morning to tell him that we were finished. Or maybe Howard called him. Either way, the next call was Dirk to me, bitching and complaining that Howard was upset that we'd left the carpet insulation. Of course, Dirk was unable to return to the scene (probably for another "trip to Disneyland"), so I had to go and do all the work myself. I dragged Chris along and paid him fifty bucks to help.

And what happened to those twin bags of Polaroids, you ask? Well, they went to the dump along with all the other smut. Dirk and I'd had a brief discussion that involved whether or not we should include all the sex stuff with Jasper's other possessions to let his mom know what a weirdo her son was. Ultimately we decided not to...it was the decent thing to do, I guess.

Still, I wished I had kept a few of those photos. Living in a fraternity house, there were all sorts of pranks one could pull with a lunch sack full of gay pictures. Fortunately for the benefit of pranksters worldwide, Jasper wasn't the only pervert who would die on my watch.

we done wrong

Because I got you to look after me, and you got me to look after you, and that's why.

—*Lenny to George,* Of Mice and Men

THE END FOR THE CRIME Scene Cleaners began with a van crash.

It was an unspectacular van crash, but I should have recognized it as an indicator of the future. The van in question belonged to the Public Guardian's office, and our latest confidante from their office, Billy, was piloting it. Billy was a goofy, fumbling, lisping man, the kind of guy that other guys would have written off as gay. His blondish mop of hair was pushed heavily to one side, as if it were the mother of all comb-overs, and he had a jauntiness that belied his actual age, which I would approximate as early fifties. And he had a really overly manicured blond mustache.

Upon arriving that morning, Billy had turned into the driveway of the target house a little too suddenly and jarred the side panel of his van into our large, rented, metal dumpster. A violent, banshee-esque shrieking ripped through the still air of the neighborhood, which was adjacent to Koreatown, causing any and all early morning passersby to stop and look.

Befuddled, Billy then backed the van up with the ragged corner of the dumpster still embedded in its side. Doug, his buddy Kool, Dirk, and I watched in shocked amazement, wincing as the reverse caused a sharper screech.

Finally Billy, lost for ideas, mashed down on the accelerator, producing a final deafening squeal that brought the last of the neighbors from their homes. The van bounced up onto the grass lawn of the home and came to a jarring stop, a nasty gash of sharply contorted metal punched in and raked along the side of the county vehicle.

Kim arrived in the aftermath, along with one of my frat brothers, Bobby G., whom I had recruited for the assignment. All of us stood in shocked amazement. Billy bounced from the driver's seat of the van, took a look at the damage, then took a look at Kim, and shrugged it off. "Not my van" was how he essentially phrased it in his lisping, goofy cadence.

The house in question had belonged to another hoarder. It wasn't one that Chris and I had surveyed together; rather, it was one that Dirk and I had looked at, watched over by the stern eye of the head of the Public Guardian's office. The house was a "get" for them, and they were taking it seriously.

It wasn't much to look at as far as dwellings go—a shoddy one-story deal in a shitty neighborhood filled with two-story homes. Behind it, the deceased's home also had five independent structures—two one-room guesthouses, two large sheds, and a large, enclosed sunroom that spanned the back of the house. This all combined to make the one regular three-bedroom, two-bathroom home into one hell of a large task.

Since we had not won the cleaning contracts on any of the lesser properties that I had spent days documenting, Dirk and I came to the conclusion that we were the Public Guardian's go-to guys for really nasty jobs. When normal companies didn't cut it, you had to call in the superstars. And this property required superstars.

Gordon Chow had been the janitor of an elementary school that was roughly nine yards away (the Jeff Klima measurement of front lawns, not the football unit). With a name like Chow and living on the outskirts of Koreatown, he'd be Korean, you'd probably guess, sight unseen. But you, like me, would have been dead wrong.

Ol' Gordon was a heavyset white guy in his eighties who'd been found dead in his bed of natural causes. Gordon was being taken care of by a woman from across the street, so even though he died alone, he didn't have a chance to rot. But just because Gordon wasn't musty, decomposing, and filthy when he was discovered, that didn't mean his house wasn't.

Whereas the majority of hoarder houses I had come across were more in line with general disarray, largely just a collective of heaped trash, Gordon's house reflected that he was a bona fide collector. Where the Sewer House had a mountain of empty beer cans, Doritos bags, receipts, leaves, and other refuse to climb over, Gordon had records. Pressed vinyl recordings of every band you've never heard of, slipped from their crates and forged by time into a large mountain of musical waste. It was like someone had prepped an anti-disco bonfire, and all that was needed was a lit match.

The smell made for a bad work environment. The house, with its ill-working plumbing, had long since spewed water into the walls and floorboards, covering the surface areas with a grainy black mold. Black mold is the really bad kind, the kind that does major damage to your health under prolonged exposure. Worse still, it had begun to creep from the fixed surfaces out onto the trash layers, giving everything a soggy, filmy texture. As a result, all the records were ruined.

In oblivious homage to *Raiders of the Lost Ark*, the house was filled with dangers and booby traps, orchestrated accidentally by Gordon's insanity. The spiders were everywhere, and shelving, weighted under impossible loads of cheap, bubbly carnival glass gave way with the slightest change in atmosphere. Towers of inferior still-in-the box stereos stretched to the ceiling, their exteriors being devoured by the mold. In hindsight, it would have been smarter to drop that lighted match after all.

Donning paper painter's masks, my crew foraged their way into the mess, determined to blaze a path back out or collapse trying. They were an expendable bunch. I was mostly there for supervisory purposes, because I was unwilling to once again risk my back by hauling out box load after box load of the structure's many curios. As such, I had the task of once more setting up my chair on the front lawn and acting as neighborhood liaison.

The usual chattering oddballs made their way across to watch and offer commentary, but with their being mostly people whose first language was something Asian, I could typically only nod and smile agreeably. One neighbor, an obese white man on his electronic Rascal scooter, zoomed over early to welcome me to the neighborhood. His was the house with the twenty-five-foot antenna looming over the backyard, and he told me conversationally that his neighbors didn't like it, but fuck them.

As self-proclaimed mayor of the neighborhood, the guy, whom we'll call "Rascal Fats," was quite opinionated about everything we were doing. Rascal's daughter had been Gordon's caretaker, he informed me, the orange pennant flag raised above his backseat flapping in the wind.

"She's supposed to get the house," Rascal continued, jabbing a sausagelike finger in my direction. "If you guys find a will in there... disregard it. Gordon promised that my daughter could have his house. That will is old...It promises everything to a sister out in Florida who never even visits him. My daughter deserves everything."

"That's for the courts to decide," I said, raising ten defensive sausagelike fingers of my own.

"I should get to pick through the trash there and see what I want to take...My daughter took care of that man, so it's practically her stuff. She's the only other person who had a key to his place...She's the only one Gordon trusted..."

Rascal started his stupid scooter toward the pile of salvageable merchandise on the front lawn, and I jumped quickly in front to block him, casting out my palm as something akin to that guy standing up to the tank in Tiananmen Square. Rascal didn't like that, but he stopped short all the same.

"Why should you guys get to steal all his stuff? We're his neighbors."

"We're not stealing anything," I said angrily, though my anger might have been directed at myself. I had had my eye on a surround-sound speaker system that would complement my room at the frat house nicely. "Anything of quality goes to the Public Guardian's office, and they auction it off. The money then goes back into the estate...so if your daughter is the one who gets the house, she'll get the money, too."

I didn't believe that necessarily, but Rascal's piglike eye sockets narrowed greedily. "Have you guys found the will yet?" he asked, suddenly friendly.

"Nope," I shook my head. "But if it's in there, we will."

Having complete freedom on the first day under the unwatchful eye of Billy was a liberty we took for granted. It was his duty to search the house for that aforementioned will as well as any other valuables. The bag of money from the mobile home had caused quite a stir in the county office.

Instead of working, though, Billy decided to flirt with Kim, grinning that loutish grin of his and making what he thought were cleverly seductive comments. Kim, ignorant, babbled on about her impending engagement and how she'd recently cleaned up a decomposing body.

Meanwhile, Dirk and the gang were inside the house scouring for cash. Dirk had made the unbelievably stupid mistake of clueing in our coworkers that if they found any cash, they were to keep it secret from Billy, and the lot of us would split it. I could see why he would tell them that. He was paranoid that they'd pocket it themselves or do the honest thing and report it to Billy, and Dirk would lose out completely. He was hedging his bets, believing that many eyes searching would yield that humongous payoff that would tide us all over nicely.

I was furious at Dirk for doing that, not because I was suddenly above stealing, but because it was a stupid way to do it. The sort of people who willingly came in and cleaned out houses infested with mold, spiders, and the potential for raw sewage were not the brightest people on the planet. It especially didn't help that it was a crew full of chatterboxes.

All I needed was an ignorant dumbass like Doug to go foolishly spouting to Rascal that we were secretly splitting up any money we found. It was like that old saying about how three people can keep a secret if two of them are dead. With a team of idiots tearing through the house in pursuit of ill-gotten gains and a snoopy neighbor poking around, I should have known that the job was one giant disaster waiting to happen.

• • •

The second day on the job saw my crew returning to the house without Dirk. They had failed to find their financial windfall the previous day, and Dirk, tenured position with the sheriff's department or not, couldn't keep missing work. Everybody else on our side happily returned, though, their feelers buzzing like metal detectors circling pay dirt. They hadn't been in on the last score, and they honestly believed that all the bags full of dirty twenties, fifties, and one hundreds had gone to the county. They had seen that money, though, and its possibility was potential enough.

Billy also hadn't shown up for work that day, even though he had the keys to the house. Wanting to make the most of the workday, I instructed the crews to start working the sheds at the back of the house.

Judging by the content of the sheds, Gordon had two true loves in life—colored yarn and ceramic tile. I didn't know what sort of zany business scheme he had ventured into that could possibly have combined the two, but it was fucking ridiculous.

The first shed, poorly constructed and rotting from the inside out, was full of several tons worth of tile. Literally several fucking tons of tile were in that shed. Boxes upon boxes had long since collapsed the shelving inside, and rain had decimated the cardboard, leaving a horrendous collection of odds and ends. The crew spent the first hour and a half just moving shredded, pulpy boxes of the square, ceramic counter tile, nearly filling the day's allotment of dumpster without even venturing into the house.

Billy still hadn't shown, and I knew something would have to change. I contacted Dirk at the police station, my voice a familiar one to all the operators there. He then did the dual tasks of contacting the Public Guardian's office and posting an ad on craigslist offering "free tile" to anyone willing to come and collect it.

The Public Guardian's office said that they would have someone right on it, but nothing seemed to come of that. But as for the craigslist ad? We were swarmed. People will climb over smaller people at the opportunity to receive something free. I would just be happy to see it all gone. Truckloads of people showed up, each clamoring to get their hands on as much tile as they could.

Of course this is America, so I was also swarmed with bitching, complaining assholes whining that it was too much work to receive free tile and that they didn't want to have to carry it all to their cars. But they all took what they could and drove off, the truck beds scraping the grounds under all the tonnage of tile, the wheel houses collapsing on straining tires, moving out much slower than they'd come in.

And yet there was still more tile, a lot more. Most of the people claimed they would be back once they'd unloaded their cars and trucks, but I knew they wouldn't. No sane person needed that much tile.

Equally as depressing, though easier to deal with, was the yarn. It rivaled the tile in quantity, leading me to wonder, "What weighs more, a ton of bricks or a ton of feathers?" What Gordon wanted with that much yarn, I could only speculate…but I didn't think the moon needed a sweater. No, Gordon doubtlessly had something much grander and far crazier in mind.

Another phone call to Dirk, and another ad went up on craigslist for "free yarn." Several carloads of women showed up, and none of them complained. They took all they needed, and still there was lots more yarn. Eventually, so many cars came through the property that Rascal took it upon himself to scoot on over.

"Have you found the will yet?" he complained, by way of introduction.

"Nope," I said, not even wanting to give him the courtesy of my attention.

"Just what in the Sam Hill [I didn't think people actually talked like this, but they do!] do you think you're doing giving away all that tile and yarn? Don't think I haven't seen you, cuz I seen you. I'm always watching." He rolled his scooter back and forth in short, lurching spurts as if that somehow showcased his ability to watch me. "I oughta call the county folks on you and report you…"

"The county is the one that authorized us to do it," I bluffed, finally looking at him and seething with irritation.

"It's technically my daughter's house…she should have the right to all that stuff."

"Listen old-timer," I said, regretting the term as I said it. "If you want any of that yarn or tile, feel free to load it up on your little scooter and haul it away. Cause I want it gone." Instead he gave me a self-satisfied little grunt and zipped away.

When the county boys finally arrived, I realized how much of a shit storm had been brewing in their absence. Several official-looking men showed up in vans and cars, and a team of government lackeys suited up in biohazard suits to comb through the wreckage.

Suddenly we in our paper painter's masks and work gloves didn't look so terribly professional. Billy had "no called, no showed" for several hours and then finally called his boss to complain that he was sick and, therefore, staying home that day. The Public Guardian's office reacted by unloading a mass of workers to tear through the house and find all valuables and the elusive will.

I attempted to play foreman on behalf of my crew and get us access to work, but I was summarily dismissed with looks of disdain from several of the county jerks. To save face, I had my crew continue working on the backyard while the government invaded the house. I stayed out front to shoo off the women returning for more yarn.

Nearing two o'clock in the afternoon, the county men emerged from the house, having knocked over every standing box, cleared off every surface, and emptied all trash onto the floor. They'd emerged with a grand total of thirteen thousand dollars, mostly in small bills they gathered off the dining room table.

Later, when I told Dirk of the money's location, he kicked himself for having neglected to look there. It wasn't his fault entirely; that house was filled to the brim with trash. Still, no will had emerged, and the county men were certain they'd done their job to the fullest and that no will had, in fact, ever existed.

Pulling off their biohazard garb, which they left for us to clean up, the men took the now-enveloped money as if it were the Ark of the Covenant, dropped the house keys off with me, and departed. As far as the suits were concerned, the house was empty.

I was overjoyed that we were once again left to our own devices and, putting my crew to work cleaning out the garage, went to get lunch. As the only one there who couldn't do any sort of heavy lifting, and relishing the chance to get away from the work site for a while, I drove out to fetch a couple of pizzas.

I returned feeling like a good foreman, eager to feed my troops, and was completely unsurprised to see the lot of them not working. This had been the case every time I had left to bring back lunch or run an errand. But while in the past they had been gathered in the shade huffing down cigarette smoke, now they were standing in the driveway clustered around some sort of parchment.

"We found the will!" Kim exclaimed loudly to me. In disbelief, I hustled over. Sure enough, when I had a look at the yellowed flap of paper, I saw she was right. They'd found the will.

How the "intellectuals" at the Public Guardian's office missed it, after looking for hours, will forever be the bane of my existence. The idiots in my crew, so amped up at the prospect of getting ill-gotten cash, had found a small safe nestled in the garage within about ten minutes of looking. In my absence, they'd also busted into it and uncovered the will. I could only wonder whether there was also money in the safe that never found its way to me.

I didn't know what to do with the will. The assholes from the Public Guardian's office had just left; I'd already called Dirk at his office more times than he was happy about; and really, it was just a piece of paper. So I set it on a shelf in the garage with a bunch of other pieces of paper that seemed equally important, stuff I'd deal with later.

• • •

The third day started off innocently enough. Since I had the keys, we didn't have to wait for goofy Billy to show up (or not show up) and let us in. We were able to set our own pace and run it fast and hard. I went around the main building, surveying the work ahead and unlocking the sets of doors as I went.

The front door and side doors were stout, heavy, windowless doors. The back door, separating the sunroom from the main house, was an honest-to-God cage. Gordon's sunroom, where he had kept an allotment of his electronics goods, was walled in securely with a sliding steel-cage door, complete with bars and a large, heavy, old-school lock.

All doors to the house were securely shuttered and fastened exactly as I had left them before, so I unlocked the place and went to whip the crew into a working frenzy. They weren't in such high spirits now that the will had been discovered, the cash was gone, and there was still much more work to be done.

They had to satisfy themselves with taking small electronics and mostly not too valuable odds and ends from the remnants of Gordon's life. I'd gotten my surround sound, of course, but I was increasingly leery with Rascal always on the prowl. Anything that the crew took from the house had to be done discreetly and with a sense of purpose, as if they were using their cars to carry the items to the county office.

In reality, the county didn't give a damn what happened to anything from inside the house. One of their men, a field tech named Oscar, explained that the value dropped so sharply on household items that even a brand-new, high-end plasma TV still in the box wasn't worth their time or effort to sell. They didn't give a damn what happened to any of the electronics. And so Dirk and I took them.

Loading the swag into the back of his Silverado at the end of every day, I would transport it to our storage for safekeeping. We told the crew that the county required that it be destroyed, so we were "taking it to a landfill so that neighborhood people wouldn't try to retrieve it from our dumpster." What Dirk and I didn't take for our own use later sold with healthy returns at a yard sale.

The third day would have ended just as smoothly as it started except for one thing: I couldn't find the will. I'd decided midmorning to place it in Dirk's truck for safekeeping, but it, and all the other papers we'd left with it, had vanished. It was bad that I hadn't called the Public Guardian's office as soon as the will had turned up, but now that it was missing, forget it—our relationship with them would be dog shit.

Searching for the documents was a futile effort, because the crew had since finished the garage and moved on, attacking the hallway and back bedrooms of the house. Immediately, I suspected that Kool, the token foreign guy, had accidentally thrown the papers away. It was a pathetically racist assumption on my part, but he was the only one of the group that I wasn't sure completely comprehended what a will was.

To be fair, he didn't really speak English, and in the hurried pace at which the team was working, shit could happen. In that nervous, foreign-guy way, as if he thought it might end with him being deported, Kool denied my accusations as well as he could gesture. At a loss for another explanation, I didn't exactly believe him. Gulping, I looked at the dumpster that was mostly full. If it was in there, it was gone.

By the end of the day, the will hadn't emerged, and I'd given it up as a total loss. I locked the house securely for the weekend, still feeling uneasy about the whole affair. But the will was gone, and if it had ended up in the trash, I was adamant that no one outside of our work team, not even Dirk, would know about its short-lived existence. Losing a last will and testament was just one of those things that you hoped nobody found out about.

• • •

On the fourth day, we were fucked.

I had shown up early to scope out the remainder of our project. It was mostly finished, except for a few boxes of yarn, several more boxes of tile, and the attic. We had deliberately saved the attic for last, because Dirk was sure he could finagle more money out of the county to clean it. In scoping through the house initially, I hadn't even noticed there was an attic, so when I presented the numbers for Dirk to compile, it wasn't listed in our original bid.

Dirk was certain that little technicality would net us an extra grand on the project. He also wanted it left alone until the end of the project, because he had a gut feeling there was money hidden in the rafters and he wanted as few fingers in that pie as possible.

When I unlocked the house, I knew instantly that I had been too hard on Kool…He was innocent. Whether it was arranged as a "fuck you" to me from Rascal and his cronies, or whether they simply got sloppy and forgot, I realized that the will hadn't innocently disappeared. Four folding chairs had been imported into the house and arranged into a semicircle in the living room with empty boxes interspersed between. A quick check confirmed that the attic had been ransacked.

I might have chalked it up to drifters, teenagers, or area drunks except for the one telltale piece of evidence. That heavy metal gate, the one with the bars and the giant lock, the one that only I and Rascal's daughter had keys to, was left hanging wide open. And I knew that I had locked it. Knowing the full tilt of the situation, I placed the call to Dirk that I hadn't wanted to make.

To his credit, Dirk was good to me about the will and my not mentioning it previously, but his annoyance was palpable. He agreed that it had Rascal's involvement written all over it, and a later phone call to Kim confirmed that Rascal had been over "innocently checking on the progress of things" when the will was discovered. And he had zipped off when he saw me driving up the street that day bringing back lunch. Being the calmer of our two heads, Dirk dictated that I write everything down and then call the police.

To avoid being recognized, Dirk was hoping that the reporting officer would be long gone by the time that Dirk arrived on scene. The house was squarely located in Dirk's division, and though it was a day off for him, he'd already been catching shit for his potential conflict of interest as an active cop cleaning up crime scenes. Most of the time he wanted that cop involvement on his side, using his background in law enforcement as a selling point to grieving widows looking for someone trustworthy. With other cops, though, his involvement was a dicey proposition.

Dirk showed long before the sheriff, a beefy new dick with gum-chewing indifference. Dirk was constantly ducking his head in the sheriff's presence and trying to appear casual, which made us look all the more suspicious. The cop started to fill out his report and then, realizing that he didn't feel like it, he stopped.

"You say he didn't take anything?" the cop queried me.

"He took the will," I offered, furious at the whole situation.

"But you didn't see him take the will?"

"If I'd seen him do it, I would have stopped him myself and saved me the trouble of calling you."

"But you didn't see him take it."

"No."

"Well, what I'm going to do, sir," he said, looking at me with the sort of disgusted gaze that I'm sure he reserved for white-trash squabbles, "is go over there, knock on his door, and if he answers, I'll tell…this guy…and his daughter…to stay away from the house. And if they have a key, I'll have them surrender it."

I rolled my eyes, not caring if he saw. It didn't help our case any, but it was clear by that point we didn't have a case at all. True to his word, the officer did in fact walk over to the house and knock on the door. A few moments later he returned alone.

"I spoke to the gentleman in question, Mr., uh, Rascal, and he says they don't know what happened to any will and that they lost their key to the house a long time ago."

"Of course that's what they'd say!" I insisted, but the cop didn't care.

"We'll send a cruiser by the house at night. If they notice any of the family trespassing, they'll arrest them. That's what we can do for you."

"Do you know Sergeant Milner?" the furtive Dirk suddenly piped up.

"Yeah, he's the desk sergeant," the sheriff responded, seeing the road this was veering toward and not caring.

"He's a friend of mine…" Dirk said, with a certain pomposity, and I could tell that it had irked him that the sheriff hadn't recognized him. "You see I'm a sheriff, too."

"Oh, yeah? I guess you look sort of familiar."

"Yeah, I work down in evidence," Dirk said, proud of that, though I could imagine what beat cops thought of cops who didn't get out in the field.

"It isn't a conflict of interest to do this and be a cop?" the sheriff asked, suddenly more animated than I'd seen him before.

"It's a gray area," Dirk admitted cautiously.

"Is the pay good?" the sheriff asked.

Even Dirk's "connection" couldn't help our case any, though, and the cop left us to fuck off. He even declined to take my written account of the events, which I had written with an author's flourish and stuffed chock-full of fifty-cent words to inform whoever it was that read such things that I was not, in fact, some hillbilly fuckup.

Dirk ended up taking the report with him and said that he would straighten everything out with the kind (and sure to be understanding) fellows from the Public Guardian's office.

The aftermath of that situation came at us hard. Dirk got his ass chewed out by the higher-ups of the Public Guardian's office, which I felt bad about because it was sort of my fault. He confided to me, though, that even after the verbal smack down he'd received, the fat cats in the Public Guardian's office had reassured him that they would still do business with us.

While we wouldn't get to finish out our work on the Gordon project—another company was going to take over—we were told that there would be future projects that would doubtlessly come our way. They were an understanding lot after all.

But Kerry had a friend who worked on the inside at the Public Guardian's office, a trusted confidante who spilled the truth to me. The truth was we were finished. Nobody would put their ass on the line to work with us; even our old buddy Mona, who'd brought us in, would no longer take our phone calls. Billy, he of the van wreck, was fired for mishandling the case and made into the scapegoat on their end.

All ties were indefinitely severed, and though no memo had circulated about it through the P.G.'s office, we were unofficial ghosts on the county's radar. Just as we'd begun to climb the mountain and achieve some legitimacy and stability, we'd cut our fucking throats.

And worst of all, after the bullshit we endured through the loss to our livelihood and reputation, the thing that made me angriest was that Rascal had won. The miserable son of a bitch got away with it. True to his intentions, the will never surfaced.

CHAPTER 19

kids don't bleed as much

Even very young children need to be informed about dying. Explain the concept of death very carefully to your child. This will make threatening him with it much more effective.

—P. J. O'Rourke

LIKE A GIANT FAUCET, OUR business simply turned off. We had been running at full speed, erasing all traces of the dead from Southern California, and with little more than a lost will we had crashed to a standstill.

I was unprepared for the transition, as was the business, and we racked up a considerable amount of debt between us. Dirk was apparently doing fine through it all between his job as a sheriff and his wife's ample paycheck. I was like the grasshopper in that fable...playing in the warm sunshine, never believing that winter would come, while the diligent ants gathered food for the brutal months ahead.

I had outspent myself, honestly believing that with the Public Guardian's office on our side we were riding a gravy train with biscuit wheels. Now that the train had jumped the tracks, I was fucking broke. And worse, I had dodged my bills for too long, setting them to the side to be paid off with future jobs, jobs that were no longer coming through the P.G.'s office.

When tax season came around, I took stock of my bank account and filed an extension. Since Dirk had me operating as an "independent contractor," sparing him from the insurance, liabilities, and tax issues on his end, none of my government tax deductions came off with my paychecks.

Not that my tax bill was that much: the previous year I had made a pathetic thirteen grand cleaning up dead people while on call twenty-four hours a day, seven days a week. It was far less than I would have earned at Beverages & More. But 2008 had been showing more promise…I'd already made that much money in just the first couple of months, and I was liable to stay on that pace—until we fucked up.

• • •

It was my fault, I knew that, and the last month or so had been an icy tribute to it. If my phone even rang, it was only Dirk lamenting our current position with the Public Guardian's office. Their unofficial disregard of us had been like a vise clamp on our jugular vein, and all work even unrelated to them had ceased. It was as if all of Southern California had stopped dying.

Of course, the news spelled otherwise. In addition to the usual deaths from gangs, police, suicide, and old age, a Vietnamese man had taken a rifle and laid waste to the rest of his family, two little kids and his wife, right up the road from the frat. A multiple murder involving children—it was my dream job.

I'd once admitted to Kim that in doing my job I wanted to achieve three events: I wanted to clean up a multiple murder; I wanted to clean up a celebrity; and I wanted to clean up a child.

It's not that I wished for a child to die…or anyone really. But as a crime scene cleaner, there was a stigma hanging over my head. You see, at parties people often asked me what it was like to clean up children and were they worse than cleaning up adults. But I'd never actually had to clean up after a child's death.

"Yes," I'd tell them, feeding into their *schadenfreude*. "Cleaning up children is the worst part of my job." It was as much a part of my need to appear "normal" as it was to feed their morbid curiosity. I wanted to believe that cleaning up a child would be worse than cleaning up a splattered, rotting adult.

Adults, for me, had grown as stale as wiping jam off the front of the dishwasher. I was tired of ordinary death; it was all so pedestrian. I wanted something new, something spicy, and this Vietnamese man, in his insane, honor-bound way had seemingly provided it.

I began to create excuses to drive by the condo, frothing over the potential that lay past the wreaths, flowers, and burning candles left by well-wishers. The truly warped had even left toys outside the front door, somehow believing that the toys might make it up to the kids in heaven or something far-fetched like that. Yeah, that and they might see a naked lady walking around with only high heels and a designer purse.

Of course, when we learned of the multiple murders, we didn't comprehend the Public Guardian's enmity toward us and were still deluding ourselves with the idea that Orange County was just unnaturally safe those days.

Dirk had even gotten word through his inner-office connections that June, the P.G. liaison on the Dollhouse gig, was heading up the case on the government side. This should have been great news. I had gotten along great with June, and in a world where redneck deadbeats and their shitty kids didn't steal wills, O.C. Crime Scene Cleaners would have sewn the gig up.

I was certain in the days preceding the murders that bygones would be bygones and that the Public Guardian's office would call "their guys" in. Those murders were practically our birthright. But as the flowers in front of the house began to wilt, and an ordinary government seal along the door frame replaced the flashy yellow police tape, reality set in. I even called June on both her desk line and cell phone at Dirk's request, placing a friendly reminder message that "her guys" were available for "any and all jobs in the next few weeks," but she never picked up or called back.

And so I got drunk. Stewed and miserable, I figured the company had run aground and that we were, professionally speaking, doomed. I was tired of being the downer of the party that night, so I cast my cigar at the nearest trash can, missed, and stumbled upstairs for bed. It was after one in the morning; I was soused; and it had been a very long and frustrating day full of nothingness, empty nothingness (which in frat speak is essentially quaffing afternoon beers and trying to bounce a basketball into a fellow drinker's nutsack).

I patted my pockets and relieved myself of my keys, wallet, and cigar paraphernalia and reached down to take my cell phone out of the cargo pocket on my shorts. It wasn't there where it always was; I lived with it at my side, always answering it with a gruff, but polite, business tone. No, I'd left it sitting beside my bed, unnoticed for the day, a sure sign of my disbelief in ever working again.

I picked it up to turn off any alarm I might have set, having no pretenses about what the next day held. As soon as I picked the phone up, though, the jarring spasms of vibration coupled with a tonal bleat in the twinning effort of a ring. I stared at it, my eyes half-lidded, unsure whether reality was intruding on my drunkenness or vice versa.

The logline said it was Dirk calling, which wouldn't have been too unusual. He'd made the commitment to our police contacts that we were at their beck and call twenty-four hours a day, seven days a week, no matter how big or how small the job was. The job was always small, miserably small.

Typically, a late-night call involved my climbing out from the comfort of my soft bed, driving across two towns mired in the head-lights of other tired commuters to spray Simple Green on a splotch of puke no bigger than a pizza slice (and often it was a regurgitated pizza slice!), a quick wipe with a paper towel. Fifteen minutes later I'd be driving back home to my bed with a whopping $37.50 for my effort.

Meanwhile Dirk, who literally lived right up the street from Orange PD, slumbered happily. It was a frustrating situation in that I was supposed to be the daytime guy while he covered nights and week-ends, but I needed the money. He didn't. And so it had become me, without the additional sources of income that he had, as the day guy, the night guy, and the weekend guy.

I continued to let the phone ring until it went to voicemail, figuring that I would take the night off. I was hurting for cash flow, but $37.50 wasn't going to solve my financial issues—and it certainly wouldn't cover the DUI ticket I would get driving into a police station shitfaced.

I set the phone down and flopped onto my bed, determined to pass out and wake up hungover many, many hours later. Immediately the phone rang again, and my head popped up, checking the logline. It was Dirk again, being persistent. This also meant little to me, as his latest trick involved exactly this sort of sleight of hand.

Knowing full well that I knew he lived right up the road from Orange PD, Dirk had become creative in his methods to get me out of bed late at night to scrub puke, piss, shit, or all three. If he sensed hesitation in my voice at the prospect of doing a night job for the police department, he would quickly tack on that it wasn't just some bullshit cop car or jail cell; it was three cop cars, or two cars, a detention cell, and a jail cell, and also an interrogation room.

Suddenly that $37.50 gig was worth several hundred dollars to me, and I'd cave in. Then, when I got down to the police station, I'd question the police about the "crazy mess in multiple locations" only to have the befuddled desk sergeant explain that it was just a small spot of urine on the backseat of a single cruiser. Dirk had pulled this stunt on me more than once, and I was determined not to fall for it again.

Drunk or not, though, I was curious to see what he said. I answered the phone on its last ring, affecting a thick, growly sort of speech that fell somewhere between sleepy and sick.

"Hi, this is Jeff," I bleated, drunkenly overdoing my confused invalid state.

"What's up, homey? It's Dirk," he added, as if that weren't the only way he ever started a phone conversation with me in all the time I knew him. "Look, I need you here, buddy… We got a bad one."

I started to beg off, making up some bullshit excuse that sounded exactly like one he'd use when he didn't want to work, but then I thought better of it.

"What do you mean 'a bad one'?"

"Dude, I need you out here…It's a multiple murder involving a kid."

"We got that one? The Vietnamese family?" I asked excitedly, dropping the croaky throat effect.

"No, this is different. This is a white guy out in LA County who kicked open the back door of his wife's house and shot up his family. Killed a kid, killed the grandma, shot another kid, and capped himself."

"When was this?"

"Right now! I just got to the scene. Coroners are still on site, and we're waiting for the clearance to enter."

"We?"

"Yeah, you and me…I told the officers that my team was on its way, so get out here."

I scribbled down directions and threw on shorts and my work polo. I couldn't stop for coffee, because the last thing I needed was to be shitting my brains out in some dead person's bathroom while cops stood around, disgusted. I drank a big glass of water, though, and hoped I was sober enough to make the trip. I couldn't miss out on a dead kid.

I had to be careful leaving Frat Row; cops were always cruising around the area, sharklike, waiting for some drunken asshole to try to make a taco run. Driving drunk around cops is like a chess match. You have to see the moves they're playing as well as the moves they think you're playing.

Do you drive fast and loose, betting that the cops will think the guy blaring his radio and pounding out the beat of the song on his car door is clearly too drunk-seeming to actually be drunk? Or do you go cautiously, keeping to the speed limit, window up, hands on the wheel at the ten-and-two model of a perfect driver? To me, this is what cops are looking for—the guy who at two in the morning is driving just a little too well.

Instead, I hummed along at just above the speed limit, arm resting casually out the window and head back against the seat, looking exhausted. I was the poster child of the late-night commuter, the bouncer just getting off work, the driver who's winding down his long, sober night of not partying. If nothing else, I was drunk enough to try to explain to the police that as a crime scene cleaner, I was really just one of them…a compadre in the line of justice, and that they should let me be.

I didn't need to try that line of reasoning, though, as I rolled through the cruisers untouched and edged the Red Rocket onto the freeway. Torrance, where the shooting had occurred, was about an hour away from me under normal conditions, but with the aid of alcohol and using the knuckles on my left hand like a gun sight to keep me lined on the road, I was able to reach the off ramp in thirty-eight minutes.

I spent the next hour driving up and down neighborhood streets, angry...futilely trying to read the directions that Dirk had described to me over the phone. I was beginning to sober up, and what may have once seemed crystal clear during my drunken haze now seemed illegible and incoherent. I was at the edge of giving up when my eyes were suddenly drawn skyward. A blossoming bulb of lights lit up the night sky before me, something akin to being in the presence of a UFO, and I was drawn mothlike to its presence.

Driving several neighborhoods east, I turned the corner and found myself in the sphere of the media presence. The glowing beams were massive light towers extending from news vans, illuminating the dark of the night in a snow-globe bulb of false daylight. Competing reporters scurried; men with both mounted and portable cameras were panning and tracking; and a multitude of uniformed peace officers stood around attempting a semblance of control.

It was the usual circus, colorful and crass, with no ringmaster to rein in the antics. Parking awkwardly, I popped a mint that had been wallowing in my cup holder for at least two years, exited my car, and walked into the center ring.

Dirk had been hanging out outside to the west of the cameras, nervously awaiting my arrival. If the newsmen so much as looked in my direction, I put on a stern stare of contempt, playing the role of the disgusted professional. Once we had the okay signal from the on-scene lieutenant who was running the show, Dirk gave me the tour.

It was a sad scene, sadder than I expected it to be, and made worse by the fact that nobody else seemed to find it as sad.

Entering through the gunman's point of entry, the garage door, Dirk gave me the tour he himself had been given by the police only moments before I arrived. It was easy to visualize the gunman's rampage, the trails of blood crisscrossing through the one-story house as the killer had shot his own family. He was upset about a restraining order his wife had filed against him and came back packing heat.

From what Dirk traced out in front of me, the man had shot the grandma, his mother-in-law, first, killing her instantly. The three-year-old boy was next, dying in the foyer of the living room, guts splashed over his toy fire truck.

"My son has that same fire truck," Dirk said softly.

The gunman shot his five-year-old daughter in the leg, but her mom managed to grab her and run out of the house through the front door and down the block to safety. Daddy, realizing that his wife had gotten away, stomped bloody footprints through several rooms looking for someone else to shoot before giving up and blasting his own head off in the dining room. It was still all so fresh.

"This is definitely a several-man job," I said, incredulous.

"I've got some bad news," Dirk said, and I had to work to take my eyes off the blood-mottled floor where the little boy had breathed his last. "Because the news is here filming, they've probably got footage of me on camera. I can't call in sick to work today; my boss might see me on TV…so I've got to go. I've got to get some sleep."

"What would you have done if I hadn't picked up the phone?" I hissed, furious but mindful of the milling cops and not-too-distant media boom mikes. This was exactly the kind of shit I was beginning to expect from him.

"I'll try to call Kim or Misty to help you out. I can stay for maybe forty-five minutes, but after that you're on your own."

Between the sheer amount of carpeting that needed to be removed, and walls and floor that required sanitizing, not to mention children's toys and furniture, it was a tall order for several people, let alone one man. One drunken man who was in desperate need of sleep.

Our suiting up got the attention of the cameras, and straight-faced, I looked past them.

Dirk and I started in on the dead kid, scrubbing at the shaped smears of blood that hinted at his tiny outline. The coroner had taken the little boy's body only minutes before I had arrived, and his blood still had its vibrant freshness. It was nice when we were able to deal with fresh blood—it requires a lot less elbow grease. Dirk wanted to clean the dead kid's fire truck, while I was of the opinion of "fuck it, chuck it." But it seemed he felt some sort of emotional victory in saving the toy.

It took him awhile, but he got it all cleaned up and looking like its owner's blood hadn't been splashed all over it. Not that it mattered much; the kid would probably be buried with the thing if it fit in his tiny coffin.

Once the fire truck looked innocent again, Dirk had to go. He promised to keep calling Kim and Misty, though, neither of whom had picked up.

I gave him the keys to my car, needing to keep the truck for all the work I had left to do. I was completely sober by that point, and my head was throbbing, begging me for water and sleep, neither of which it had coming.

Using my razor blade, which had dulled from cutting apart many a mattress in times past, I had to saw through the carpeting, enduring "Looks like you need a new razor" comments from any cop who wandered by.

As the hours passed and I worked in silence, the police presence began to dissipate. The more work I did, the less the house looked like an interesting crime scene. The higher-ranking officers got bored or tired and departed. And as they left, some of the media followed, to my relief. It was awkward having them filming and making commentary every time I lugged something out to the truck. ("He's bringing something out of the house, Jim…It looks like…more carpeting… We've got another section of carpeting.")

By the time I started cleaning up the dad's outline smear, which was the worst mess of the lot, the attitude at the house had lightened up considerably as the remaining cops hung around watching the news footage on a large TV in the den.

"Wanna see me become a TV star?" one of the grinning cops asked me. He briskly walked out through the garage door, unhooking his flashlight from his belt. Sure enough, a moment later there he was on the big TV screen, anxiously training his flashlight through the planters in the front of the house, his face one of intense police seriousness.

The news cameras, of course, ate it up, filming him as if he were on the trail of something hot. ("Jim, I can only speculate what they're looking for out there...He looks intent on finding something. Perhaps it's some sort of clue that will shed some light on this gruesome scene!")

When he came back inside, the cops were all enjoying their cama-raderie, laughing it up like some tight-knit club, and I felt the envy scorch me from my place on the floor.

"They should make you guys a reality show," I said with a shuck-and-jive grin, indicating that I was in on the joke. But instead of laughing, they turned back into serious policemen and went back to their work. I returned to scrubbing, reminded that I was just a lowly janitor.

Miraculously, at 6:00 a.m. Misty showed up, looking tired, and I tried to convey to her how I hadn't slept all fucking night. The work was mostly complete by then, but she had arrived in time to help scour some baseboards and furniture of residual splatter. At that point I was exhausted and my head was throbbing; I needed sleep. And then Dirk called.

"Hope you're not too tired," he said, sounding cheerful and rested, the bastard. "A Motel 6 in Compton called. They've got a suicide."

I approached Misty delicately, hoping that now, after the three or four crime scenes she'd helped with, she'd be game to tackle one alone.

"I've actually got to get to my other job..." she said with a shrug. "If I call in sick and my boss sees me..."

"Yeah, yeah, yeah," I interrupted, cursing the news media once more. I was alone once again.

We finished the murder house by 7:00 a.m., and I gave Misty the shitty job of scrubbing the blood out of the front-porch bricks where the mom and daughter had fled the scene. I was worried about staining, due to the porous nature of the grout, but of course I wasn't too worried, as we'd included my standard clause in the contract.

As we packed up and left, it signaled to the media that the show was leaving town and they, too, packed up, scavenging after their next kill. I spit on the front lawn at their departure. They'd probably at least have some downtime before their next breaking story. Lucky bastards.

• • •

As I drove alone to the Motel 6 in Compton, the bed of the truck already filled with stained carpeting and bags of blood, I was happy for the work. We'd pulled down a nice paycheck on the homicides; Dirk had at least done that right before leaving me hanging. And the Motel 6 gig, while not exactly a sizable payday, well, I was just grateful that ol' Tom Bodett didn't know anyone from the Orange County Public Guardian's office.

I thought about stopping for breakfast, because my stomach was growling over the sound of the radio, but I knew my finances couldn't yet account for that. I was a pathetic, hungover, exhausted, and broken sight, having just cleaned up multiple murders, and I didn't have enough pocket change to buy a Sausage McMuffin, hold the egg.

In the daylight Compton is not such a bad place. It is a classic low-income area with all the trappings—worn-down people walking aimlessly up and down the sidewalk, escaped newspaper inserts blowing up and down debris-spotted streets, and rusty chain-link fences keeping trespassers out of dirt patches where factories once stood. Now even weeds didn't last there. In the early morning it doesn't seem like the dangerous stomping ground of legend from so many rap songs, more like a dying town that cultivates only weary unrest. Now, I'm sure there are certain areas of Compton that I would be foolish to navigate even in the daylight, a goofy white man out of his element, but none of that was on display.

While it wasn't the location the company put on the front of their brochure, the Motel 6 at least looked hospitable. There was no violence there, rather, just everyday suicides. I cleaned up the room quickly, finding a nasty-looking syringe between the mattress and the box spring. It wasn't the first one I'd found at a Motel 6, and I wondered if it wasn't their version of the mint on the pillow.

The guy at least had the good sense to kill himself in the bathroom, which was easy on cleanup. Motel 6 clearly had learned over the years to use nonporous material in the bathrooms and easily removable carpeting in the rest of the unit. Like moths to a flame, so go the despondent to off themselves at Motel 6.

I didn't have to take the mattress, which I vocally thanked the dead guy for; by that point in the morning, I couldn't exert a single bit more energy than was absolutely necessary. I was past thirty hours of no sleep, dehydrated as hell, worn down from my hangover, and ready to drop.

I called Dirk from the parking lot, intent on asking him if I could just drive his truck home and swap him vehicles many, many hours later. I was already going to have a bitch of a time getting from Compton back to Fullerton in the traffic of the 105, which seemed to last all day, rush hour or not.

"You're not going to believe this," Dirk said, his happy-go-lucky cadence sounding to me like dripping shit. "Corona PD just called... Someone threw up in the back of a cop car...They need you, man."

• • •

Torrance to Compton is not a bad trek, but West Compton out to Covina was about the length of civilized Southern California. My eyes fluttering from exhaustion, I nosed the truck for the long drive east.

We had our contract with Corona PD, so it wasn't just a simple case of "Can't do it; see you on the next one," and I knew that. I also knew that it would be a small miracle if I made it out to Corona without crashing the boss's truck. I might even have done it on purpose, but with no personal insurance and no company insurance, if I got hurt on a job, Dirk and I used to joke, we'd have to bury me in the desert.

They say there is truth in every joke, though, and I repeatedly slapped myself in the absence of caffeine to stay on the road. (That can't be something you want to see driving next to you: a scraggly looking motherfucker with a truckload of bloody carpet and trash bags, jabbering aloud and slapping himself as he tears down the road out to the middle of nowhere.)

Corona PD, if I haven't told you, sucks. Aside from their having a bunch of asshole cops and an uncovered parking lot where the patrol cars bake in the desert sun, they only called us out for the really nasty work. Whereas Orange PD once called us out over a prisoner spitting on the back window of a patrol car, Corona PD made sure that whenever we were called out, we worked for our money.

I've cleaned up vomit before, many times, in fact. I'm not quite the connoisseur of puke that I am of poop, and I was extremely tired and already at the end of my rope, but let me assure you that none of that held sway when I looked in the backseat of the cop car and realized that this was, without a doubt, the most heinously violent, chunky, rancid, smelly, wretched, slimy, multihued vomit that has ever existed on this planet.

Honest to God, I should have saved a cup of the stuff just to convince the naysayers and beat all claims to that title. I cannot imagine the putrid demon soul that unleashed this nightmare hose of chuke (chunky puke) across the backseat, windows, floorboards, and beneath the plastic seat dividers up into the front seat, but for your benefit I will try.

I imagine it was a woman, black widow-like, because I'm sure that some of the upchuck consisted of hunks of former mates and bits of her offspring that didn't crawl out of the nest fast enough. She was a big lady—had to be to contain the sheer amount of hurl that was spread rich before me. I imagine that she had ratty, dirty, long, curly hair; wicked pustules threatening to burst off her overstretched cheek meat; and an incredibly surly, loud, and brazen disposition.

Anywhere else I might have considered her as a candidate for a biker skank who nobody wanted on the back of their chopper, but this was Corona, and there was a good chance that she was the mayor of the city. Also she was wearing a straw cowgirl hat. Why? Why not.

I set to work scooping, yes, scooping up the volume of throw-up. I worked tirelessly under the blazing sun to do so, constantly averting my head, willing my nostrils not to pick up the scent of the cooked barf.

One time at the frat house, we found some of Phil's mom's home-made chunky turkey soup left over from a Thanksgiving that had been several months ago and rotting in the fridge. Instead of leaving it in its large plastic bag and properly disposing of it, we instead emptied it into a bucket, where the smell of the stuff made several guys retch.

Of course, any and all puke was collected in the bucket, as well as the urine of all present parties. One guy even took a shit in the bucket, creating a revolting mixture that we all somehow forgot about and left sitting on the patio when we went off to drink. Several days later we remembered it was there and threw it into the street for the street sweeper to slop up. I will forever remember the way that mess churned and sloshed as it was collected in the spinning brush of that street-sweeping machine. And yet the puke in that cop car in Corona was way worse.

I finished hours later, the remnants of the stink keeping me alert for my drive over to Dirk's office to retrieve my car. It had been a long day, too long, and made worse by my drinking. I had cleaned up four bodies and some insanely bad yak, but I had survived.

That night, I tumbled into bed feeling complete, like I'd done a day of honest work, and rest would be the greatest reward. It was how I imagined farmers and firemen and other hardworking blue-collar joes felt at the end of a long day. I could feel a measure of pride in myself as my eyelids slipped shut and sleep came.

My cell phone woke me up early the next morning, yanking me from deep slumber. I was refreshed, having slept from 4:30 in the afternoon until that jarring, irritating ring, but it interrupted me from a scummy, lascivious dream where I was a sultan and in command of my own girls' roller-derby team. Let's just say that I made them keep their skates on…Where the dream was actually headed, I'll probably never know, because goddamned Dirk woke me up.

"The guys out at Corona PD want to have a word with you," he said.

Me being me, I naturally assumed they wanted to congratulate me on a job well done, so I called them with an air of bravura that was quickly shattered.

Forty minutes later I was headed out to Corona to reclean a cop car free of charge. Apparently the cop driving the car the previous night became sick at the horrible smell still lingering foul as ever in the car and had puked his guts out. So now there was more to clean.

I never was able to get the smell out and told the men that if they couldn't put air fresheners in the car and deal with it, they would have to rip the seats out. Only then would I come back and clean again. Lo and behold, they ripped the seats out, and I went back a third time at my own expense to deal with that bastard car. *Now maybe you'll believe me when I tell you that it was hands-down my worst puking job?*

I don't know if that car was put back into service or not…I can't believe it was. But they never called us again. That feeling of pride that had enshrouded me earlier was gone, replaced by a feeling more appropriate for a jerk-off in my position. Reality is a bitch.

So when people ask me these days how it is to clean up a kid, I don't bullshit them talking about how you can feel the sorrow and the pain, the profoundness of the moment. I just tell them the dirty truth: cleaning up kids is better, because they bleed less.

child molesters don't last anywhere...

Molesters do not wear an ugly mask. They wear a shield of trust.
—Patty Rase Hopson, activist

I WAS FEELING VERY FRUSTRATED by the whole crime scene experience. If it hadn't been before, it was now crystal clear that we were on the Public Guardian's shit list, and that revelation was unhinging Dirk. Also, it didn't help that a rival crime scene cleaning company had filed a complaint with the city that Dirk, being both a sheriff and a crime scene cleaner, had a conflict of interest. Dirk, in response, began lashing out at anyone he viewed as a "traitor" to our company.

As far as I was concerned, he told me that I was not a very good manager of other people when we had large projects. According to him, I let people slack off, which caused the projects to take longer, lose us money, and make the Public Guardian think less of us.

Of course, since he needed me, he didn't personally tell me that I was so ineffective. Instead he went to my crew members and individually consulted them about taking over my job while retaining me solely for crime scene work. My role would switch to that of worker drone. Of course, my guys relayed this information to me. Rather than consulting Dirk about his actions, I stayed silent, just watching to see what else he had in mind.

Taffy Spears, Dirk's pal from the Public Guardian's office, the one who'd hooked us up with them in the first place, became some sort of evil entity in Dirk's burgeoning delusional state. Using his sheriff position, he ran a background sweep on her, only to find out that she'd recently bounced a check to an auto mechanic's and that they were threatening legal action against her unless she paid up.

Dirk decided that the most sensible course of action to restore our good graces with the Public Guardian's office was to blackmail Mona. He literally wanted to call her and threaten to release her personal information if she wouldn't give us work. Tempted as I was to see what trouble Dirk could wind himself into with this, I had to stop him.

In the meantime, against all belief, work, sans the Public Guardian's office, continued to find us. Dirk called me with an early evening gig that came through the City of Santa Ana police force, not the sheriff's department. Dirk's constant badgering of fellow officers had finally managed to put some food on our table.

The police were still on scene when we reached the courthouse building in Santa Ana. We drove the truck straight up on the sidewalk, because the placards on the side of the truck now read "Crime Scene Cleaners" with our embossed company logo and the tacky "Integrity. Respect. Compassion." tagline that Dirk thought was so poignant. It would have been more fitting had it read "Dewey, Cheatem & Howe."

We drove along the walkways and up to the police cars, cruising past awestruck junior officers until we found a sergeant who coolly clued us in on the details. The dead man was yet another child molester. Waiting to be formally charged with child molestation the next day, he had been up on the eleventh floor of the courthouse for some bullshit reason.

Deciding he didn't want his soon-to-be fellow inmates to do the job for him, he ran for the open-air veranda and pulled a swan dive off the balcony. Surprisingly, a pursuing cop managed to snag his leg as he leapt, but the cop couldn't hold on. Down, down, down the Chester went, eventually making like Humpty Dumpty all over the pavement walkway. The general consensus of all policemen present was that they wouldn't have made a grab for the jumper, lest his weight pull them over, too.

A person falling from a great height is one of the messier jobs in the crime cleaner's repertoire. This guy, like his prison counterpart, had bounced but, unlike his prisoner counterpart, had also truly exploded. Whereas the prisoner's head had cracked open and splattered brain everywhere, this current son of a bitch had me hunting up huge chunks of his liver and other innards in the dark of the night. He'd really done a number on me, firing bits of everything everywhere, splashing hunks of his stomach and skull in a blast zone that radiated out about thirty-one feet from impact.

Dirk had a real reluctance to buying tools for the business, as evidenced by the company truck he'd been promising me for a year and a half before I got it. There was also the matter of a power washer; my frat brother had moved and taken his power washer with him, which was too bad, because it would have come in handy on a slew of outdoor jobs we took on.

There was the old man who'd died from falling off his concrete porch and smacking his head open on the business end of a rake, or the job I did at a Motel 6 in Fontana where a man, knifed in the gut, had dragged himself along a hundred feet of walkway and rounded a corner before finally collapsing by the stairwell.

Stuff like that required serious equipment to do the job correctly, equipment that Dirk didn't want to shell out for. Instead, he believed in his method of using a small furniture-scrubbing brush like a glorified toothbrush and scrubbing the blood out inch by inch. Of course, he usually wasn't the one out there doing it.

We also lacked the proper lighting for any sort of outdoor work, instead relying on a building's atmospheric lighting and a single box light that I'd purchased on impulse for a different job using my corporate credit card. We'd called Kim out for that job, and she had come eagerly at Dirk's request, though I was a little sketchy about using her or anyone from the will fiasco. It was nice to have a third party working there, though, and she was great leverage in helping me convince Dirk that we should stay and do the work that evening rather than having us abandon the job in the absence of light.

That way I wouldn't have to come back early the next morning to finish by myself before any federal employees showed up for work around 5:30 a.m. (That was another strategy of Dirk's whenever the hour got late: "I think what we'll do, Jeff, is have you come back early tomorrow morning and finish up.")

A week or so later, such things happening in twos and threes, I got a call from the Orange police department for our second non-scrub job for them (the first had been that old man with the rake). The second was another jumper, though not a child molester this time. But she, too, had done a good job of making her effort a fatal one. I had become openly mocking of any crime scene call that didn't involve a fatality (such as that poor Motel 6 bastard who caught a screwdriver in the eye). Consider it the cynic in me.

That second jumper was a middle-aged woman with financial woes. I could certainly relate. Fortunately for me, the lady had the good sense to kill herself in the late morning, so I was able to get in gear by early afternoon and take full advantage of the light. She'd jumped off the four-story parking structure of an executive building and down onto its driveway, blocking all the Mercedes and Lexuses housed within from leaving until she had been cleaned up. Everyone has his or her own way of striking back at "The Man," I guess.

I spent a lot of time on that job just jawing back and forth good-naturedly with the policeman who had to stay on scene until I was finished, the scene technically being a city sidewalk. I had a lot of empathy for the guy; since he was the low man on the totem pole, he got stuck with all the shitty jobs. I could definitely relate.

Hanging out and listening to the stuff he'd had to deal with as a policeman, just the bullshit civil stuff, the wife beatings, the kooks who called in complaining about missing wills. It gave me a certain respect for police officers everywhere...until I had to clean one up.

Dirk had cultivated an acquaintance with the lead homicide investigator for the Orange County Sheriff's Department, and that friendship had yielded us a somewhat touchy gig from the department. The head investigator was allowed to assign a company to come out and do the work on the proviso that the job stay under a grand. Over a grand, and he'd have to legally offer it through a bidding process. The sheriff's department had caught wind of how we'd stuck it to the local cops when we cleaned up the courthouse jumper.

The sergeant on scene didn't give a damn what we charged, so we stupidly ratcheted up the price an extra two grand. He signed off on it, ensuring that the police department would be furious at us for hosing them and costing us what could have been a fruitful relationship with local police. And yep, they never called us back again.

Eager to extend a favor to his fellow sheriffs, Dirk offered the homicide investigator our services for the rock-bottom price of nine hundred dollars. It had been awhile since we'd worked for so little, and considering that I was doing all the labor, I wasn't too excited about that.

I met the investigator at a nearby tow yard, where the job was being done discreetly, out of view of the public or professional eye. We had to clean up the interior of a detective car, which didn't have all the molded plastic and steel separating the front and back seats.

The detective in question was a sheriff who'd had a long and positive relationship with his department, making many lifelong friends during his tenure. But then they discovered that he'd been sexually abusing a boy for several years. The sheriff, hearing over his police radio that there was a warrant out for his arrest, drove to a Denny's parking lot in South County and ate a bullet.

"Have you ever cleaned up a car?" the investigator asked, eyeing me suspiciously when I arrived.

I nodded casually as if it were old hat for me. The investigator, who looked like Wyatt Earp, would know if I was lying—I was certain of that—so I decided against it from the get-go. He had those piercing eyes that have seen through the souls of murderers and people more practiced in the deceptive arts than I. Fortunately, I'd done that drive-by job, so I wasn't lying.

His presence made me uncomfortable, and I hoped that he would leave after I'd given him his copy of the contract. But he made no motion toward the exit. Instead, more than any other client I've ever worked for, he seemed keenly intent on helping me.

This was particularly unnerving, because lately I'd had a stretch of guilt about how we'd conducted ourselves, knowing full well that we, and our technique, were largely superficial bullshit. If anyone would see through that, it was this rangy, observant law dog.

His interest in my work seemed based in curiosity, though, as he helped unbolt the seats of the car for me to take out, accepting of my lame explanation as to why I didn't have a bolt set of my own. Rather than reveal that Dirk was too cheap to splurge on such necessary items for the business, I simply gave my standard excuse for not having a piece of equipment.

"Oh, we have that, but if I towed every piece of equipment along to every crime scene, I wouldn't have any space left in the back of the truck for hauling bloody stuff." This worked with fast-food restaurants when I needed to use their mops, brooms, or other cleaning items, always assuring them that I'd sanitize the tool before giving it back. Like my standard contract clause, it had become just another excuse to keep our business alive.

But as it turned out, my lack of a bolt set didn't matter. Police cars all employ a special star-shaped nut in their units to prevent convicts from smuggling in standard tools for use in their escape. The investigator hunted one down, and we fitted it over the nut, me having to first dig out the dried blood that had molded into a clay consistency inside the nut housing.

Once all the seats were out of the car, I used surgical blades that Dirk had smuggled out of his job to cut through the floor fabric and rip that out, taking the car down to its reinforced chassis. I didn't even stop to consider that the investigator, who worked with Dirk, might recognize the style of blade and make a comment, but he stayed silent, eyeing my cuts with a surgical precision of his own.

I scrubbed and rescrubbed every inch of the car that I could reach, because Dirk had been adamant that this was one of those jobs that had to go exactly right. I wasn't allowed to give it the "nine-hundred-dollar version," which largely involved just making sure nothing major was visible.

When I was finished with the car, I extended my hands outward as if I were a model on *The Price Is Right*, showing the investigator what he'd won.

"What about the seatbelts?" The investigator sliced through my daydream with a question he'd probably been waiting several hours to ask. In typical idiot fashion, I hadn't even considered the seatbelts, especially not the one the detective had been wearing when he blasted a hole through his noggin.

Looking like the goofy fucking amateur that I was, I pulled the seatbelt out of the retractable holder, revealing dark stains already leached into the mechanics of the thing. I grinned my usual shit-eating grin, felt like crying, and got back to fucking work.

Finally, and with a considerable amount of disgust at my ineptitude, the investigator suggested that we should just cut the seatbelts out and forget my attempts to scrub them, as I'd been getting nowhere for the last half an hour. I'd already tossed both of the surgical blades away, and my standard carpet razor still had that same dull blade, which was of no use to me on the seatbelts. So, with one last pathetic, pitiful appeal, I asked him, "Can I borrow your knife?" I assured him that I would clean it off before I gave it back to him.

Last, but not least, the dead man's service effects, namely his radio and his badge, were resting on the hood of the police cruiser. The radio had been attached to his belt at his death and thus had been spared the brunt of the mess. The badge, though, had been clipped to the pocket of his polo shirt, and streams of blood had curled through the ridged contours of the gold shield that was supposed to stand for law and order.

I got the radio cleaned easily enough and put it in a bag with the items from the sheriff's trunk. The badge, though, had been sitting awhile, and not all of the blood came off. I'd never held a policeman's badge before, and that one, streaked in blood, seemed like a bad one to start with.

All the while, the homicide investigator watched me silently scrub at his dead coworker's effects, judging me. When I was finished, he thanked me for coming on such short notice, and I couldn't tell if his abruptness with me was due to my barely capable performance or if it was merely in regards to the situation. He never called us for work again, so I figured I had my answer.

• • •

I'd cleaned up enough criminals, so it was inevitable that somewhere in the mix I'd eventually come across a dead cop. I suppose he was a criminal himself and largely no different from the others, but I couldn't help wondering, standing there with that tainted symbol of justice in my hand, if I stayed with the crime scene business long enough, would anything else ever shock me?

I didn't have the intelligence to recognize it then, but a seed had been planted.

kill me last

Funny how gentle people get with you once you're dead.
—*Joe Gillis*, Sunset Boulevard

MY FAMILY HAS A BEACH house in Aptos, a sleepy little community of rich beach bums and retirees at the north end of Monterey County. It's a beautiful two-story house midway up Monterey Bay, on a private beach that keeps the "townies" out. One of the big shots at Yahoo is our closest neighbor. My family has gone there every summer since before my birth to relax, sit on the sun-warmed patio, swim in the ocean, and forget life's cares. It is absolutely my favorite place to be; every time I'm there, I'm convinced that there is no better place on earth to savor a cigar and imbibe a glass of port than on the deck of your own beach house.

Now, I'm not telling you about the beach house to brag, but rather to illustrate what I contend is a valid point. To have your own little slice of paradise and then to just throw it away—to me, you deserve worse than death.

I wasn't born rich. My family isn't "from money," and most of my life has not been spent in the lap of luxury. My great-grandfather, who was evidently a very smart man, bought a sizable chunk of the coastline of Monterey Bay when no one else was out there.

He built a large three-story home with views on the top floor of the entire bay, from Carmel to Santa Cruz. The house had an indoor pool and an elevator. (When I was young, we took a tour through the house, and I remember seeing the indoor pool…it was amazing. I can think of few things cooler than to be a kid in a house with an indoor pool and an elevator.) Years later, my great-grandfather built another home next door that he lived in while the kids and nieces and nephews had the other home as a sort of playhouse.

When my great-grandfather died (years before I was born), the next generation was riddled with debt and ended up parceling off the rest of the land. Then they sold the three-story mansion, which went through several owners, one of whom had the elevator and the indoor pool removed. The Yahoo guy lives in that house now, and I can only wonder about how it looks.

My family managed to keep our house though a collective of aunts, uncles, cousins, my mom, and many, many other relatives I've never met. Each family uses the house for one week a year, renting it out when it's not being used, almost like a time-share.

If it's not rented, it's fair game for the family. I've used that house many times for parties and weeklong bacchanalian retreats with friends and strangers alike. (Some "townies" have even found their way in there, much to my chagrin. Poor or not, *nobody* likes "townies.")

My family doesn't exactly fit in with the rest of the neighborhood. We're dirty, we're poor, we're loud and silly, and we arrive in caravans of dirt-stained minivans and cheaper-end sedans. The rest of the neighbors and other renters enjoy their SUVs, their Cadillacs, and their sports coupes.

We used to get challenged on the beach to games of touch football by handsome, fit families of fathers and sons with strong Ivy League jawlines and mothers and daughters who filled out bikinis without overfilling them like my family does. Those games of touch football or beach volleyball would usually start with the other family racking up huge points on us and end with us fist-fighting among ourselves while the other family looked on in disgust and shame.

We were rough-and-tumble, from areas where people would literally kill to have beach homes. Yet the house was such a part of my existence that I was honestly surprised in fourth or fifth grade to find out that not every family had their own beach house somewhere.

We were very, very lucky, and I now fully appreciate what a blessing it has been for us to get that taste, even if for only one week a year, of what privilege is like. And to think, some people have the opportunity to live in a luxurious, multimillion-dollar beach house fifty-two weeks a year, basking in the sight of the ocean.

I know people live like this, because I cleaned some of them up.

• • •

The Targus family, three generations of Turkish immigrants, lived in a hillside mansion in palatial San Clemente, in the exclusive southern tip of South County. San Clemente was part of a world I couldn't relate to. Down in South County, potholes were filled before they had a chance to become potholes, everything was clean and green, and most cars were sleek and European-made.

Dirk and I rolled down the broad stretch of the five-lane freeway with our newest employee sitting in the crew cab. Dirk had hired his cousin Russ, a mortgage guy who, like the rest of the nation's mortgage guys, was feeling the sharp chop of his own ax. So while his job destroying ignorant people's credit scores was circling the toilet, Russ decided to hop on board and see what our little train ride was all about.

Dirk had sworn up and down the block that he was going to retire in a few years and the whole company would be mine. Now, with his cousin as a partner, my slice of the pie got that much smaller. I was courteous but aloof to Russ and spent most of the trip down staring pensively out the window.

The police department in San Clemente had called us out—how they got our info, I'll never know. I wanted to believe that Dirk had done his part to scare up business, but like our first several jobs, it was more than likely just some big mistake. Doubtlessly, we'd do our damnedest to make sure they regretted choosing us.

I didn't know anything about the Targus family when we pulled off the freeway and down into the thick of the beachside city, but then I typically never knew anything about the victims ahead of time. If they lived in South County, though, the odds were good that we'd be able to charge whichever one was still alive decent money to clean up the one who wasn't.

It was still early morning for me when we reached the gate to the private community. A guard checked in visitors, which ensured that there was money to be made. I was a realist, though, and knew that the kind of money we might make wasn't anything like the money these people made on a daily basis. Still, any cash we earned we'd spend just fine back in dirty Fullerton.

The Targuses were a family of five living together in a small white mansion that had a gorgeous, raised view of the entire South County chunk of the Pacific Ocean. While the spread wasn't as vast as some adjoining it, spreads that were worth many millions, it definitely was still very valuable property. From the short driveway, which boasted standard European automobiles, I could see the angular side of the house sloping downward as if it had been constructed onto the face of the hillside.

The busted glass panels on the French-style front doors indicated that we were indeed in the right place…that and the swarms of police officers buzzing in and out of the house in protective face masks.

Stepping out of the truck accompanied by Dirk and Russ, I could easily discern the reason for the face masks. The air, rich with salty sea freshness, had a rancid undercurrent of spoiled flesh. For us to catch wind of it out on the driveway, I knew that either whoever was dead was close by, or the scene was going to be a bad one.

"They're all down in the bedroom…" a local cop filled us in from behind his breathing filter. "It's a bad one," he confirmed.

The news reports that emerged in the wake of the deaths all focused on how tight-knit and private the family was. The twin girls, just graduated from college, dressed alike, acted alike, and preferred to hang out with each other rather than anyone outside their family. Their grandmother, from the Republic of Turkey, was living there on an expired visa and apparently mostly stayed inside the home.

The mother dabbled in real estate and ran a jewelry store at the mall. The father of the twins was a PhD who experimented with thermal energy and was an expert witness for the state of California on car-crash statistics. He worked out of his home as a consultant, which seemed like sweet work if you could get it.

Neighbors were quick to offer their own accounts of how incredibly closed off the family was, even in the midst of a community that seemed to pride itself on being closed off. Of course, neighbors will say any fucking thing that might get them in the newspaper.

Every crime scene I've ever worked had some neighbor coming around with that wide-eyed, cautious demeanor, as if he or she were a squirrel contemplating granola in an outstretched hand. They were always eager to give me their version of the dead person's hang-ups and peccadillos, as if I were hiding a journalist in my pants.

Usually I was polite, offering up the occasional "No, kidding?" every time there seemed to be an unnaturally long pause in their speech. Most would finally run out of blather on their own accord and mosey off to find some new idiot to unleash their version of the story on. I'm convinced that the need to tell bullshit stories and borrow cups of sugar was the catalyst for the first neighborhood.

What actually happened to the Targuses varies, depending on which account of their death you believe. When we first arrived, the police were chattering about how the entire family had been murdered in retaliation for some shady mob shit the father's relatives had been involved in back home.

Even the contract entomologist whom the detectives sent in found it odd that so many differing species of maggots (six, to be specific) were present at the crime scene. That, of course, led to the speculation that some of the bugs had been "trafficked" into the scene as a message.

But the coroner officially ruled cause of death as suicide. I personally agreed with that assessment, since I'd already cleaned up a mass murder and I'd never before cleaned up a mass suicide. Media speculation differed, of course, but it helped the coroner's case that each member of the family was dressed head to toe in matching black outfits when they were found.

While the reasoning for the group suicide was never publicized, the inner-circle theory alleged that the family was financially fucked by the mortgage fiasco. Coupled with the fact that they felt an immense amount of shame over the twins' inability to get into the medical school of their choice, the financial problems drove them over the edge. It seemed like an extreme end to such a temporary disappointment, but death means different things to different people.

Bidding the job was easy. The brother of the dead man absolutely did not want to be on scene for any part of what we were going to do. I told Dirk to charge at least ten thousand, maybe twelve...cleaning up mansions should never be a lowball gig. He went seventy-five hundred for five bodies, though, and the guy gobbled that price tag right down.

"You shoulda gone for fourteen," I chided Dirk.

It also killed me that we had settled for an oral contract instead of a written one. The rotted-guts removal business isn't exactly a service that can be undone with failure to pay. Though one time Schmitty, our silent company owner to the north, actually threatened a non-paying customer with exactly that.

We'd scraped up a little old grandma out of her apartment where she'd collapsed and rotted away in the span of carpeting between her recliner and her TV. The landlord didn't feel like paying up, so Schmitty threatened to dump the old woman's guts back on the landlord's porch and smack a mechanic's lien against the property.

The tightwad paid. But that little scenario was an exception to the rule. Realistically, once the guts were gone, all we could do was continually harangue property owners with nagging phone calls. Russ, the soulless ex-mortgage guy, eventually took care of those.

To make the cops feel like sissies and assholes, I descended into the catacombs of the mansion without a mask on. Dirk was of the opinion that we should side with professionalism when dealing with a new police squad, but I wanted to show off.

I was impressed with the elegance of the house. Expensive painted portraits of the family grimly observed me from their ornately framed place on the walls. At my parent's house, unflattering photographs taken at Sears were hung in plain frames. (Of course, we're also still alive, so score one for us!)

Rugs that looked to be out of some movie about Turkish royalty covered the floors, and the overall house had an impressive state-of-the-art look to it, highlighted by decorative ethnic accents.

Down sharp-angled tiled stairs, curved hairpin-style, were all the bedrooms. It would have been a bitch if we had had to haul a bed out of there. The girls' bedrooms were simple, decorated as if still occupied by small children instead of the twenty-year-olds who had inhabited them. A mess of long, green straw led from one of the bedrooms and up onto the stairs. Small mobile patches of it were scattered along the house's white marble floors. Curious, I picked up a small clump of it.

"There were six bodies found in here." A policeman answered my quizzical glance. "The family had a pet bunny that died a few days after they did."

I grimaced slightly and dropped the hay; a human's dying didn't do much for me, but it hurt my heart when an animal bit the dust.

Once the last of the cops had exited the master bedroom, I poked my head inside cautiously. What was left of the bodies had already been removed by the coroner's office; the detectives had concluded their cursory examination of the scene, and all that was left for us jack-offs was to scoop up the remainder—and do what we could about the smell.

By that point in the game, I was no stranger to the rank odor of rotting people, but this was something entirely new. Whether it was because fluids had been sealed into the bedroom since they weren't able to leach down through the marble or the collective mass of humans rotting together, the smell was devastating. I could feel it seeping into me when I sweated, and I knew that a simple shower wouldn't be enough to shake the musk. I actually had to swallow repeatedly and force myself not think of Phil's mom's turkey soup to keep my four-burrito lunch down.

I was excited to see the new guy walk into the room. If I was used to the smell of a dead body and this got to me, I was betting Russ would fall to his knees, the sound of exiting vomit echoing through his chest cavity as if it were from a high-pitched cannon. Big, stinging tears would drop from his eyes, and he would gasp frantically for nonexistent fresh air. Or better yet, maybe, just maybe, his face would fucking melt right off, like the Nazis at the end of *Raiders of the Lost Ark*. Whatever the reaction, it was certain to be a beautiful sight to behold.

At this stage in my career, I shouldn't have been so affected by disappointment, but I was when Russ walked in carrying a milk crate full of his brand-new supplies and went "Phew!"

That was fucking it. From having kids, he was probably no stranger to bad smells, but come fucking on. I had waited eagerly in the funk of the master bedroom, simmering in the noxious fumes for ten minutes only to get a generic "Phew"? Dirk was in the next room, and cousins or not, I could tell that he, too, was a little sad that Russ hadn't puked his guts out. So much for hazing the new guy.

The scene itself definitely contained all the grandeur and spectacle one would hope to witness in a mass suicide. Aside from the nasal abuse, the assault on the eyes was equally marvelous. That cop out front had been right—it was a bad one.

The twins had died on the parents' Cal King bed, which was far larger than any Cal King I'd previously seen; it took up half of the enormous bedroom. A perfect outline of the dead girls would have been preserved in the thick down comforter spanning the bed, but the maggots and other larval insects had picked away at the remains, scattering thick trails of grease outward from the bodies and distorting their image. The level of decomposition was so great in the insulated bedroom that the coroner had once again taken only skeletons and left us the remainder.

Most surprising to me was the grandmother, who'd died sprawled out on a chaise lounge, copping a pose from the Scarlett O'Hara School of Dramatics. The stifling air of the bedroom had coupled with time to create a most unpleasant effect on her ancient, saggy body, which had turned to slime and forced itself through the layers of the lounge chair.

She was evidently a big woman as well, because surrounding the legs of the chair and pooling outward into a corner of the room was a congealed lake of salty, mustard-yellow fat, a puddinglike skin thick across its surface. I'd never seen anything like it. Getting down on my hands and knees to simply be closer to it, I surmised that it was about two inches deep at its thickest point.

I wish I could say that seeing that woman's ass, thighs, and midsection reduced to a stinky, quivering lake made me rethink my life and the fast food I was sure to imbibe over the remainder of it. But alas, I felt certain that many more cheap burritos were in my future.

We saw the parents last, as they'd isolated themselves in their huge walk-in closet, which was separated from the main bedroom by a private bathroom with a large two-person Jacuzzi tub and a separate shower, also built for two. Maybe that's not a big deal to you big-city folks with your washboard abs and your remote-controlled cars, but when I saw that, I nearly dropped my testicles out my asshole.

While the rest of the group had opted for poisoning themselves (with what, I don't know…but if I had to guess, I'd say tacky jewelry), Ma and Pa had taken the bullet ride to Brain Island. They muffled the sound of the shots with enormous comforters, but the reality was that the sheer amount of clothing and accessories in the closet would've been enough. The two of them were equal in their affinity for fashion, and the closet was split down the middle—expensive fur coats and designer dresses for her, custom-made suits and Missoni sweaters for him.

When we began the work, I called dibs on Grandma, eager to tackle a problem I'd never encountered before. Dirk and Russ went to work on the parents, which was no easy task, surrounded as they were by the regal couture that had absorbed the stench of three weeks' decay.

All the clothing, handbags, shoes, and accessories had to go…but not by us. We had strictly defined ourselves as crime scene cleaners and couldn't be bothered to deal with stinky garments, so all apparel went into the bathtubs to be discarded by someone else.

The comforters that the parents had draped about themselves added a degree of difficulty as well, since they'd essentially been transformed into humongous Brawny paper towels with super absorbency. I don't know what a heavy down comforter weighs normally…maybe twenty pounds? With all the good stuff that used to be people soaked into them, each one now weighed in excess of a hundred pounds. I had to abandon my Granny escapades to help the others load the two comforters into Hefty bags, which then had to be carried up the narrow stairs.

The potency of the offensive smell increased with the removal of the soggy blankets, and the gagging began. Finally, all three of us had to resort to wearing our industrial gas masks to stay in the room. Much of what had been in the comforters had splashed out onto the ground, leaving a mulchy brown, bilious glop across the closet tile.

Worse still, the mom's innards were particularly corrosive and had melted away the sealant coating of the marble flooring. In some manner of unholy osmosis, the fluid had sucked its way into the white tiles, rendering them a garish color that might best be classified as vermillion. I wanted no part of that and wandered back to my salty sea.

I began my attempt meekly, first tapping one of my small hand towels into the fat at its shallowest point. I might as well have been trying to clean up the goo with a stick of butter for all the good that my cloth towel did. No, with Grandma's fat, my thinking needed to be done outside the box.

I grabbed all the parents' bath towels that I could find. They were monogrammed Egyptian cotton with a ridiculously high thread count, so I figured the absorbency would be ample. Throwing them into the midst of the lake, I stood back to watch. Lo and behold, the yellowed mass with a top like crème brûlée held firm against the lightness of the towels.

What the scene needed was three hundred pounds of human to push the towels through the crust. In my white bunny suit, I took the leap, soaring thoughtlessly into the thickness, not realizing that a huge portion of the fat was really just slippery, slippery grease. I hit the towel and went down hard, my hands and knees saved from the unyielding marble by the years of breakfast treats the lady had indulged in.

Landing largely past the safety of the Egyptian cotton, my gloved hands and knees were yellow with the sticky, waxy fat surrounding them. I scooted back, disgusted, onto the crumpled safety of a towel that, like an island in the sea, was sinking into the abyss. Standing slowly, I chose what I hoped was the lesser of two evils and stepped back into the grandma, my size 13s carving footprints into her lard, which left untouched, would've been an important fossil find many thousands of years in the future.

Back on the safety of clean marble, I stripped out of my bunny suit and changed into a fresh one. All the towels were marooned in the midst of the mess, and the eye of the storm was yielding little effect. I had to try something else.

The largest of the woman's fur coats was next. I formed a mink bridge between the clean tile and the bath towels and, from there, crouched down and gathered up the towels, scooping up layers of fat with them. At that point I learned one of the tenets of life that should be passed on to one's children and their children: *mink does not soak up human remains.* No, human remains just make a ruined coat more ruined. (Remember that rule, and you're three-quarters of the way toward being a crime scene cleaner yourself.)

Once the towels, the mink, and the comforters were all safely in Hefty bags, along with the rest of Grandma (who finally came up with a snow shovel and a shit ton of degreaser), we tore apart the bed and the chaise lounge, which was filled with sharp tacks.

Attracted to the bed frame, I seriously considered taking it home and swapping it for the Murder Bed. The frame was mostly clean and constructed out of a rich, heavy, light-colored wood hand-carved into a contemporary and pleasing design. I nixed the idea when I realized that I would never be able to find a mattress that could fit such a massive frame. We'd sawed the original into stained pieces, and since Tampax didn't make a panty liner for Paul Bunyan's wife, I was shit out of luck. Anyways, Dirk and Russ didn't want to help lug the headboard up those impossible stairs, so I dropped the idea.

We'd gotten a fair shake from the property association and the police in regards to the paparazzi, because none were allowed past the front gates of the neighborhood. Instead, they had had to set their cameras on the land far below, in a shopping center across from the rugged hillside. From the balcony where I copped fresh air and stared enviously out at the span of the Pacific, the reporters down on the public land looked like the squirming, crawling maggots we were paid to vacuum up.

One or two reporters tried to get the scoop and managed to get past the old codger guarding the front entrance (an impressive feat, considering that he gave us, in our giant fucking truck adorned with crime scene cleaner decals, a bitch of a time before he let us in).

As we were setting bulging Hefty bags of human flesh out in front of the garage door, a cameraman came running up, filming, and attempting to outmaneuver and out-guff the police. Finally, under the threat of arrest and without being able to film anything more than my fat ass carrying out generic trash bags, he scampered back into his car and left.

We gave up the ghost shortly thereafter with Dirk bitching about how tired he was. He wasn't used to working on actual crime scenes (ooh!), and I had urged him to push on, knowing what the eventual outcome would be if we didn't finish the job in one day. Sure enough, though, I would be returning the next day sans Dirk to finish what we had started. To his credit, Dirk talked an unenthusiastic Russ into returning with me.

At dawn the next morning, while the early birds were still at home dreaming about the worms they would catch, Russ and I made our way south in Dirk's truck to finish the job. The mansion was just as we'd left it, with plywood nailed over the hole smashed in the front window by the initial police responders. Using a key one of the cops had found in the dead wife's purse, we opened all the doors and windows to once again blast the neighborhood with the scent of unchecked privacy.

The sea that day was serenely calm, and only a few straggling reporters remained down below to capture the action that they couldn't see. Standing out on that balcony in the early morning, basking in the solitude, I decided that I liked cleaning up rich people.

I used the absence of a police presence to really explore the house. Several massive flat-screen TVs took up wall space throughout the home. I might have taken one or three to adorn the walls of my frat bedroom under the auspices that they'd "been contaminated," but Russ's anecdotes on the drive over about his good Christian values had put a halt to any large-scale thievery. I couldn't imagine that he'd last long in the job, with the way Dirk and I conducted business.

Instead, I involved myself with a stack of bound manuscripts, heaped six high, on the edge of a nightstand. They were screenplays, all written by the father. Eagerly, I thumbed through the top one to get a feel for what Mr. Targus had to offer. It was an action pic, as seen through a sort of Bollywood-esque simplicity, kind of an Indiana Jones adventure with soap-opera melodrama packed in. I was not unsurprised to see that it hadn't sold, as had none of the others—all of a similar vein.

But the title of that top screenplay, sitting there for weeks surrounded by a decomposing family, caught my eye: "Kill Me Last." I was certain that the father was trying to send a message of his own to a certain dashing and intuitive young crime scene cleaner who worked outside the law, solving cases no one else would touch. But as I was neither dashing nor intuitive, I got my fat, lazy ass back to work.

After several hours of intensive labor, sweeping and vacuuming up many maggots, we finally had to address the issue in the closet. While Dirk and Russ had scrubbed laboriously the day before, they had simply been unable to get that vermillion stain out of the marble chunks.

We weren't about to come in with jackhammers under the original bid (though I would have, just for the experience), so Dirk, against his better judgment, called Schmitty for advice. Schmitty was a bad call, because any project we worked on that Schmitty caught wind of meant he would want his cut. And I wasn't about to let him get a piece of our mass-suicide plum.

Dirk finally came up with the idea of posing a hypothetical situation to Schmitty: if we ever had to scrub a dead woman's guts out of marble, what should we use? Schmitty suggested muriatic acid.

Muriatic acid is pool acid, used to clean the decks and walls of swimming pools, and found only at the right swimming-pool stores. Fortunately, we were in the rich part of Southern California, which was a haven for swimming pools, so such a store was nearby.

We bought a five-gallon bucket of the stuff and, not knowing any better (still don't), dumped a good measure of it in concentrated form on the affected tile. Instantly a thick, white, acrid cloud rose from the tile as chemicals reacted with one another in the poorly ventilated closet space.

We beat feet out of there, fearing the long-term effects of that gas cloud. When the smoke finally cleared, the tile was as vermillion as ever, and we were in possession of a useless three remaining gallons of pool acid. The stain left by that lady wasn't coming out without that aforementioned jackhammer.

I'm fairly sure she's still in that house to this day. Our saving grace was a line item in the contract: "Due to porous nature of the affected area, residual staining may occur."

CHAPTER 22

drunken madcappery no more, goddamnit!

False friends are worse than bitter enemies.

—*Scottish proverb*

THE GOOD TIMES HADN'T LASTED at the frat house. In the time that I'd injured my back and stayed in my room for months recuperating, I'd gone from beloved housemate and dedicated fraternal bro to "that old guy who is past his expiration date and heavily in debt to the chapter."

A new group of brothers had come into the house and taken over, and I was no longer part of the club. Sure, I still hung out and partied with the herd, but I was no longer an invited presence to outings away from the house. My time had passed, my legend had faded, and I was just another pathetic asshole trying to cling to his glory days.

Even the cops took notice. One night during a bit of hard partying and beer ponging with the stereo blasting, we were rolled up on by the police. This was a regular occurrence, and I'd gotten to know most of the police officers through wisecracking and smart-ass comments that most of them good-naturedly endured. This night, though, I opened the front door of the house to encounter a police officer I'd never met before.

"Aren't you a little old to be a frat boy?" the cop asked me with genuine shock. No "Hello," no "Keep it down, motherfuckers," just surprise at my age.

I affected mock disgust for the benefit of my party mates and said something to the effect of, "Why, Officer! How old do you think I am?"

"I don't know...twenty-three?" he responded, shrugging and guessing the oldest age he could imagine that some dickhead would still be hanging around a frat house. I was twenty-six.

Chris had moved out in July of that year, in what had to be the hardest blow to my happiness. Finances finally had overwhelmed him, and, up to his throat in debt, he had loaded up his electric-blue El Camino, which was more lemon than automobile, and made his way back home to Mom and Dad. It was the best thing for him, really, but I was crushed to see him go. Through it all, he'd been my best friend, and we'd weathered many a storm together.

Now I was alone in the frat house. Anthony, the guy who'd brought me in, had moved out; Christian, the cat-eating insane guy, had moved out; and most of the guys I'd come in with—or had really grown close to—were long gone. Even Donkey Kong was planning his exit to join the military. It had become a place I didn't recognize.

The house was just coming off a massive probation that we'd incurred for underage drinking. (This means eighteen- and nineteen-year-olds, not eleven-year-olds, okay?) To celebrate, we decided to have a party. It would be the last one that house would ever see.

The party started innocently enough with just the dedicated few whooping it up lightly in anticipation of the crowds. Some nights the house was so clogged with people that you could hardly get through the maze of grinding girls, wrestling guys, nerds, drunks, and other revelers. That night's party wasn't expected to be any different.

We'd hung a black tarp across the front entrance to the house, giving us a "reasonable expectation of privacy" per police standards, and there were still beer cans hanging off strands of Christmas lights from our last shindig. Everything was gearing up for the hordes to come charging in and breathe life into the house.

A little after nine, a ripple went through the few in attendance, noting that the cops were outside and that we were to keep it down. It wasn't a real concern, because cops lived on the row on Fridays and Saturdays, and it wasn't unusual for them to run random checkups.

That night, though, the police decided that we had in excess of three hundred people at our house, when in fact there weren't more than thirty. The cops never exited their car to make this determination; instead, they ballparked it horribly and shut us down early as a result.

Since most everyone there was a bro or girlfriend of a bro, we didn't ask anyone to leave but instead turned away most would-be partiers as they arrived. I stayed up for a while having a cigar and being "that weird old guy who keeps trying to look down girl's shirts." Kerry was tired and went up to my room to fall asleep. An hour later, I went upstairs and joined her.

Sometime after 4:00 a.m., Donkey Kong's brother, Napoleon, who was visiting, came and woke me. "Jeff, it's bad," he slurred, sounding alarmed. "There's some guys downstairs starting trouble, and Dan punched one of them and they won't leave."

I knew it had to be bad for tough Ernie to come and wake me, so I ran downstairs. I was usually the guy contacted for such emergencies, as I'd been in the midst of a few of them before.

When I got on scene, I saw two things: 1. Donkey Kong stalking back and forth in a state of severe frustration, and 2. three frat guys holding back a stranger whose face was gushing blood. I didn't know what the stranger had been thinking, because Donkey Kong had at least fifty pounds of hard muscle on the guy and a whole heap of wrestling knowledge.

While this was a surprising matchup, it wasn't a surprising situation—when you're in a fraternity, drunk people often show up looking for a fight. We're sort of a proving grounds for those goddamned townies.

I knew we had to get the stranger separated from the group, several of whom were beginning to get less interested in restraining the frothing bleeder and more interested in pounding his ass. Also being restrained in the scrum was the bleeder's friend, a loudmouthed guy who kept screaming, "Don't hurt my friend," at anyone who would listen. I had size on everyone there, so I stepped in and put my arm around the bleeding guy, leading him politely but firmly off the property.

"Fuck you, fuck you, fuck you," he screamed in my face, spitting blood across my cheeks. He tried punching me, but I was used to handling drunks from my club days and kept him away. His friend followed behind us, now almost crying and begging me not to hurt him.

I yelled back that I wouldn't clobber the guy, but that he had to leave the frat house or he would get hurt. The friend was sober enough to comprehend that and attempted to plead with his blood-soaked friend, whom I'd marched out to the sidewalk.

Not being happy with a forced exit, the bleeder jumped back on our lawn and charged me, calling me a faggot and trying to entice me to fight. I could have beaten him to the ground—not because I'm a badass, but because he was drunk and I was sober. The upper hand was easily mine. Instead, I pulled out my phone and called the police.

In the past, I never would have done such a thing. But life had taught me that it was simply easier and smarter to just call the police and save myself the headache. Maybe I was too old to be in a frat after all.

Explaining to the dispatcher that a bleeding drunk was trespassing on our property and making threats, I started to give her the house information when the bleeder came to his senses and allowed his friend to take him off the lawn. I canceled the cops and hung up. Down the block, we could hear the guy punching car windows as he was dragged away.

"He was in my face," Donkey later confided. "He was screaming at me, and he wouldn't leave. I kept pushing him away, and he kept coming back and talking shit to me…Finally, I hit him."

"How many times did you hit him?" I asked, the guy's blood still spattered across my face.

"Just once."

Several months beforehand, I'd had Donkey Kong punch me as hard as he could, just to see how hard he could hit. It fucking hurt a lot, and that was in the arm. The bleeder's senses were probably dulled by liquor that night, but I had to bet he'd be in agony the next morning.

Calm settled over the inhabitants of the house, so I showered and went back to bed, chalking it up to just another night on Frat Row.

On Monday the events started coming back to haunt us. In the beginning it was only the party, which hadn't been "cleared" with the school. Then it was the cops showing up and "finding three hundred people milling around." The actual story didn't matter to the Greek liaison (a school-hired intermediary between the Greek system and the campus), a prick who was new to the job.

He was still deliberating our punishment when a call came later in the week from the bleeder's mom. Furious that her son was now missing his two front teeth and had a broken nose (that sounded about right), she was thinking about suing the fraternity for medical damages and going after Donkey Kong personally.

When the frat leaders had initially told their side of the story to the Greek liaison, they'd neglected to mention the punching incident. They figured that it was an isolated event and that hopefully the bleeder would be man enough to accept that he'd gotten drunk in a place where he had no allies. (He was a friend of a friend of a bro, but neither the bro nor the friend was at the party.)

In a different frat house and without my intervention, he could have gotten a lot worse. Instead, he whined to his mom, who whined to the school, and a lot of fuel got added to our fire. The Greek liaison, in his determination to make a statement about how he wouldn't tolerate such conduct, immediately decided to come down hard on us.

It was a dark time around the frat house. Already morale was at a low from our previous suspension, and we were certain to get the book thrown at us. We figured it couldn't get much worse…and then came the allegations of hazing.

Sigma Nu was founded as a non-hazing fraternity, a place where men behaved like men. We didn't force guys to consume dangerous amounts of water, alcohol, or anything else. All the activities we engaged in were silly, harmless, and mostly non-degrading.

There is a difference between "hazing," which puts people in challenging situations to foster brotherhood while building respect for the institution, and harassing, which makes naked men walk in single-file lines each grabbing the cock of the guy ahead of him through the guy's legs (that "elephant walk" I told you about earlier). Or leaving people out in the desert to walk home with no shoes on. Shit like that is just mean and sometimes deadly.

Harassment is what gets frats bad publicity, and everyone suffers because of it. We never harassed our guys, but unfortunately, one of the bros didn't feel that way. We'll never know which of the group betrayed the herd (some of us had our ideas), but an anonymous phone call was placed to the school when we were at our weakest.

It was definitely a bro, as the caller spilled information that only a bro would know, such as specific incidents and our rush activities. Not happy with the way we'd done things, rather than address the chapter the Judas spilled it to the school, which then got the Sigma Nu national governing board involved. It was looking like Sigma Nu wasn't going to be a chapter at Cal State Fullerton anymore.

After national came through and met the guys, surveyed the charges, and assessed the situation, they decided that the situation was overblown. We weren't guilty of hazing, which they took seriously and for which they had closed down numerous chapters in past years. The national representative made his recommendation to the school that our punishment not be severe.

But the school went in the other direction and handed down the most severe non-expulsionary sentence in its history. Our ties to the school as a social organization were cut for three years. No rushing, no promoting, no partying, and no participation in any Greek events. If any other Greek organization associated with us, they, too, would be punished. We were lepers, as far as Cal State Fullerton was concerned.

The message was clear—while they weren't kicking us out, with no fun and no recruiting for three years, we would wither and die all by ourselves. We'd be eligible for review in a year, but by that time we'd see our numbers diminish significantly. We'd toed the razor line of expulsion and walked away, and this time the fraternity was determined to clean up its act. In past years we'd ignored any punishment we got and partied harder. Now we were dead in the water. With only enough members left to cover the cost of our house, the actives began looking for alternatives.

I'd been ready to move out for months, giving my thirty-day notice and then redacting it when it became clear that the house couldn't go on without everybody there chipping in their rent monies. It was bad enough that I was in debt to the guys for over a grand; I should have been kicked out for all that back money owed. But that was when the house wasn't hurting for brotherhood and I was still a god.

Now I just looked like some freeloading asshole. My money owed wasn't affecting the present status of the chapter and I was paying the rent currently, so I had a stay of execution, but the earth beneath my feet was eroding fast. The trust was long gone.

• • •

Kerry loved me and, not recognizing a sinking ship when she saw one, offered to move out of her parents' house and get an apartment with me. We'd been together for three years, and she'd put up with all of my shit. More and more, she seemed like she was The One. Maybe it was just that I was a user and saw a good person willing to bail me out of a bad situation, but I like to think it was love.

A good deal came down the pipeline in December of that year. A two-bedroom house with a big yard, a driveway where the street-sweeping police couldn't hassle me, and very reasonable rent came to our attention. It was a wonderful situation, because the landlords were friends of Kerry's parents and didn't run a credit check on me. I had no intention of being a bad renter, but crime scene cleaning had taken its toll on all aspects of my life, financial and otherwise.

I went back and forth with my frat brothers, trying to get an answer out of them about our current situation. One minute they were intent on renting a smaller house; the next they were going to stay at the frat and work to make ends meet. I couldn't move my stuff into Kerry's and my rented house yet, because new carpets were being laid and we were going out of town to celebrate the New Year. I needed an answer, but they couldn't give me one.

So, with a day left before our trip, I called my cousin Brad to meet me with his truck to get what I could out of there. We moved almost everything—including the arcade game, the kegerator, my bed, and a standing suit of armor that Brad and his father had gotten me as a gift one Christmas—into the garage of the new house, working in the rain. (Who said it never rains in Southern California?) We worked until the night got too dark and then had to give up. I left town hoping that the rest of my stuff would still be at the frat house when I came back.

It was New Year's Day when I found out the frat didn't have a house anymore. The few brothers left had made the snap decision to up and move out, basically telling the landlord as they shut the door behind them. I still had friends among the new bros, and they had grabbed what they could of my stuff, but other than that, what was left had been stolen or destroyed. This included my high-school yearbook. What kind of a sick fuck steals a person's high-school yearbook?

Walking into the frat house the morning I came back hit me hard. As part of their exit strategy, the new brothers had hacked apart or thrown off the balcony most of the furniture and mobile components of the house. Toys, games, books, and kitchen essentials had been ripped apart, thrown, and smashed.

Two big restaurant booths that had facilitated many drinking games and poker nights had an ax taken to them, not as some beautiful gesture of release, but as an act of anarchy and chaos. Scavengers from the neighborhood and other fraternities had looted the house as we'd once looted another expelled chapter's house.

The landlord was understandably furious about the mess we'd left and the way we'd disappeared and threatened to sue. Alumni weren't notified or asked for help in saving the chapter. When they showed up expecting to drink and hang out, to bond with the new guys and swap stories of pussy had and pussy lost, they were angry. Everyone was angry. The frat had been through far too much for these youngsters to just give up the fight and walk away. They'd all gone back home to live with their parents. They weren't men of honor, just boys who didn't give a shit.

Personally, I think it was all the fault of old guys like me. We'd been stopping the hazing to a certain degree with every new generation, because we didn't want to lose pledges, but it had come at the cost of their brotherhood. They weren't molded into men who'd bend over backward to help one another, who'd come pick you up in the middle of the night to keep you from driving drunk. Some might say that real brothers would never put one another in that position, but hey, shit happens.

The young ones were sheltered whiners, never understanding what that frat house and a band of brothers could mean to someone like me. We never broke through their emotional walls and made them believe in the liberating splendor of true brotherhood, as had been done with us. In the end, non-hazing cost us our home and almost our chapter.

CHAPTER 23

pray for death: redux

Do what we can, summer will have its flies.
—*Ralph Waldo Emerson*

OUR NOW SWORN ENEMY, THE Public Guardian's office, was pissed off that we'd cleaned up the Targus house. Apparently they bitched to whomever would listen that our being in there before they could secure all the valuables and assets meant we'd "compromised the integrity of their work."

It eventually worked in our favor, though, because the residual smells of the downstairs bedroom were compromising the integrity of their noses. I had to run back out there one day and deploy a bunch of deodorizer bombs. The rotted smell had taken up residence in the walls, seeping in like some low-end paint.

I did my best to warm up to the Public Guardian representative and look professional, despite showing up in the Red Rocket, which could barely crawl up the massive hills to reach the house. She looked sorely out of place among the Mercedes, Porsches, and BMWs.

Hell, a Lexus would have looked out of place up there, and Red, with her numerous scrapes, dents, and overall cheapness, didn't do our company any favors. She was over ten years old, which was like being 109 in car years. But she made it to a gasping stop in the driveway, and I patted her dashboard appreciatively.

Apparently I made a winning impression on the guy from the P.G.'s office. He was new to the game and possibly didn't know our reputation yet. I acted professional and pretended that I knew what the hell I was talking about when it came to odor neutralization. He seemed to respond positively enough, even telling me he'd call me the next time he had a gig. He would learn our shady history soon enough, I decided, but I gave him a business card to use until he did.

Dirk was starting to learn something about quality-control issues himself. On the Targus job we'd actually used a biohazard-removal company to pick up the bags of soiled material we'd taken from the house. Typically, the bags of blood and guts would end up at the dump, preceded by us removing the magnetic business decals from the side of Dirk's truck. The signs at all the disposal places definitely read "No Dumping of Biohazardous Material," but due to our white skin and innocent faces, no one had caught on.

There was too much waste on the Targus job for us to get away with disposing of it illicitly—and the stink of it all was far too obvious. So Dirk called a local company that we'd used a few times before, just to keep anyone from getting suspicious about what we did with biohazard. It was expensive, and it came out of our bottom line, but the fact that there had been a job was good enough for me.

Summer, if the previous year had been any indication, would be a bad season for us. It was hot, dry, and somehow devoid of death. One would think that with that whole "hot temperatures raise tempers" notion there would be a buttload of summer-related murders—or even just old folks keeling over in the dusty heat. But that wasn't the case.

I was going to make good money off that suicide, though, and like a squirrel storing nuts, I was planning to sit on that paycheck and make it last the whole summer, if necessary. I felt like I was beginning to understand the ebb and flow of the death business. Sure, we'd had our problems in the past, but that was all part of the learning curve.

In the wake of the mass suicide, I was feeling very up about the crime scene business and had begun to assimilate a deeper philosophical meaning to it. I'd come to think of those of us who cleaned up dead bodies as survivors of some bigger scheme. Like we were a cosmic force sent to deal with the horrors of death, and that in dealing with it, we would emerge stronger for it. I thought of us as a unit, banded together in the face of misery and despair. It was about then when I had an incredibly moronic epiphany: *we should all get tattoos.*

I promptly set about designing an emblem—something that would strike fear in the hearts of weaker organizations, something that would show our solidarity and our dedication to the cause. It had to be dangerously original and yet ominously familiar…something akin to a pirate flag or a shark fin.

I started toying with the idea of a giant biohazard symbol. With its jagged corners and rounded intersecting half circles, it certainly looked foreboding. It was subtle, yet it sent a message that we were not to be fucked with. It was perfect. And then I found out that homosexuals who were HIV-positive often got a biohazard tattoo. That was not the kind of message I was looking to send. While we did frequently work with AIDS blood…no…no…it was just a bad idea.

I revisited the idea of the pirate flag and, with enough cobbling and the help of the oh-so-basic Microsoft Paint program, created our logo. Based on the Jolly Roger's skull and crossbones, instead of generic crossed bones it had crossed mops! But those crossed mops weren't merely decoration behind the figurehead of our skull; instead they were slammed through the skull, penetrating it from all angles like violent spears. And there was blood. A whole fucking mess of blood, splattered over the skull, emanating from the four points of impact and out onto the surrounding area of the wearer's skin. It was dark yet colorful, dangerous and yet funny, clever but not nerdy.

Below each tattoo we would get the date of our first cleanup inscribed. For Dirk and me, that would be March 14, 2007, the day that old lady put the shotgun in her mouth, sounding the death blast that gave our company life. For Misty it would be a slightly less impressive start: Happy, the dog that had been gunned down by police officers. For Kim it was the gay guy who jammed a knife in his heart in the Miami Beach–style hotel. Russ would have the mass suicide— not a bad one to pop his cherry on. Hell, even Doug, whom I hadn't spoken to since that debacle with the will, could be in on it. He would list the date when he'd arrived to help clean up that creepy doll lady's house, a solid decomp, if there ever was such a thing. We would all be united for life, a team fighting together against the corrosive elements of death. All we needed was a name.

When I presented the tattoo concept to Dirk, he was genuinely honored that I wanted to get a lifelong brand that would celebrate our work. While he adopted a "wait and see" aspect regarding tattooing himself, he gallantly stated that the company would pay for any one of us who wanted to get the tattoo ourselves.

I got mine done before he had the chance to change his mind, using my company-issued credit card to pay for it.

"The Dead Janitors Club?" the tattoo artist asked, reading the name arcing just above the skull. "What's that?"

I proudly told him about the unity and friendship borne out of being a "dead janitor," and the risk and reward of being a human vulture. I think it impressed him.

When he was finished, on my left arm just below the shoulder was a large and beautifully wicked-fresh tattoo, just as I'd envisioned it. "There'll be other people in here to get this same tattoo," I promised the artist. Kim had already committed to getting one, and I knew that once they saw it on my arm, the others would be swayed as well.

I guess I should have known better.

• • •

Summer hit Los Angeles with a vengeance. The Red Rocket had been going on four years without any sort of AC or fan inside her, and it was close to unbearable. Whenever I had the kind of spare money I could have allocated to fixing her air conditioner, it was during much cooler months, when I'd forget how oppressive the heat was.

Since doing the Targus house, I had the money to fix the AC. But there was a new problem: I didn't actually have the money. The brother of the dead man, pissing and complaining after the fact about the amount we charged him, had not yet paid the bill. And if the company didn't get paid, there was no money to pay me. And so I was more or less in the exact same situation that I'd been in the previous summer.

Although everyone said they liked my tattoo, all of a sudden nobody else actually wanted to stain their body with one. And since the company was momentarily bankrupt, Dirk's offer to foot the bill was null and void. Not that that mattered—even Kim, who had been so gung-ho, suddenly got silent about the notion of actually putting needle to flesh. I was in a very lonely club of one, and with money owed but no money forthcoming, I wasn't so warm to the idea of being in the Dead Janitors Club myself.

The summer months passed and the bills piled up, and still there was no money. Russ was involved in a game of phone tag with the Targus brother and his wife, Dirk being reluctant to turn the matter over to Schmitty, who'd then demand a fourth of what would be a lucrative pot.

The money I owed to the frat, to the hospital (which had since declined my back injury forbearance claim), and to all the student loan institutions that I'd hoped to pay off with the "six-figure yearly income" I'd read about in that newspaper article so long ago all came overdue at the same time. With no prospects other than blind hope, I told them all that they would just have to be patient. There was to be no blood from this stone.

A long, hot two months passed by with nothing in sight. The brother still hadn't paid up, though Dirk assured me he would soon. But his promises to me mirrored mine to my creditors, and I knew that none of them could be trusted. I had just enough money left for a third of a tank of gas; after that I'd be just about dead in the water. My one ace in the hole was the company credit card. My own credit cards had been suspended for delinquency, but I knew if worse came to worse, I could charge gas or food to the company card, and Dirk could later deduct it from my paycheck, whenever that came.

And then a miracle happened, like spotting a seagull after being lost at sea. Orange PD called us. It was only to clean up a car, but still that was an extra $37.50 in my time of need. Where once I'd sneered at the prospect of driving all the way down to Orange PD in the dead of summer for a pitiful $37.50, now it seemed like luxurious work on a shaded oasis. And it's cyclical, I convinced myself, believing that I could see a pattern based on all the jobs of the past. Where there was one job, even a tiny one like puke in a cop car, others would come. We would be saved after all.

I drove out there, stopping by a Home Depot to pick up some supplies that we were out of, and handed the clerk my company credit card to pay for them. She handed it back just as quickly; my ace in the hole was declined. Just as my personal credit cards were delinquent, so too was our work account. I used the rest of the money in my savings to pay for the supplies so as not to look like the pathetic loser I was.

After I finished the police car, I stopped by Dirk's house to deliver the invoice and my Home Depot receipt so that I could be paid back when the company caught up financially. I wasn't going to press him, since I was sure he was under as much financial strain as I was. Sure, he and his wife both had other jobs—full-time, stable, secure jobs, but nonetheless, they certainly had more expenses than I did, what with the kid, the big house, a pool, and multiple cars. All that cost money.

Hell, I decided, Dirk is probably as bad off as I am. He'd told me often enough that he was flat broke, and the credit card being declined, like a busted poker hand on the table, proved it. Still, I always believed his repeated vows to get me some money one day. And then he unthinkingly opened the garage to get me some additional supplies.

You see, Dirk had stuff in his garage that I couldn't pick up at Home Depot, like our biohazard suits and our special disinfectant enzyme. So when he opened the door to get them for me, there in the midst of the garage, gleaming and proud, polished to a T, and unavoidable as an STD in a Vietnam-era whorehouse, stood Dirk's brand-new cruiser motorcycle.

"My wife got that for me…for Father's Day," he said quickly, noticing the look on my face. "I didn't even want a motorcycle," he babbled on, but the damage had been done. I just nodded silently and ignored whatever else he had to say. My famine was his feast.

• • •

Weeks passed after the cleaning of that police car, and my belief that more jobs were coming diminished with each passing day. We were a busted company that had ruined our relationships with other companies that could have offered us salvation.

Kerry, now long past the "I told you so" phase in our relationship, simply wanted me to find new employment, any employment. Shit, *I* wanted to find new employment. Dirk, apparently not having anyone else to confide in, called me every so often to reveal his exciting exploits in his motorcycle-training classes and, as a side note, to empathize with me and my tough times. You never realize how much you can hate a person until you are poor and they are boasting about all the fucking fun they are having not being poor.

But "when it rains, it pours" was part of the pattern I'd seen in crime scene jobs of previous months. So it was no surprise when one day out of the blue we got a call to clean up a suicide at a Motel 6, and two other calls came in concurrently. One was for a stabbing outside an apartment complex phoned in by our buddies at Orange Police Department.

The other was for a suicide at a mansion in the upper reaches of Beverly Hills. Excited that we'd cracked the "90210" zip code but not at all sure how we'd done it, Dirk and I both knew we weren't about to miss that one. We called in Russ to handle the Orange call while we raced from the motel up to the good side of Los Angeles.

We'd handled numerous calls in Los Angeles County before, but never one for the richy-rich, and at a Beverly Hills mansion, no less. Heath Ledger had died in January of that year, so we ruled his body out as the scene we were going to service, but the whole way up, Dirk and I listed every other celebrity as a distinct possibility. It made my dick hard to think of driving past the throngs of onlookers and news reporters as we made our way through the police barricade and inside the mansion's likely massive steel gates en route to the house.

My guess was that it was Ian McKellen, star of *X-Men* and the *Lord of the Rings* trilogy. Something in his eyes made me think "suicidal" whenever I saw him on-screen. Dirk was of the opinion that it was a Steve Guttenberg type, some once-prominent actor who had long since slid into obscurity and taken the cheap way out. I thought his guess was too broad and kind of a cop-out, but then again, I didn't have a motorcycle. It had to be someone of note, though, to live so grandly way up in the heart of the hills of Beverly.

The day had already been a long one, but the thought of achieving my crime-scene-goal trifecta (mass murder, scene involving a child, and a celebrity) had me amped up enough for the work ahead.

"What if it's Oprah Winfrey?" I said excitedly.

After circling round the curved roads leading past immense steel gates and leering security cameras, we reached the address the man had given us over the phone. Twin gates taller than the cab of the truck stood impassive before us, thwarting lookie-loos and casual passersby. Two older men calmly opened the gates for us. Certainly these were the handlers for our celebrity, his PR flacks or whatever.

Outside the gate, there were no mourners, no news corps, no camera-toting mobs angling for a view, but this only got me more hyped. Clearly we had been brought in ahead of all that. We'd scooped the world! My mind reeled with possibilities: Quentin Tarantino, of a drug overdose? David Bowie, of a self-inflicted gunshot wound after a drug overdose? Rosie O'Donnell falling into a wood chipper...a big wood chipper? Sylvester Stallone, of old age? All of it seemed gloriously possible in the suddenly magical heat of summer.

The house, up a short driveway, though sizable and impressive with its gorgeous view down into the city below, wasn't exactly enormous.

Definitely not Oprah Winfrey, I thought, a little discouraged.

"Thank you for coming on short notice," said one of the men, a bespectacled fellow in his early sixties, nodding appreciatively.

"No problem...under ninety minutes, that's our motto," Dirk fairly stammered, and I could tell he was nervous as well. The closest he'd ever gotten to a celebrity was confiscating some of the guns belonging to Jesse James, the car-repair guru. I'd once seen a guy who looked a lot like Eric Roberts eating pancakes at a restaurant in Eureka, but that was about as close as I'd ever come. *Maybe it was Eric Roberts!* I thought.

The bespectacled man led us into the house while the younger man stayed outside, doubtlessly to ward off all the soon-to-be-arriving, grieving fans.

The décor of the house was nicer than that of any house I'd ever been inside before, but had an old-person vibe to it. I started thinking back to Ian McKellen. There were pictures on the walls from various decades, but we passed by them too quickly to recognize any faces.

The man led us up a stairwell inside the master bedroom (ooh-la-la) to the second-floor office of the homeowner. A massive wooden desk with ornate, antique metal objects at each corner stood beneath a large painted mural of the MGM logo. I tried to remember if Steven Spielberg had ever done any work over at MGM.

In front of the desk, spilling out of the chair and onto the carpet, was a big pulpy bloodstain, very similar to the one created by the minister with the DUI and the spill at Dodger Stadium. I'd seen variations on it in my time with the crime scene business, but never one with such a massive, gelatinous chunk collected in the center of the blood. I now knew enough to be certain that it wasn't brain.

Dirk nodded, looking around the house. "This is a nice mansion," he said, fishing for information about the owner.

"Can you do the work?" the older man said curtly, unwilling to provide us with juicy details. My mind soared toward murder and a cover-up, but the bespectacled man dashed my sweet imaginings. "My father-in-law was sick and shot himself. My wife is downstairs with her mom."

When it came time to quote a price, Dirk nearly fucked it up for us by severely overestimating what we could charge someone in a fancy house high up in the fancy hills, and then having to drop the price several thousand dollars to keep us in the game. It was a stupid mistake, but one I probably would have made myself. After all, clearly the star was dead; these were just the in-laws, clamoring for as much of the estate as they could get.

After we embarrassed ourselves and agreed on a much lower price, the man signed off and left us to our work. I'd been hoping that when he signed off on the contract, his name would offer a clue, but as a son-in-law, of course it wouldn't.

"I recognize that picture…" Dirk said pointing to a hanging black-and-white portrait photo of an old, bearded man. "The guy we're cleaning up used to be the head of MGM."

I knew what Samuel Goldwyn looked like and knew that he'd died many years ago, as had Louie B. Mayer, who also looked nothing like the man in the photograph. So if Dirk was to be believed, then surely we were cleaning up the elusive and seldom photographed "Metro" of Metro-Goldwyn-Mayer fame. It had to be him; the mural was painted on the house like a tattoo.

We had to watch our comments and our speculation, because the son-in-law was a creeper, silently ascending the stairs at odd moments to watch our work and trying to catch us stealing something. I would like to have had a souvenir from the place, but I figured the son-in-law would make us empty our pockets on the way out.

After the usual four and a half hours of cleaning and scrubbing, we were finished. Dirk even ended up taking a drawer from one of the cabinets, one that wouldn't come completely clean. He promised to "clean it at our s" and mail it back. It wasn't the sort of thing that we did, so I think he felt especially awkward about trying to scam the guy.

While it wasn't a celebrity per se, I couldn't deny that cleaning up "Mr. Metro" was an accomplishment, and he would have to count as my celebrity in the trifecta until Ian McKellen did cap himself.

I was soaking with sweat, exhausted from double cleanup duty that day and eager to get home to the comforting embrace of the Murder Bed. Dirk, though, had other plans. We were in Hollywood, home of movie stars and celluloid magic, so we couldn't go just yet, according to him. Instead, I got the long tour of locations from various films he liked, places where someone had once pointed a movie camera and yelled "Action."

Most disquieting was a trip into a filthy, shaded parking lot behind a porno store. He let the truck run as seedy, curious homosexual men looked on from their places in the alley.

"They filmed scenes from *8mm* here," he said referring to that pseudo-snuff film he liked so much. "Now it's a popular homosexual hangout." He let the truck idle there in that dark alley for a moment.

"What's going on?" I asked, glancing out at the shadowed figures hunched in corners pretending not to be curious about us.

Dirk slid his moistened fingers across the tightened fabric of my shorts, hands moving cautiously, his eyes rising to meet mine. I placed my hand atop his, producing an electric crackle as flesh met flesh.

"Your first mistake was that your eyes were bigger than your mouth…" I said, reaching in a controlled motion for my zipper. "Your second mistake was in thinking that you would be on top."

Okay, okay! So nothing happened. Dirk's not gay, and if I were gay, it certainly wouldn't be for a guy like Dirk.

But seriously, I know that in reality that anecdote goes nowhere. It's boring. Dirk just showed me some boring, fucking alleyway. I guess I don't have one of those crazy lives like people who write good, compelling memoirs…I'm impressed you stuck it out this long.

• • •

The money from the mass suicide finally came in, and along with the check from the Beverly Hills cleanup I had just enough money to pay off chunks of my overdue credit card bills, some back rent, and a piece of my hospital bills. And then I was right back where I'd been all summer long: flat broke.

Kerry kept at it, nagging me about getting out of the business altogether, but I was resolute. We'd made it through the summer, and if the previous year had been an indicator, we were priming the money pump and ready for a big payoff. Statistics had been correct about the lean summer; surely they would also be accurate about the bountiful autumn, rife with death and despair, right?

Fuck statistics.

Eager to tell people that I'd cleaned up a celebrity, I scanned the online obituaries for any mention that would confirm our cleaning of "Mr. Metro." It took a couple weeks for his obituary to pop up, but then I found him. "Mr. Metro" was actually some mid-level accountant (a well-paid mid-level accountant) for MGM and not at all the highfalutin studio mogul that Dirk was certain he was.

Devastated, I relayed the information to Dirk, who took it worse than I had. We'd both been hoping for someone of note to add to our cache. What good was living in Southern California if you didn't clean up someone famous? I was glad I hadn't stolen anything from the house—how embarrassing would it have been to get caught shilling some mid-level accountant's antique crap on eBay in the guise of "Mr. Metro"?

Autumn gave way to winter, and all too soon we found ourselves staring down the barrel of a gun called Christmas. I was poor again—really, really fucking poor. And I was going on a trip with Kerry to visit my folks in Eureka for the holidays. I had no money for any of it. Kerry knew this and offered to pay for the trip, but there was still the little matter of gifts. Everyone had gifts for me, and I couldn't show up, the big brother, the son, the important crime scene cleaner, empty-handed.

Kerry said she didn't care if she didn't get anything, but that was a bald-faced lie. If a girl ever says she doesn't care if she gets a Christmas gift or not, no matter how cool or bohemian or Jehovah's Witness she might seem, she's a fucking liar. Women want gifts, and they will fuck up your existence in the wildest ways if you don't provide them.

From big shit like withholding sex or cutting off your wiener or divorce to little shit, shit that you wouldn't even think was intentional, a woman without presents will calculatingly ruin your life. I know this seems like a misogynistic generalization, but, fellas, it's not. Once they're sure they have your love, girls want gifts.

So I had to do something. I started applying for seasonal stuff, or even just doing odd jobs for people, but it was all too late. The mortgage crunch assured it would be a very lean Christmas for everyone, and even in Orange County there just wasn't any quick money floating around.

The week I was to leave on the trip, I actually reduced myself to attempting to make gifts out of wood or paper or found objects. I was pathetically untalented, though, and most of the gifts were shaping up to look like smaller, rougher versions of the objects that they'd been previously.

It was at my most pathetic, my most poor, my most desperate wishing-on-a-star moment that one of those mortgage brokers who had helped ruin the economy found himself ruined, put a gun in his mouth, and pulled the trigger. His kid's presents "from Santa" were hidden in the attic compartment above his bedroom, so they didn't catch any blood…not that his kids would be having a merry one anyway.

The broker had made a plenty big mess of his bedroom, though, and it had been paid for by credit card, so we didn't have to worry about waiting for anything to clear, like we would with a check. Dirk was able to hand me a nice fat paycheck before I left town that I could finally buy gifts with.

It was my Christmas miracle.

CHAPTER 24

something doesn't ad up here

Don't tell my mother I work in an advertising agency—she thinks I play piano in a whorehouse.

—Jacques Séguéla, adman

I SAW THE FIRST BUMPS on my arm a day after cleaning up another dead gay guy in a hotel room. I'd cleaned up AIDS, hepatitis C, and so many other biohazards that I'd grown invincible...or so I thought.

When I first started the job, I always wore my complete bunny suit the way I'd been taught. But the ones Dirk bought were so flimsy that they would rip and shred under our bending, moving, and straining, usually to the point that having them on was more ridiculous than not.

When the first summer heat wave hit, I made the executive decision to tie my protective suit off around the waist, like I was a goddamned house painter and not someone interacting with deadly viruses. That style stuck, and both Dirk and I wore our suits like that when we didn't have clients around whom we were trying to impress with our "professionalism."

Soon I was leaving my bloodstained suit on when I broke to eat, forgetting it was even there. Sometimes in my gorging I'd drop a fry or piece of burger down the front of my shirt and then pop it into my mouth without a second thought as to where it had been.

Being fearless in the face of death became a badge of honor, and soon I was leaving my gloves off while cleaning up small areas or spots I'd missed after already shedding my gloves.

One time a bathroom sink had become blocked and had filled with blood and water. The ratio of blood to water was enough that it was impossible to peer through the water. Since blood was present, we were responsible for cleaning it and unblocking the sink. Dirk decided that one of us needed to reach a gloved hand down into the bloody mess and fish out whatever was blocking the drain.

I never thought of taping my gloves to my sleeve, so when I dipped my hand into the depths of the red mess, I felt it wash against my naked wrists, the still liquid heavy with pulp. I was lucky that there weren't razor blades or needles down at the bottom blocking that sink instead of the paper-towel wad that it turned out to be. Considering the nature of that particular suicide, razor blades and needles would have been far more likely.

"Sometimes you gotta get messy to do the job," Dirk said when I came up with bloodstained wrists. It became his credo from that point on. I was just happy something had finally replaced "Sexual Seduction."

With all the safety precautions we either ignored or outright didn't know, it should have come as no surprise to me that I was putting myself at risk for something serious, something life-threatening. And not just me, either. I had a lot of loved ones and innocents who were directly in line to suffer from my incompetence. So when I saw those small blisters popping off my flesh, my first thought was, "Oh, fuck."

Sad to say that exclamation wasn't so much for my loved ones or even for me. Instead, it came from the realization that I still had no health insurance and a long overdue bill from the one hospital I knew that would even accept someone with no insurance. My back injury had resurfaced to screw me again.

So I did the only other thing I could think of, given my circumstances. Using a sterile razor blade, I sliced the bumps off and went about my day. When they reappeared days later in different places, I hacked those ones off and went on ignoring them.

Secretly, I was freaked out, worrying that I had a serious health problem on my hands. I was already spooked by the fact that I had been smelling death everywhere I went.

Crime scene cleaning wasn't that old an occupation so no studies had been done on the long-term effects of repeated interaction with blood and guts on a janitorial level. Of course, coroners had been dabbling in the messy arts for years, but my job was different, less safe.

It didn't help any that somewhere along the way Dirk had learned that the gelatinous mound that we'd dealt with at so many jobs was in fact the spinal-cranial fluid from victims with severe head wounds. It was where most of the really nasty diseases could be found in bodies, both living and dead. It wasn't brain after all; it was disease embodied, and I'd dealt with it far too carelessly.

• • •

It wasn't just the physical and mental baggage from cleaning crime scenes that I was dealing with, either. My emotional compass had vastly skewed in the last two years. I'd lost my compassion for people.

I've always prided myself on being a "people person" in the sense that I always saw the individual along with the big picture. Empathy was one of the positive traits that I'd picked up from my mother. In high school it didn't matter who you were—nerdy, cool, fat, ugly—I'd be nice to you. Not because I expected anything for it, but because it was the right thing to do. We were all on this crazy planet together.

And then at some point in my crime scene cleaning adventures, I'd just stopped liking people. Retail work had weakened my empathy; crime scene cleaning killed it. I'd begun to break people down into market segments and to see them as walking piles of money. If the person paying the bill, the survivor, had a really nice car in the driveway, I was very comforting and falsely sincere, listening to their stories and memories with a child's sense of wonderment. In turn, they would compliment my kindness and understanding, and pay my exorbitant fees.

If the car wasn't as nice, or the home didn't reflect an economic status that would mean more money in my pocket, I was a gum-chewing asshole, bored with life and straight to the point. Especially when it came to a suicide call in the heart of Compton.

Unnaturally hot, the clinging warmth seemed to collect over the ghetto like an impenetrable bubble. Climbing out of the truck, I felt like a heat lamp was pointed directly at me. Dirk had begged off on accompanying me once again. That in itself was frustrating enough, but to make matters worse, the house bearing the address I was seeking looked poor. I'd cleaned mansions in South Orange County and Beverly Hills; what the hell was I doing risking life and limb by walking into some shithole shack on the dirty side of Compton?

A shy teenager answered the door, and I thought about being nice to him on the off chance that he'd be in the NBA someday, but the reality was that he wasn't tall enough. And he wasn't stocky enough for football.

"Is the surviving owner of the house available?" I asked, chewing hard on my gum and really letting my lips smack together.

"My mom's here," he said, clearly used to my type of personality. Without an invitation, I stepped past him into the house, with the sort of swagger typically found on some government asshole.

The mom, dressed to fit her surroundings, was on the couch trying to look strong for the children whom she probably could no longer afford to feed.

"What's the nature of your problem?" I asked gruffly. If there had been a Range Rover in the driveway, she probably would have gotten a hug.

"My husband is dead," she pointed. "Out back, in the garage."

"There isn't some crazy big dog that's going to attack me if I go back there, is there, ma'am?"

She shook her head "no," and I toted my clipboard along through the kitchen and out the back door, which was actually a sliding plastic panel. I drummed my fingers on my clipboard and wished I were cleaning up some high-end hotel. At least they could pay me what the job was worth.

I hoped that the dad had done the family a favor and died in a six-foot hole in the ground, because that looked to be all that they could afford to have me clean up. I would kick some dirt into a hole for a month's worth of food stamps.

Some paint was peeling from the side of the garage, and I flicked it off in front of the woman, watching as a bigger chunk than expected flew off. If she disapproved, she didn't say anything. She stopped at the entrance to the garage.

"I can't go any farther...please...he's in there."

I scrutinized her for a moment, trying to determine if I was being played for a fool. I wanted to ask her if she was setting me up to be killed, like it was some gang initiation or something, but she had started to cry and I figured those tears were probably legit. She turned and walked back into the house, and I, sweating under my personal Compton heat lamp, walked into the garage.

Posters covered the windows of the garage, making the room unnaturally dark. I could make out the vague shapes of engine parts strewn about the murky darkness. The place had probably been a chop shop before the dad bit it, I reasoned.

Shadows of inanimate objects gave the room an ominous feel; it suggested the sort of scene where you flick on a switch and all your friends and family jump out and yell "Surprise!" But if my friends and family were in here, I knew they were already dead. I searched for a light switch, fanning my hand across the drywall, hoping I didn't connect with a black widow spider or a broken forty-ounce bottle of malt liquor.

Finding no switch after a brief search, I left the oppressive heat of the insulated garage and went back out into the Compton sun. From there it was a short trip back into the living room where the family was still huddled, as if in prayer. I rapped my clipboard against the doorframe twice to get their attention. I was wearing my sunglasses indoors now, having put them on just before entering the house.

"I can't find a light switch...I won't go back there without light. It's a safety hazard."

"I'll turn it on," the teenaged boy volunteered from his place in the prayer huddle.

"No!" The woman barked sharply, making both the boy and me jump slightly. "You shouldn't have to see that mess."

I glanced around the innards of the house, with its brown color scheme and picture frames I recognized as being from the Dollar Tree.

She kept the place tidy, which was nice, but it was probably also an indicator that she was a stay-at-home mom.

"Are you a stay-at-home-mom?" I asked point-blank as she led me back out to the garage.

"No, I work," she said quietly, proudly. I could see that she was indeed seriously affected by having to go inside the garage.

She opened the door and, reaching into the darkness, flipped on a switch and then stepped quickly back out into the yard, desperate not to see.

"That light switch is pretty far in from the door; I wonder if that's up to code..." I mused aloud and pretended to jot something down on my clipboard.

"Smells in here," I felt it necessary to add, though I'd smelled worse; he was probably still pretty fresh. I rounded the corner into the garage and stopped short. "Holy Toledo," I exclaimed, unable to suppress my surprise. Dad hadn't done his poor Compton family any favors.

It had been done with a shotgun, but it looked more like the work of a grenade...or several grenades taped to a larger bomb. If there had been anything for the coroner to take away, I would have been surprised. It seemed as if I could account for just about every piece of the man, blown into portions no larger than a Bazooka Joe bubble-gum wrapper (and just as colorful).

The unfortunate part of his situation, other than leaving a wife and kids to fend for themselves, was the engine parts. Because he had engine parts scattered around his garage when he pulled the trigger, the chunks of him flew far and hard, embedding themselves into every nook, cranny, and chink available. The carpeted garage was oversaturated with the familiar red, lumpy mush.

Impressively, he'd managed to overkill himself. Somehow, some way, pieces of his brain had found a way to curve a corner, landing hard around a fabricated inner wall eight feet away. Stalactites of dripping guts hung from the ceiling in scattered rows. The wall posters had absorbed their fill, and worse, the flies had gotten to him by that point in the afternoon, and the air was thick with their buzzing.

I stood over engine parts rife with flesh, imagining using an unwound coat hanger to scrape biohazard from the intricate inlays of the metal, because a toothbrush would be too big to reach down and in with. It would involve multiple days of intense work, and it would have to be done cheaply, because there was no way the family could afford to pay me what it was worth in my mind.

I just couldn't justify it. I had recently pocketed a thousand dollars to clean cocktail sauce out of the carpet in a posh Los Angeles hotel because the managers thought it was a bloodstain. (To me, the shrimp tails tossed on the floor nearby were a dead giveaway that it wasn't.)

I had made another grand cleaning up an advertising big shot who killed himself in the bathroom of his boutique, beachfront Venice Beach agency with a high-powered hunting rifle. He had pulled the trigger and blown most of his head off. Apparently that hadn't done the trick, because he had had to pull the trigger again to take the other side off.

He had attempted to kill himself five years earlier, but when that failed, he had bought a life insurance policy that covered suicide…if he didn't kill himself within the first five years. The second that clause was nullified, *blam*…and then, I guess, *blam* again!

I had made decent money on those jobs. The ad guy was a lot of work, but even still, he was nothing compared to what I was seeing in that garage, and there was no way I'd be seeing adman money on this job.

Even more frustratingly, the garage was cluttered with bulky and heavy odds and ends that had been splattered with grisly human pulp, and the contents of several open cardboard boxes were effectively riddled with bio. Disgusted with the man's lack of consideration for me, I spit into one of the open cardboard boxes and left the garage to call Dirk.

Dirk, of course, was still unavailable to help, but he was also adamant that we needed the money and should bid really, really low to get the contract. Dirk had recently spent a good amount of cash on an ozone generator for the business, which was essentially an industrial machine that filtered the bad smells out of the air by somehow drawing odor to statically charged panes of glass like magnets. To me, an ozone generator seemed about as necessary a purchase and as practical as magic healing stones or a wool baseball bat.

We finally ended up using it (and charging the customers extra for its use!) on a decomposing body scene, though we didn't use it to get the decomp scent out of the air but merely the smell of cigarette smoke out of the garage. We left the machine running for two days straight, and it didn't do a fucking thing. At least we could have used the wool baseball bat like some sort of half-assed wall sponge.

I knew that the family was in a bind—the Compton cops had made them call a company to do the cleaning, and they happened to choose us. So I had them over a barrel as far as the work was concerned. But whether I wanted to deal with a payment plan stretched out over the next twenty years was something else entirely.

I could have done the work cheaply, something like a pro bono case, or because it was the sort of thing that good people did. Instead, I popped a new piece of gum in my mouth, pushed my sunglasses up on my nose, and with one thumb keeping a beat on my metal clipboard, walked back into the house.

"That is a mighty big mess your fella left you with…" I said, sounding more like a Southern sheriff than even I had meant to. "Yes, sir." I shook my head for effect, as if I had just seen some war atrocity. "The bottom line is you can't afford my company."

The widow looked at me; her kids looked at me; and through a single, small mirror hanging over the couch like wall art, I looked at me. And I hated what all of us saw. And they hated me too…at least the mom did, knowing full well the intent of my words.

"I'm not even going to offer you a price here," I shrugged, "except to say, 'Picture the most money you could imagine me charging to clean something like this. Now quadruple that.'"

I felt like a bastard as I said it. And yet, I meant it. Old Jeff would have helped them out; New Jeff just wanted to get the fuck out of there and over to a nicer zip code.

In the end, I recommended that they call Might-T-Clean, our biggest competitor. Maybe those assholes would take on a charity case.

During the long drive home, I called Dirk and told him that I bid the gig fairly, but that they wanted to "entertain some other offers." I could hear the desperation in his voice as he hoped they'd choose us. The idea of him sitting beside the phone waiting for a call that wouldn't be coming made me laugh.

It wasn't funny, though, that we frequently charged people a grand more than our competitors (from what we could gather from follow-up calls to those clients who'd declined our services) to do work that potentially would be of much lower quality. But if private citizens had it bad, private companies had it worse.

I remember heading out to clean up a nonfatal shooting incident in the parking lot of a major fast-food chain that we had an account with through our corporate headquarters. Since Schmitty had dispatched the call to us, he was entitled to his cut, and he wanted his cut to be big.

The fast-food chain was on a "per job" basis, meaning that each scene carried its own price tag (unlike our Motel 6 account, which had a flat rate for all services rendered). Schmitty thus gave the order to Dirk, which was passed verbatim on to me: "Charge the fuck out of them." Contracted account or not, I was to fleece them for all I thought I could.

Granted, in business the philosophy is that something is only worth what someone will pay for it, but this was one step beyond. We had an exclusive contract with the corporation, so the local franchises didn't have any choice but to pay what *we* thought our services were worth. And according to Schmitty, our services were worth a fuck of a lot.

I set out with the notion of charging them at least fifteen hundred dollars, but when I got there I was shocked to see that the job didn't require anything more than quickly wiping up a couple tiny blood spots and sweeping up some windshield glass in the parking lot. The job took me maybe ten minutes, and I used their broom and dustpan to do it—and charged them twenty-five hundred dollars for my time. This left the franchise owner furious in my wake and bitching about how one of his employees could have done it for "seven dollars an hour." I gave him my "welcome to capitalism" wink and was on my way.

But that sort of thing was in the past—that was the kind of thing that someone without freaky bumps polluting his body could do. I'd begun a sort of metamorphosis into something else, something I hoped would resemble a better kind of person.

CHAPTER 25

mr. klima goes to washington

The villain is the hero of his own story.

—Unknown

THE JOKE IN CRIME SCENE cleaning is "If we die, who is going to clean us up?" Our clients, feeling clever, say this to us frequently, each believing that they are the first one to consider it. Hell, we say it ourselves conversationally to break the stress of what it is we do. In cleaning up the deceased, we have to separate ourselves from them and not consider how easily it could be our body on the slab and a different batch of assholes wrist-deep in what was once our face.

And yet with those bumps on my arm and no money to have them looked over by a professional, the "industry joke" was anything but. My anxiety overwhelmed my sense of invincibility and forced me to weigh the possibilities of my own demise. I have to admit that I didn't like the conclusions I came to.

As much as I don't like to consider myself "expendable," I certainly am. I don't have any dependents to care for; the fate of the world doesn't necessarily hang on my shoulders; and if I blipped off the map tomorrow in a plane crash, few outside my immediate family would mourn me for an extended period of time. In short, I am as human (in the most negative connotation of the word) as the rest of you.

I've never fooled myself into believing that human beings were anything more than self-aware animals, ranking above the rest of the fauna only because we believe we do. I'd like to believe in heaven; it seems like it would be a comforting place. At the same time, though, I don't like to believe in hell. The two of them together are so intimidating that I find more solace in the notion of just ceasing to exist. I will slip out of consciousness at some point, and that will be that. No heaven, no hell, no pearly gates or divine being sitting in judgment.

Do I like this idea because, with the way I've lived my life on earth, I think I am in danger of going to a "hell"? I don't know. With my health scare looming, it wasn't so much "hell" that I was considering so much as: 1. How would I go? and 2. What regrets do I have?

If the bumps on my arm turned out to be AIDS, cancer, or a series of tumors that were devastatingly inoperable, how long would I endure? Because I don't currently believe in life after death, that means I don't believe in any religious repercussions of suicide. And that belief is a freedom unto itself. I just know that if I'm fucked anyway, I'm not going to waste something as potentially hilarious as my life. I've seen too many wasted lives, both professionally and personally.

But strictly professionally speaking, I've also seen too many wasted deaths. Your death is your last chance to do something profound, something that resonates…something that endures. If you perceive yourself as worthless in life, don't make your exit vanilla as well.

If my bumps turned out to be fatal, do you think I would take a razor to my wrists in the bath? Do you think that I would do anything as mundane as allow the disease to consume me? Fuck no. As some figure from my past, notable only for their motto, once uttered to me: I don't want to be laid in my grave; I want to slide into that mother-fucker sideways!

Ten-four to that! We should all truly aspire to such an entertaining exodus. If my bumps turned out to be the end of me, I decided, I would pack myself with dynamite and candy and then go down to the steps of city hall with a megaphone.

Now I wouldn't do anything as selfish as taking anybody out with me. (How I've changed from the days of my youth when I thought about becoming a serial killer!) But I would make it a point to gather a large crowd to bear witness to my final moments.

Stripping the whole affair of any seriousness, I would do some stand-up or sing a silly song, something that would make people say, "Hey! Troubled or not, this guy has a fun-loving personality…we should invite him to our next barbecue." Then I'd hope a police sniper would notice that underneath my trench coat, I was packed to the gills with dynamite and Tootsie Rolls, rigged to go off when he shoots me between the eyes.

About a second later the metropolitan downtown would be a confetti rain of Jeff and Tootsie Rolls. (No, I'm not going to spring for expensive candy if I'm going to kill myself.) There is just something wonderful about the knowledge that some asshole in the crowd would gather up some of that candy to snack on later.

Now, since you have not heard on your local news that some LA fat ass painted the cityscape with hunks of his viscera and budget candy, you have probably surmised that the bumps on my arm were not, in fact, fatal tumors sapping the life out of me.

No, I broke down and had them checked out, and they turned out to be chemical burns from using the heavy concentrations of cleaners and solvents so instrumental to our work. Because I was not wearing my protective bunny suit correctly, I had exposed myself to my own unsafe tools. Whether my foolish actions will resurface down the road in the form of more serious health problems remains to be seen, but for the moment, I'm fine. When I stopped using the chemicals, the burns went away and haven't resurfaced.

But my brush with what could have been a brush with death sobered me to my position in life and gave clarity to the second of my concerns: What would I regret if I knew I was going to die?

As it stood, my single biggest regret in life was not mailing that letter several years ago—the one that would have exposed Dirty Pete, my boss at the porn shop, for the piece of shit that he was. I regretted letting Christopher's death be nothing more than a minor inconvenience in Pete's day-to-day activities.

Even if nothing came of it, I told myself, I would feel better about me. It is too late to mail that letter and have an impact for the better on the lives of those involved, but now I had an opportunity to make a difference once more. I was through with being a weasel; it was time for a new perspective in life, even if that new perspective meant being a rat.

I realized that I wanted something consistent in my life, something that I could believe in. Policemen, firemen, paramedics, doctors, nurses, all of these positions function first and foremost as guardians of human frailty. These are the people whom we need in our hours of terror and uncertainty. Above all, these are the strangers whom we should be able to trust implicitly with our well-being.

The people who undertake these assignments should be above reproach, not tainted by the characteristics that we associate with used car salesmen or lawyers. And what I should have realized much earlier was that the crime scene cleaner, while he doesn't have the same responsibilities as a police officer, also serves people at their most fragile.

I had been allowed into people's homes and trusted to do a job well, recognized as a professional who eliminated dangerous biohazards for the benefit of remaining loved ones, and it was all too clear to me that I had failed. Dirk, and even Schmitty, who from his perch up north was more than happy to collect the checks we sent him, never instilled any sense of morality or quality control. We had all blown it.

I can't speak for our competition. I don't know the standards by which the other crime scene cleaning companies of the world govern themselves; I only saw them in action on jobs where cheapskates called us in collectively to outbid one another. Based on their appearances, though, and by the caliber with which they conducted their search for biohazard, I would say that those companies weren't much better than we were.

Crime scene cleaning is a new industry, and it still has a lot of bugs to be worked out. Most people never even know our industry exists until the police mandate that they call us in to erase a loved one from their walls and carpet. The kinds of people whom crime scene cleaning attracts as employees (me not withstanding) are pathetic. I'd put us on the same level as "carnies." We are the dirty, wretched refuse of society who have no qualms about cleaning up the dead.

Hopefully, O.C. Crime Scene Cleaners was the worst of them. Our ignorance and our indifference toward our job and its responsibilities potentially endangered us and other people, innocent people who foolishly trusted us without ever stopping to check for certifications that we didn't have. It scares me to realize that any jerk-off who wants to make a lot of money fast can go to a hardware store and walk out with a dangerous new career for less than thirty dollars.

Some spray bottles, a few basic household chemicals (Simple Green and bleach), gloves, paper towels, and a trash bag or two is all it takes in most cases, and for that and the price of registration on the list of biohazard remediators in your state, any unscrupulous asshole can enter your home at the behest of the police department to wash away your loved ones. The police didn't even stick around in most of our cases, and when they did, if I ever asked what they thought of my level of quality, all of them would essentially shrug and say, "You're the expert."

To handle blood or infectious waste in the state of California, legally you are required to "have formal training in blood-borne pathogens, operate under a written blood-borne pathogens plan, have use of approved safety equipment, been offered hepatitis vaccination, and be provided with sanctioned methods of transporting, storing, and disposing of biohazardous waste."

I didn't know any of that. I had to get it off the website of a rival crime scene cleaner (whether they actually adhere to those standards themselves, I couldn't say). And while I certainly liked Dirk as a person, I could no longer let him endanger innocent people in his pursuit of early retirement. So one day I placed a call to OSHA.

OSHA, for those of you living on Mars with your head up your ass, is the U.S. Occupational Safety and Health Administration. They are the federal government entity that regulates companies to ensure the safety of both workers and the general public—in other words, people like you. OSHA had been our unseen nemesis for two years, a threat just past the horizon, never catching wind of our actions and likely oblivious to the crime scene cleaning industry at large.

It was a scary call for me, because I didn't know what the result of my actions would be. Would I go to jail? Would I get slapped with a fine? Would Dirk go to jail? He was married with a kid and a solid career as a sheriff, so the last thing I wanted was for him to end up in jail. I would have preferred to go to jail to have spared him from it; I didn't have a family, much less a young, impressionable son or a career in law enforcement. But I knew that it had to stop. Once before I'd done the wrong thing in a bad situation, and my emotional well-being had suffered for it. This time there would be no mistakes.

Dialing, I felt like the king of the rats. I tried to summon Marlon Brando's character in *On the Waterfront* as my role model, but all I could manage was Elia Kazan, the director of the film. He had gone before the House Committee on Un-American Activities, chaired by Senator Joseph McCarthy, and provided names of suspected Hollywood communists. Allegedly, Kazan made *On the Waterfront* to paint his stool-pigeon antics as something heroic. I certainly didn't feel heroic.

After two short rings that even sounded governmental, a gruff voice picked up. He didn't bother identifying himself, only asking what he could do for me, the rat.

"I want to lodge a complaint against a company."

"Go on," he said as if he'd heard it all before, and likely he had.

"It's a crime scene cleaning company."

"Crime scene cleaning, huh?" his voice raised slightly. Maybe he hadn't heard them all before. "What is the nature of the offense?"

"I've got a laundry list of complaints, sir."

"Go ahead."

"Well, to start with…I've worked for the company for over two years and never had any sort of training ever, me or anyone else. Nobody knows what they're doing over there."

"Okay."

"Are you getting this?"

"You hear that?" he said, stiffly, and in the background I could vaguely hear a light scratching sound. "That's the sound of me writing." He was probably scratching his nutsack. "What else?"

"We throw biohazardous material away in normal trash cans, take it to the dump, and just toss blood-soaked stuff out most of the time.

I've thrown AIDS-infected stuff into the trash cans of rival fraternities, that sort of thing."

"What else?"

Suddenly I stumbled. What else was there? I promised the guy a laundry list of complaints, but I was so anxious about making the call that I hadn't actually written any of our offenses down. The stealing wasn't his jurisdiction, nor was any of the other bullshit that came to mind. In desperation, I blurted out: "Brain fell into my eye. That's how we decided we needed to get goggles."

He kind of laughed at that and then took the company info down, as well as my name. My visions of helicopters, foot soldiers, and doors being kicked down dissipated after that laugh, and I wasn't at all sure if that made me happy. While I didn't want to get Dirk into trouble, I felt bad for everyone who would continue to be at risk from the company and its habits.

The G-man's promise to "send a letter" that would "request details of the company's safety practices" didn't sit well with me at all. Dirk wasn't stupid; he would squirm out of it and clean up his act for a while, but then he would go right back to how he'd done things in the past and I would be left to fuck off.

I didn't know what else I could do, though. I wasn't sure I wanted the responsibility of crime scene cleaning in the hands of the government. They fucked up my mail delivery on a near-daily basis, so I could only imagine what they'd do when it came to cleaning up my grandma. That thought alone was almost more than I could bear.

At the same time, private corporations doing the work had led to the creation of our company and likely others just as unscrupulous as we were. In the end, I did what any other person does when they want to bring light to some bullshit self-serving cause: I wrote a tell-all book.

Fuck it; let America decide if they want to let the Dirks of the world thrive off their misfortune. All I can do is push the issue to the forefront and enable you to make up your own mind. Maybe you're someone who has more knowledge, more power, or more courage to act than I do. Maybe you're not. Maybe you're just some dickhead reading this the same way that dickheads the world over read the graffiti on bathroom walls. But that doesn't matter to me. The fact that I've gotten you this far convinces me that, for once, I did something right.

omega

If you do not change direction, you may end up where you are heading.
—*Lao Tzu*

AFTER TWO YEARS IN THE crime scene business, taking money from grieving widows, experiencing the wonders and pains of being on call 24/7 and the highs and lows of my personal finances, I was done. I was still comfortable with the work itself, but the emotional baggage that came from being in league with Dirk had brought me to the point where I could no longer cope.

Another dry spell early in 2009 (usually busy months for us) had Dirk bewildered. To me, it made perfect sense. We'd fucked over and chased away the business connections in Southern California that had sustained us the previous year, and there simply wasn't anyone left to give us work.

I took a hard look at my life and was disgusted by what I saw. I hadn't paid my taxes in two years; I was flat broke—in serious debt to the fraternity, to the school, and to student loans. I'd maxed out my credit cards trying to keep afloat, and there was no quick income in sight. At least with BevMo I had known when money was coming. Dirk once again owed me cash, and once again couldn't afford to pay. I wasn't such an alpha male that I was going to break his legs over it. Instead, I knew it was time to find a new job.

None of the crime scene cleaning companies in the area were hiring, which was probably for the best, as I was more of a liability than anything else. I turned to what I had been studying all those years at college: advertising. But by that point the economic downturn was in full swing, and I was competing for scarce jobs against people who had decades more experience than me or with a sense of ambition and family connections coming out their assholes. I reeked of burnout and had the surly, disenfranchised demeanor to go along with it.

Adamant that whatever job I took offered all of the perks and none of the negatives associated with crime scene cleanup, I was going to be tough to please. I required a job that I could mostly do from home, where I could set my own hours and make a lot of money. I wanted a consistent paycheck. No more phone calls from indifferent police officers wanting me to mop up drunk puke at three in the morning and then again at six, and never, ever again would I have to cold-call on any business for anything.

Incredibly, I got an audition from a high-powered lawyer seeking a brilliant copywriter (his words) to revamp his company websites and press releases, of which there were thousands. I guess he thought they would be valuable in wrangling in new business; I didn't question it, as he was the multimillionaire and I was the slacker wannabe.

Through emails and phone calls, we both agreed that my copywriting skills were superlative and an ideal fit for his company. I passed his numerous written tests with flying colors, which pleased him. Flexible about the hours I'd work, he was agreeable to a large salary, plus he was a big Lakers fan, which pleased me. It would have been perfect.

But somewhere along the way, I had picked up some stupid-ass notion of loyalty. Looking at Dirk, I saw a business that had struggled through its existence for two long years. I knew I should have stepped away gladly, leaving a sinking ship for one with real potential. And yet, I couldn't.

I was Dirk's first mate, and while I wasn't exactly prepared to go down with the ship, Dirk had taken a chance on me at a time when no one else would. I didn't feel like I owed him anything, but I couldn't just leave the business high and dry. I was certain that without me, what was left of O.C. Crime Scene Cleaners would collapse. And while that would have been best for the denizens of Orange County, I had helped to build that pathetic company from scratch, and that counted for something, too. I even had a tattoo to show for it.

And so the copywriter job that everyone agreed I would be perfect for fell through in the way that anything one has mixed feelings about usually does. Missed emails, an incoherent live interview, and an overwhelming abundance of self-worth sent that job packing. The lawyer paid me generously for my time, and once again, I was left to fuck off.

• • •

Dirk had the notion that, as a business, we were not dead in the water; a sudden growth spurt could quickly realign our trajectory back into the black. The first step of his plan was to change me from the "independent contractor" he had claimed I was so that he wouldn't have to provide medical coverage, tax information, or a 401(k), to a vice president of the company.

It was the same old trick he'd used way back at the beginning of the business, the bait and switch to screw me out of whatever he didn't want to pay for at the moment. Except now he wanted me to make even less money—never mind that he already couldn't pay me what he owed me.

I might have considered that a fair compromise had there been genuine logic to it, some semblance of a plan to increase the overall revenue stream, thus balancing my loss. No, he whined, it was because he wasn't making enough money from *his* business. When it was about weathering the hardships, it was *our* business; when it was about income, it was *his* business.

In exchange for my lowered income, though, he said without irony, I would have the eventual right to stock options in *our* company. As if we were somehow going to split off from Schmitty and one day soon go public. I nodded seriously, as if genuinely considering the offer. But I felt like the biggest fucking moron on the planet, he who deserved all manner of bad things to happen to him, the loyal company man.

Dirk's second plan for the salvation of the company was location.

We had pigeonholed ourselves professionally by relegating the business to Orange County when, really, we were so much more than that. We were Riverside County and San Diego County, and most importantly, *we were Los Angeles County*. We'd done large amounts of work in those other counties, and yet we were potentially ostracizing them by considering ourselves "Orange County."

And so, with the speed that spurred all of Dirk's ideas to fruition, we had new shirts, new hats, and a new logo, all of which proclaimed our true intent: *Southern California* Crime Scene Cleaners. Like Alexander the Great and Genghis Khan before us, we were expanding our empire.

An empire needed troops, though, foot soldiers to do its bidding, so Dirk turned to that most unreliable of employment centers—craigslist—to once again bring about our salvation.

Dirk was certain, in that way that people who aren't even a little bit fucking certain always are, that he could find people willing to buy their own equipment and do their own legwork to collect clients, all under our banner, and that these "entrepreneurs" would pay us 50 percent of their take.

Dirk would divide Los Angeles into sections; each new hire would then control a section and respond to the multitude of calls that were certain to blaze up from their respective area with just a bit of applied promotion. Once we had the Los Angeles leg of our business in order, we would then branch out to Riverside.

I agreed that growth would help us. Maybe even a business plan with a series of long- and short-term attainable goals would do the trick. But did I think that we would find souls willing to, in effect, start their own biohazard remediation business and turn half their proceeds over to us? Hell, no.

So you can imagine the size of the crow I ate when Dirk's posting received more than three hundred enthusiastic responses in the first hour. It seemed that I had vastly miscalculated the impact of the recession, for apparently Los Angeles was teeming with eager business investors.

Incredulous, I asked Dirk if he had mentioned in his post that people would in fact be paying up front for their employment, aware that what he was proposing was essentially a pyramid scheme. And as Dirk once again fumbled for the words to explain that he had not exactly conveyed this to any of our would-be hires, I again nodded politely and made a mental note to kick my own ass.

Dirk was adamant, though, that our good intentions would shine through and we would find diamonds in the rough, the building blocks of our empire. He proceeded with his plans to conduct two separate group interviews with the candidates he handpicked from his list. At my urging, he at least implied that there would be some costs involved.

We finagled free conference-room use from an apartment complex where we'd (unbeknownst to them) thrown away much of their biohazard and set up the two meetings where we hoped to find the cream of the crop. Hating my life and unwilling to stake my financial future on "stock options" or pyramid schemes, once again I secretly began a search for a new job.

I'd blown it with the lawyer, and no real advertising firms were beating down my door, much less sending me emails confirming that they'd received my résumé. With Kerry paying all the bills for both of us, I decided I needed to broaden my employment horizon.

On the day of Dirk's job seminars, I slipped out at the break to turn in my résumé for a job as a repo man. *This is what my college degree has gotten me*, I thought. *I'm going to have a career repossessing property from other deadbeats.* They never called me back. Even the losers thought that I was worthless.

Dirk's seminars had attracted seven interested candidates, including a hot chick with big tits. Many more people had been invited, but after Dirk had revealed his true intentions about "some costs being involved," we no longer had the cream of the crop to choose from.

But I watched as Dirk spun the same line of bullshit he had pulled on me, showing everyone the same article mentioning the six-figure income—only now his speech had become more grandiose and profound, as he had experience to draw on. Their eyes, as mine once had, glazed over with the idea of lavish consumerism. They too would be screwed over by Dirk, which wasn't his intent. He was genuine about everything he said, but he was also genuinely misguided in his ambitions. Of course, he also knew how to spin some lies.

I listened dispassionately, feeling like I was wasting my time, and only broke in once, in disgust, to correct Dirk's claim that we'd cleaned up "several celebrities" but due to "contractual obligations" were not allowed to reveal their names. Dirk was hurt that I shot him down in public, but our future franchisees had at least the semblance of a right to know what they were actually getting into.

At the end of the day, we had three people clamoring for the work, costs be damned. Both of us were delighted to see that the hot chick was among them. She was an older broad named Penny, a total fucking MILF, as the hipsters would say, though it looked like any kid who had breast-fed off her had caught a mouthful of silicone (not that it wouldn't have been totally worth it).

The other two, from different sections of LA, were an old woman from Brooklyn (by way of Beverly Hills real-estate brokering) and a doughy middle-aged guy who seemed good with numbers. The Brooklyn dame, Bitsy, had a sharp tongue and was oblivious to tact. I pushed for her because I was curious to see how she would react to decomposing flesh. I was betting that she would hurl and then make some off-color remarks to the widow.

I was against Melvin the dough ball from the start, because he immediately started spouting his love for Jesus, which would have been fine if he were auditioning for a job as a priest. I'd always had back luck with overly religious types and never quite found the restraint not to mouth off a bit around them. Dirk wanted Melvin badly, though because he seemed like he had the acumen to make a buck or two.

We sent the three out with a promise that we would hold a training seminar for them, the same training seminar that I had never received. In the meantime, if we got a call in one of their sections, they could tag along.

Needless to say, we never trained them, and all too quickly the first call came in for a decomp at an Extended Stay America hotel in Melvin's zone, early on a Sunday morning. A fireman staying in the room had died while working on loan from Utah. I was quick to point out to Dirk that Extended Stay America was a corporate account through Schmitty and not something that Melvin had produced. Dirk was quick to point out that he himself couldn't make it, probably because he was busy sitting around drinking coffee and staring at a wall.

Alone and fuming, I called Mel on my way out, anticipating that he'd meet me there. Mel refused to show up to his new job until church services were over. Needless to say, I wasn't going to hang around a stinky hotel room waiting for God-boy to finish up. Dirk for once agreed, and so Mel was fired before he was officially hired. And then there were two.

Bitsy, the tough-talking New York woman, pissed and bitched that she couldn't deal with the headache of setting up a business after all and decided that instead of working for us, she was going to move down to Florida to live with her sister. And so, all too quickly, from that initial list of more than three hundred, there was only one.

Dirk was eager for the hot chick to work out, so he talked up her new career as best he could, enticing her to stay. Penny was married with children, but if nothing else, she was eye candy for the business. Dirk half-joked that we could make extra money by releasing a "Girls of Crime Scene Cleaning" calendar. With Misty, Kim, and Penny, I had to give it to him—it would have been a bestseller.

It took several weeks, but finally we received a call out for another decomposing dead body at another hotel. This one was a girl, dead of a drug overdose, who'd expired on the mattress. Dirk gave me the call out to go with Penny and train her in the mystic arts of scrubbing and cutting. He couldn't make it to this one either, but this time Dirk truly sounded remorseful.

I had been turning in another résumé, this one to a strip club (as a bouncer, I swear) and ended up being two hours late for my rendezvous with Penny the MILF. Driving fast in the work truck and cursing up a storm, I was already irritated by having to do a training gig. So when I rounded the corner, the tires of the truck squealing, and saw some dickhead with a video camera pointed at me, it didn't help matters.

It turned out that Penny with the big tits wasn't as interested in having a career in crime scene cleaning as she was in having a career in reality television. She was an attractive woman living in Los Angeles, so that should have been obvious to me, but go figure. She was going to use the day's footage to secure a production deal with some "industry connections" she had.

The dickhead with the expensive video camera was her husband, a Eurotrash type with a goofy accent and a penchant for low-angle "power" shots. Even as I called Dirk to bitch about the Eurodork's presence, he was filming and lisping for me to "act more natural."

I climbed back into the cab of the truck and slammed the door. It wasn't the thought of being on camera that got me. Dirk had once conspired with Schmitty to bring in a crew from the National Geographic Channel to film an hour-long special on us. The film crew never materialized, though, and I finally had to chalk it up to Dirk being Dirk. It was for the best that they hadn't appeared anyway, because we were going through one of our slow periods and the National Geographic Channel would have ended up with a one-hour special about crime scene cleaners playing cards.

Now, with a camera actually on me, a more pressing concern had materialized. None of what we did complied with any state legislation concerning the handling of biohazardous materials, and I was ill-equipped to teach someone else how to clean up a crime scene. If any true crime scene professionals saw footage of me attempting the work, I would be crucified.

Dirk, of course, sided completely with Penny and her massive tits. The work would be filmed, regardless of whether it was done correctly or not, because, as he didn't have to tell me, he wasn't going to be the one doing it.

To my enormous satisfaction, the hotel employees had drastically overstated the horror of the scene, and Penny found her camera filming little more than what appeared to be a small pee stain on the sheets. It was a beautiful crash course for her in how the job was occasionally nothing more than glorified janitor work. Still she scrubbed at that minute stain with all the phony zeal of your typical wannabe actress.

I wanted to laugh, but I'm embarrassed to admit that I got caught up in the excitement of filming and didn't want to ruin a take. I even uttered some on-camera platitudes that would make Jerry Springer cringe with embarrassment, all in the name of "show-biz." The European said it was all "great stuff" with his unidentifiable accent and even had me stick around to film a segment where I spoke directly to the camera, just identifying myself and making a comment about some of the gnarly stuff I'd seen.

He said I was a "great character" and would definitely be a regular on the show as soon as it got picked up. Apparently Penny's first job didn't provide compelling enough footage to impress her "industry connections," though, because I never saw her or her goofy husband again.

The money from the hotel job wasn't nearly enough to set me back on track or convince Kerry that she should continue to pay most of the bills on the small house we were renting. After I had shown myself to be completely inept and unable to land another job on my own, her father took pity on me and got me a job as a medical courier, picking up blood, urine, and stool samples along with the occasional biopsy or Pap smear. It wasn't glamorous or interesting work, but it was full-time and would get me out of the crime scene world.

I wasn't man enough to tell Dirk straight out that I was throwing in the towel, thereby damning the opportunity that he had hoped would be his path out of law enforcement and his nest egg for retirement. He deserved to hear I was making a clean break, but I was spineless and ashamed, and waffled through the whole conversation.

I assured him that I was still as available as ever…except for the forty hours a week from early afternoon to late evening when I would be completely unavailable. He was understanding and claimed that he would get Russ, Kim, or Misty to fill in when I couldn't work.

That was more bullshit, and I knew it even if he didn't. Misty had been in a bad car accident and was recuperating while relearning how to walk. (We sent her a cookie basket!) Kim had taken another job out of necessity and didn't have the freedom to work on-call anymore, and Russ's wife wanted him out of the biohazard business, period. He had young kids to think about, and she didn't like the deadly disease aspect of our industry. Dirk couldn't possibly do full-time either, and if he didn't realize that the company was doomed, he would soon enough.

• • •

The last job we worked together was a doozy. Yet another mortgage lender in South County had run out of people to fuck over in the burgeoning recession and had gone a little nutty. After driving home, presumably from drowning his sorrows at some bar for smug former mortgage-industry pricks, he smacked into his neighbor's car with his convertible. Evidently, that was the last straw, because he drove from the scene, parked his car in his garage, and shut himself up inside his house.

When a sheriff and a tow truck driver approached with the intent of towing his car, the mortgage nut made the lifestyle-altering decision to shoot at them; this action begat the arrival of the SWAT team, who were only too happy to shoot back. They filled the house full of gas pellets and PepperBalls, which were horrible sensory-impairing grenades full of an overpowering pepper-smelling dust.

When the SWAT team finally charged the house, they found him bleeding out of his skull with a self-inflicted gunshot wound. He'd been hiding in one of his large closets, surrounded by material possessions that weren't important enough to display throughout the house but too expensive to throw away.

The SWAT team dragged his barely alive body down the carpeted stairs and out of the house, away from the foggy whiteness of the exploded gas pellets and the choking air of the PepperBalls. The mortgage nut finished dying in the street, under the watchful eyes of attending paramedics and curious neighbors eager to tell each other their own versions of the events.

The whole street had been cordoned off with yellow police tape, but Dirk and I drove straight through, snapping the caution line for the amazement of the neighbors and the attending press. It was our last hurrah together, though at the time, Dirk didn't know it.

Driving up on the scene, I hopped out to start scrubbing at the sizable bloodstains amid the gauze wrappers and disposable suction cups (for the EKG monitor) littering the street. We'd actually arrived earlier, but the body was still on-site. We couldn't do anything while his remains clogged up our workspace, so we went for tacos and returned an hour later ready to rock 'n' roll. Dirk haggled with the available officers, trying to find a detective willing to put his name on the contract and sign his ass away.

One of Dirk's police friends had come through yet again, keeping the company from absolute ruin once more. We had the ugly habit of being on the cusp of utter ruin and then getting snatched back from the edge by some fortunate misfortune.

For too long I had used such events to stave off Kerry's "I told you so's," but as bitchy as she had sounded, she had been right. Maybe I had been right about the potential of the crime scene business, and maybe it had saved me from retail. Maybe given enough time with an outside source of income, one day far down the road we even would have become a profitable company. But those were far too many maybes.

Finally, Dirk found a willing detective to sign, but that detective wasn't stupid enough to agree to a contract that would let us completely clean the house. A contract guaranteeing that might have even given Kerry pause about my taking my new job. The payoff for a chemical scrub was substantial.

Essentially, the entire interior of the house and all the dead man's worldly possessions had been destroyed by the presence of the gas, which could never be effectively scrubbed out of anything porous. It destroyed his many giant flat-screen TVs, his amazing sound system, his wall art, and everything else he had thought would help define him.

Even the convertible was ruined. A gas canister fired from a SWAT bazooka had punched a hole through the metal garage door and splintered the shatterproof glass of his windshield before deploying in the front seat, its noxious gas saturating the car's interior.

The city would foot the bill only for what was done outside, meaning the blood stains that led from the front door of his impressive home, which giant fans were trying in vain to aerate, down into the sloped gutter of his fancy street. In death he had created a perfect metaphor for his life.

As I scrubbed at the blood and disposed of spent gas canisters, a scratchy burning sensation suddenly overwhelmed me. I coughed sharply several times, but the burning intensified and spread to my eyes, which were wet with tears. In their attempt to clear the house, the fans had deployed the effects of the gas on me. Choking with the bitter sensation of pepper, I crawled from the scene, gasping.

After that we donned our masks, not only to complete the work but to hide the embarrassing flush on our faces that was due only in part to the aftereffect of the gas. Several cops also caught a face full of the stuff and had to relocate, so my shame quickly abated and I didn't feel so much like the greenhorn.

While the city wasn't going to pay to clean up the house, they realized that they couldn't very well leave the place with all the windows shot out and gas seeping from the openings. A new contract would be created to hire us to board up the windows. Dirk was certain that the two of us could do it, but I insisted that we needed to subcontract this one out. We didn't have ladders, any other requisite equipment, or even the know-how to do the job, particularly under the watchful eye of the detective who'd warily agreed to sign off on a contract once more.

We had never met the window man Dirk subcontracted to, but Dirk vouched to the on-scene police superiors that he was our "regular guy" and someone we used all the time for such work.

"He's a real professional, just like us," he reassured them.

While waiting for the guy to arrive, Dirk and I wandered through the house, the haze of thick smoke lying on top of the air, threatening to choke us if we removed our masks. It was heartbreaking to see all of the man's perfectly beautiful electronics wasted, and it just made me angrier about my own situation.

I'd had an opportunity to crack into the upper echelon by writing copy for that lawyer. I had been guaranteed a regular salary and even benefits. I could have been a successful and productive member of society instead of wandering through a dead man's house wondering if anything worth stealing had been left unaffected by the gas.

The window man himself was a spectacle. The sort of man who played Santa Claus at Christmastime, he was rotund and old and didn't look as if a ladder could support his ample presence. And though he had the physical characteristics of Santa Claus, his personality was more in line with the Grinch. The mopey teenager he had as an assistant seemed to agree with that assessment.

From the moment he clambered out of his truck, the old-timer was spitting out invectives about what he would and wouldn't do, and how much it was all going to cost. Dirk took that number, doubled it, and sold it to the police authority. It was our typical method of operation for the business, and if I'd stuck around longer with the company, I'm sure I would have seen the tactic come back to bite us in the ass again.

Our window man hadn't been up on the ladder long when suddenly he started sputtering a form of vernacular that could be best described as old-man-isms. It was the sort of shit that Yosemite Sam blubbered when he got angry, the "hornswoggle this" and "consarnit that" speech that hadn't been uttered by a human in nearly sixty years.

He, too, had become a victim of the SWAT gas. From his perch high on a ladder, he was now gasping, red-faced and frantic. I didn't feel bad for him; we'd offered him a mask, but he'd rebuffed us with something like "Real window men don't need such contrivances."

As the old coot cried, cursed, and blindly attempted to make his way down the ladder, I turned in time to watch the on-scene detective walk away from it all in frustrated disgust. It was a familiar emotion to me, one I had seen on many law enforcement officers' faces after they realized they'd hired the Orange County equivalent of the Three Stooges to do their work. I wouldn't have to see that look much longer, though.

The house was to be turned over to the Public Guardian's office until next of kin could be established, so I knew that the chance of Crime Scene Cleaners getting a call to do the major work was nonexistent. They would already be furious just knowing that we'd been in the house compromising the integrity of their property. Smiling through my gas mask, I left a business card on the table right by the entrance. When the smoke cleared enough in a few days and they could finally enter, seeing that business card in the midst of the scene would really piss them off.

• • •

My last job for Crime Scene Cleaners came in the form of a favor. A drunk man had wandered out on the highway and been splattered by a car. The sister of one of Dirk's police coworkers was driving the second vehicle to hit the drunk. In a way, she had it worse than that initial car, because the drunk had flipped over the first car and exploded beneath her car, his body getting caught in the axles.

She dragged what was left for the fifty or so feet it took her to come to a complete stop. Her car was a little sedan, low to the ground, so the chassis and the paved highway had acted like a blender, spraying pieces of the man up into the hot engine parts, where they sizzled and stuck.

Dirk and his fellow officer had taken the car to a do-it-yourself car wash and sprayed water beneath the car to wash off what they could. But much of the man had cooked onto the metal, and so they called me. Dirk wanted to do the gig for free, but the other officer was adamant that he would pay me a couple hundred bucks for the work. He drove the sedan down to the police yard, where it was raised on a mechanical lift, bringing me face level with what was left of the unfortunate guy.

While I flicked and picked at what I could from the burning metal undersides of the sedan, a loudmouthed cop, too overweight for a street assignment, hung around to relentlessly heckle me. Somehow it was a fitting end to my career as a janitor for the dead.

• • •

I wasn't happy about the way it all worked out; it wasn't exactly on my terms that I said good-bye to the business I had helped create over two years. Worse yet, while I thought it would fail in my absence, Dirk adopted his never-give-up approach and replaced me instantly. Apparently craigslist had no shortage of capable talent.

I had been so naïve. I didn't think Dirk could train anybody to be the new me, but to think that was not to know Dirk. The new me was a young, stupid-looking kid, completely hungry for a change and completely ignorant about such things as proper training and safety regulations. Just like me, he had nothing better to do in life but to wait for the phone to ring and to leap at Dirk's beck and call.

Dirk went through the motions of calling me for the first couple of jobs that came along, but we both knew I was working and couldn't take them. Worse yet, the Public Guardian, months after we'd cleaned the street outside the gas house, finally turned the property over to the dead man's ex-wife. On a table near the entrance of the now-fumigated house, she found a business card for a crime scene cleaning company and called them up. My cut would have been almost eight grand for a day and a half worth of work.

Soon enough, the phone calls died off altogether and I was done. I still have my crate "just in case" something comes up, but it sits in the backseat of the Red Rocket collecting dust. As a courtesy, my cell phone's voicemail still has the information where police officers who have my business card can find a number for the company's twenty-four-hour-assistance hotline. I'll change it one day, but not just yet.

● ● ●

My new job pays me eleven dollars an hour. I make less in a month than I used to make in a couple of hours. Sure, it's regular work, but I'm miserable. Day in and day out, I remind myself that it is good, honest work and I should be thankful for that. Do I think about back-sliding into some of my old habits? All the time...There are a lot of ways I could make money with the private medical information of Orange County's cultural elite, but I don't. I'm a good guy now, and that thought alone makes me happy.

I just hope it lasts.

about the author

JEFF KLIMA IS A DEVILISHLY handsome jack-of-all-trades *who makes love like a banshee*. If that frightens you, perhaps you'd be happier reading something a little less awesome. *The Dead Janitors Club* is Jeff's first book, and when he's not speaking about himself in the third person, he's writing other books to make himself more money. By the time you read this, hopefully he no longer lives in Orange County. Oh, and his favorite drink is milk.